# BRIGHT IDEAS

*Inspirations for* CROSS-CURRICULAR PROJECTS

Published by Scholastic
Publications Ltd,
Villiers House,
Clarendon Avenue,
Leamington Spa,
Warwickshire CV32 5PR

© 1993 Scholastic Publications Ltd

Written by Colin Hughes,
Winnie Wade and Jack Wilson
Edited by Magdalena Hernas
Sub-edited by Jane Wright
Designed by Anna Oliwa
Series designed by Juanita
Puddifoot
Illustrated by Nick Ward and
Chris Saunderson
Cover design by Sue Limb
Cover artwork by Nick Ward

Designed using Aldus Pagemaker
Processed by Pages Bureau,
Leamington Spa
Artwork by David Harban Design,
Warwick
Printed in Great Britain by
Ebenezer Baylis & Son, Worcester

**British Library Cataloguing in
Publication Data**
A catalogue record for this book is
available from the British Library.

ISBN 0-590-53030-5

# CONTENTS

# INTRODUCTION

# Cross-curricular projects

This book explores the process of implementation of aspects of the National Curriculum core and foundation subjects within the context of the thematic approach – frequently referred to as topic or project work – which the majority of primary schools have developed over the past two decades since the publication of the Plowden Report in 1967.

A new debate has extended the range of variables that the 1988 Education Reform Act requires schools to consider. Schools and teachers have put a great deal of time and effort into developing the statutory orders of the National Curriculum within the framework of the whole curriculum policies which the majority of schools, implicitly or explicitly, already had in place. Many schools would, however, admit that the debate about 'areas of experience' and later, the core and foundation subjects that were to form the curriculum, had shown up defects in school planning. It became clear that breadth, balance, relevance, progression and coherence needed further thought, both in the planning and in the evaluation of the curriculum on offer. Indeed, the debate about the relationship between the statutory proposals and what was already in place has been one of the aspects of the National Curriculum, and the discussions that have surrounded it, from which everyone, not least teachers, have benefited. It brought into focus the question of what schools did well and should retain, what needed to be modified and adjusted, and what needed to be changed.

# BACKGROUND

### The National Curriculum debate

National Curriculum proposals were, to a large extent, initially concerned with the content of the curriculum, what was taught and what pupils could be expected to know and do at various stages during their school career. This discussion about 'what' ended with the publication of the statutory orders, but local educational authorities and schools continued to focus on the 'how'; many wished to retain those approaches which encouraged active learning, discovery methods and the child-centred ethos advocated in the Plowden Report. The new debate challenged the efficacy of these methods.

Criticism of the Plowden ethos is by no means new, but we must bear in mind that this document was commissioned by the government of the day in 1963 and given whole-hearted approval by the government who published it in 1967. In its time, which for many teachers may not be over yet, the Plowden Report was as powerful an influence on curriculum design as the 1988 Education Reform Act and the National Curriculum proposals are today. Teachers, not unnaturally, interpreted such phrases as 'At the heart of the education process lies the child...', and '...we stress that children's learning does not fit into subject categories...', as having authoritative influence on curriculum design and implementation. Such statements had a profound effect on methods used in the initial and in-service teacher training and consequently, on what happened in schools and classrooms.

### An integrated approach to learning

One major consideration of the Plowden Report's contention that children's learning cannot fit easily into subject categories, was the adoption of thematic and topic work approaches to curriculum delivery. These approaches attempted to integrate a number of subject areas so that they were studied simultaneously, with the knowledge and skill inherent in each subject area being brought to bear upon a problem or a coherent sequence of problems in order to find a solution. If the problem or problems identified were 'real' ones, they were unlikely to be solved satisfactorily within the limited context of something labelled 'geography', 'science' or 'mathematics'. Where schools selected 'real' problems relevant to the pupils' environment, then the ideas and methodology (often themselves overlapping and transferable) of each of the above subject areas, together with those from other subjects, needed to be employed.

One example of this is a study of the economic activity

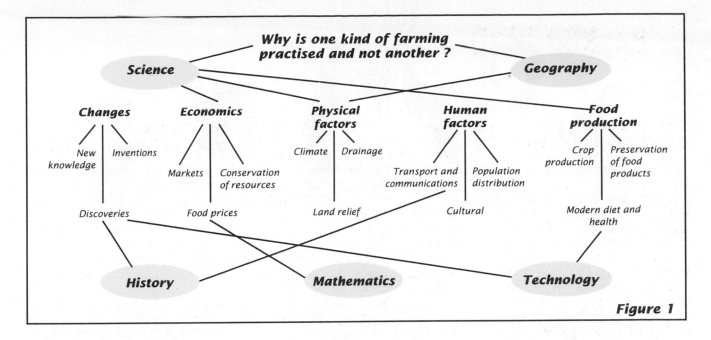

**Figure 1**

in the locality of the school within the theme of 'Food and Farming'. This type of study raises a whole range of questions which might usefully be explored and which certainly would be relevant to National Curriculum aims and objectives. If we took farming in the area as one focal point, the following questions could be asked:
• Why is one kind of farming practised and not another?
• How is the produce transported from farm to consumer so that it arrives in good condition?
• In what ways have production, distribution and consumption changed over the years?
• How have these changes affected producers, distributors, consumers, the locality, the region and the nation?
Other questions could be added to this list and all, or some of them, could form the basis of a worthwhile project. They are not, of course, in any

particular order of sequence or importance, nor are they raised in the context of a particular academic subject. They are simply questions worth raising in a study of the locality and not specific, isolated subject knowledge. The relationship between the questions asked, the relevant ideas and related subject areas is indicated above in Figure 1.

Many important questions have been raised and answered; a great deal of geography, science, history and technology has been learned and a range of National Curriculum targets have been met. This knowledge will have been learned and attainment targets met within a thematic and integrated approach which has a natural logic and coherence that makes it a good basis for curriculum design in the hands of a skilful teacher.

In the first place, the questions raised in the example above are real ones that pupils need to consider if they are to understand and participate effectively in their

own locality. What is more, these questions and the process of finding answers are transferable to any other locality or region. This provides not only for simple comparisons, but also for an understanding of the existing similarities and differences, why they exist and how people all over the world develop their cultures as they react to their environment.

Secondly, any success in finding answers will depend upon the extent to which a range of fundamental concepts, ideas and generalisations are encountered and an understanding of them developed. The relationship discovered between, for example, land relief, prevailing wind, condensation and rainfall, vegetation, temperature and growth, animal adaptation, pollution, and conservation will all have to be integrated at appropriate levels of sophistication to facilitate understanding of just some of the issues raised.

## Cross-curricular learning skills

The skills of discovering these kinds of relationships and outcomes will need to be practised. Concepts, ideas and generalisations do not develop in children's minds unless the children are required to reason out for themselves the significance of the variables and of the interaction between them. This means that pupils must be asked not simply to recall and describe what they experience and discover, but to identify similarities and differences, to infer causes and predict consequences, to interpret and make hypotheses, to evaluate and make judgements, to express informed opinions. These are the characteristics of the educated and informed person who shows the ability to think both critically and analytically, to see the relationships between the variables in a problematic situation and to make rational judgements about how a solution might be found. In addition, as these qualities develop, the growing knowledge and understanding, and the increasing skills are transferred to new problems as they arise, so that the overall problem-solving ability increases and progresses. All this is implicit in the objectives of the National Curriculum which clearly identifies at the appropriate levels the knowledge and skills that children should acquire.

The main emphasis of this book is on making integrated curriculum planning work. The activities within each theme involve children at all levels in the process of identifying and addressing transferable ideas, concepts and skills which are exemplars of National Curriculum content. Learning pursued in this way will have relevance and coherence and will therefore be more effective than the linear approach of separate, timetabled subjects. In addition, the thematic approach does not place restrictions on the mode of delivery or classroom organisation. Whole-class groups, teacher-led sequences and chalkboard summaries can be as appropriate as small-group activities, individual work and note-taking. This book enables teachers to combine the tradition of thematic teaching with the structured approach of the National Curriculum. This must be part of a whole-school curriculum plan.

## What is in this book for you?

This book illustrates how to develop systematically a thematic approach to teaching and learning in the primary curriculum, offering examples drawn from selected areas. It does not preclude other forms of curriculum organisation. However, whatever decision is made about the curriculum, it must be carefully planned and taught to ensure that all the National Curriculum objectives are achieved through a whole-school plan. It must also satisfy teachers that it encompasses a method of learning which is effective and meaningful to children, not because 'we have done it since Plowden' or 'it says so in the Alexander, Rose and Woodhead "Three Wise Men" Report', but because it works and has been evaluated as having worked.

Chapter 1, 'Cross-curricular planning: philosophy' provides a philosophical basis on which a curriculum audit might be developed to assist whole-school curriculum planning. Such a plan takes account of curriculum coverage, breadth, depth, relevance, differentiation, progression,

coherence and an appropriate balance of time for each curriculum area.

Chapter 2, 'Cross-curricular planning: implementation', illustrates this approach to curriculum organisation using the deliberations of teachers and advisers from one local authority, and describes how the aims and objectives of the National Curriculum can be achieved within a carefully devised whole-school plan. This is placed within a framework with agreed time-scales for each curriculum area and is based on sound long-term, medium-term and short-term planning. Examples of planning grids are given, clearly indicating the projects, topics or themes to be covered and the National Curriculum coverage. A clear rationale explains the choice of project and curriculum areas within each project.

Chapters 3 to 9 consider seven projects commonly associated with infant or junior classrooms, taken from the whole-school curriculum planning grids. While the titles of these projects may not mirror your own, they will nevertheless include activities you might consider in your own planning. Two projects, 'Local study' (Chapter 3) and 'Earth, weather and seasons' (Chapter 5), address both Key Stage 1 and Key Stage 2. 'Local study' offers 42 activities and 'Earth, weather and seasons' offers 18 activities. The other five projects (Chapters 4 and 6–9) will focus on a particular key stage or part of a key stage (for example, Key Stage 1; lower part of Key Stage 2 [Levels 2-4]; upper part of Key Stage 2 [Levels 3–5]). All the activities within the projects indicate their relationship to the National Curriculum programmes of study and statements of attainment. The sample grids and the

suggested activities provide the type of support that primary teachers, with their responsibility for teaching a wide, in-depth curriculum, need. Each activity suggests appropriate group size (though teachers must ultimately make this important decision), lists resources required to carry it out, and gives detailed advice on implementing the activity, questions to ask children, an explanation of the relevant knowledge, understanding and skills, further possible activities where relevant, safety guidance where appropriate and references to the National Curriculum attainment targets and statements of attainment. Teachers can then use this information to select the activities of their choice within the framework of their own whole-school planning grids.

Chapter 10 includes planning webs for mini-projects which teachers may also wish to incorporate into their planning. These may relate to an individual class, school, event or time of year.

Chapter 11 offers suggestions of criteria for evaluating the success of a chosen topic before and after teaching and learning. This uses examples from a project described earlier in the book. It also offers methods of recording children's achievement and their assessment.

Chapter 12 lists details of some of the resources and books described earlier. Photocopiable pages at the back of the book enable teachers to implement more easily those activities

requiring complex paper resources.

This book is designed to help busy teachers, co-ordinators and headteachers, at a time of rapid change in schools and to think about, discuss and organise whole-school planning so that it includes breadth, balance, differentiation, progression and coherence, as well as covering the National Curriculum. While this does not rule out other forms of curriculum organisation, it ensures the rigour in 'topic/thematic' planning, allowing children to be taught in a way most likely to secure effective learning about the world in which we live.

# CHAPTER 1

# Cross-curricular planning – philosophy

The introduction of the National Curriculum has led to a reappraisal of curriculum organisation and teaching. As the process began and the first statutory orders were received, local education authorities responded in a variety of ways to help teachers meet the legal requirements. Science, one of the first National Curriculum documents to be published, was an area in which teachers felt a lack of knowledge, understanding and skills, and needed strong support.

Many local authorities provided in-service training which addressed this need.

Humberside Local Education Authority, for example, suggested an organisational planning model which clustered the science requirements under major areas of study. Using these areas, schools developed long-term plans, based on a two-year cycle, which ensured coverage of statutory requirements and systematic revisiting of the concepts, skills and knowledge of science.

An unfortunate consequence of this was that many schools concentrated on the teaching of science so that the curriculum breadth and balance began to suffer.

Many schools taught less history and geography, and in some schools subjects such as art, music and PE became marginalised. With the publication of orders for technology, history and geography, it became evident that there was a need to look once again at the whole curriculum and to examine the principles on which any effective curriculum planning should be based. Humberside's intention was to provide guidelines which could be applied by any school in the context of its own particular circumstances.

# BACKGROUND

The resulting curriculum policy document stated that the curriculum should reflect the following characteristics: breadth, balance, relevance, progression, differentiation and coherence.

Schools which had a clear understanding of these terms as defined below could underpin the organisation of their curriculum with sound, relevant and effective planning principles.

## Breadth and balance

Breadth requires as a minimum the inclusion of National Curriculum core and foundation subjects, religious education, cross-curricular themes, dimensions and skills as identified in *The Whole Curriculum* (Curriculum Guidance 3, NCC, 1989).

Determination of whether breadth and balance are achieved requires a detailed curriculum audit. This should examine the proportions of time allocated to particular subjects and the extent to which an effective balance has been achieved. This process should become an integral part of management planning, curriculum planning and evaluation. The only way to ensure breadth and balance is through detailed long-term, medium-term and short-term planning. It is recognised that breadth and balance in the long term can only be achieved over a year, a two-year or a key-stage planning cycle. This presents very specific challenges for teachers working in integrated year groups, particularly in small schools.

Breadth and balance can be achieved through a variety of approaches. These range from projects focused tightly on one subject, through those with a strong subject focus, to the integration of some, but not all, subject areas, and finally to projects involving all subject areas.

## Relevance

If the curriculum is relevant, there is likely to be increased motivation and hence more effective learning. Relevance for children is the extent to which a project relates to past experiences and to the problems which they are seeking to solve. Such learning initially stems from first-hand experiences where children begin by working in a concrete, hands-on way; but as knowledge, understanding and skills develop, learning will move from the concrete to the abstract, from the known to the unknown. Relevance is further enhanced by real learning contexts to which children can relate. For example, learning about the human geography of a distant land is made more relevant if the starting point is the human geography of their own locality and region. The concept of human geography, like all concepts, transfers as it develops from known to unknown, but *similar* situations. It is likely that thematic and integrated approaches, in contrast to teaching through discrete subjects, increase curriculum coherence and relevance for children and heighten their interests. Children are interested in human behaviour, human achievements and human dilemmas. Their own natural curiosity will seek explanation and interpretation that may need to draw on the knowledge, understanding, skills, feelings, attitudes and values from across the curriculum – using that word in its fullest sense. For example, a child looking at a contemporary large-scale map of his/her village may notice that, compared with a similar map of one hundred years ago, the individual fields on a local farm are much larger. This is a historical change – but the study of its cause and effect draws upon a range of understandings that exist in what National Curriculum literature may place under discrete subject headings.

Causes may have to do with the development of technology, with inventions and discovery, with notions of labour saving and efficiency. The effects are wide ranging and might include unemployment, destruction of habitats, the erosion of food chains, the interruption of life cycles and concerns for conservation. Confined simply within the history syllabus that initial observation is constrained. Where the curriculum approach is more flexible and integrated, aspects of technology, history, human geography and environmental and biological science can all be addressed and a real problem, a real consequence of human behaviour over time, explored and explained. Drawing on curriculum knowledge from a wide area provides for coherence, finding explanations increases interest, and relevance is promoted because in such integrated situations real problems can be addressed and a real problem-solving approach needs to be used. This involves children in asking questions, identifying needs, seeing problems and suggesting hypotheses or solutions which can be tested and evaluated using evidence. Where this process is applied to real situations the purpose becomes clear to the child.

## Progression and differentiation

The fundamental purpose of any educational curriculum, however it is structured and delivered, is to provide a suitable learning context and relevant opportunities for the progressive development of worthwhile knowledge, the understanding of key ideas, the ability to apply a wide range of intellectual, practical and social skills, and appropriate attitudes towards learning situations.

The acquisition of factual knowledge and information will increase as the curriculum provides the learner with access to a wide range of information and activities, leading towards an increasing capacity to acquire such knowledge independently.

Key ideas, concepts and generalisations are general responses to specific experiences which exist at all levels of thought. Children learn through the formation of conceptual understanding which leads to the ability to analyse situations and solve problems. Key and fundamental ideas spawn and are inclusive of minor or subordinate ideas. The key idea that people are affected by their environment cannot be fully understood unless, simultaneously, children are also developing their understanding of such subordinate ideas as climate, seasons, soil, rock, vegetation, latitude, longitude and many others. Concepts, therefore, are constantly refined, extending children's range of understanding. It is a crucial aspect of curriculum planning that the concepts learned are clarified and made explicit.

Acquiring information and developing understanding is only valuable in educational terms if the curriculum also provides for children to undertake tasks associated with the knowledge and understanding they already have. Such ability is referred to within the curriculum areas and objectives as 'skill' and can apply in the physical, intellectual or social domain. Skills, however, cannot exist on their own – knowledge and skilful reorganisation of such knowledge towards the

development of understanding is the bedrock of the curriculum process.

The development of attitudes is a further outcome of a well-planned curriculum process. Together with knowledge, concepts and skills, attitudes provide the ethos which fosters learning. Attitudes towards the learning situation manifest themselves through the extent to which a child exhibits curiosity, is willing to co-operate, shows independence and accepts responsibility.

However, all these attributes of the well-planned, appropriate and relevant curriculum develop in individual children very slowly and at different incremental rates. It would be as unreasonable to expect a young child to have a well-developed sense of responsibility as it would to expect the same child to understand abstract ideas. Similarly, it would be unreasonable to expect every child to progress at the same pace and in the same way. Progression in development

and differentiation of tasks are, therefore, functions of the curriculum experiences which provide the following opportunities.

• To acquire knowledge through activity and experience, through practising increasingly sophisticated library and research skills and through working on a wide range of information storage and retrieval activities.

• To return frequently to the key and subordinate ideas that are essential to the understanding of the world in which children live. This revisiting of ideas – the spiral curriculum – must be a fundamental aspect of curriculum design if conceptual understanding is to be refined in the course of concrete experience with a limited number of conceptual relationships to consider. Later consideration of the same concept will be in more complex and abstract situations, with many and more subtle relationships to handle simultaneously.

• To go beyond the simple description of their experiences and the problems they are trying to solve towards the increasing ability to approach situations and

problems from different perspectives. This means using information not simply in a descriptive and unchanged form, but to use it to categorise, make inferences and predictions, to extrapolate from the known to the unknown, to evaluate, assess and form opinions. In this way, information is reorganised and the relationship between one aspect of the available information and another can be teased out. It is the understanding of the cause and effect of these relationships that allows the children to form and develop ideas and concepts.

• To acquire appropriate attitudes. Curiosity and co-operation, for example, are not necessarily attributes that children bring to school with them. The curriculum must foster them by providing opportunities for children to be co-operative, moving from situations in which taking turns and sharing are encouraged towards situations in which agreement and co-operative ventures are decided by negotiation and by the good of the wider group being put before personal interests and preferences.

• To engage in open-ended tasks at their own present stage of development.

Progression and differentiation then are closely related to the design of the curriculum, to its aims and objectives, to its content and process, and to the evaluation and assessment of outcomes. Progression and differentiation will manifest themselves in a variety of ways across the full developmental spectrum, including the following abilities:

• To cope simultaneously with a greater number of variables

in problem-solving situations;
•To analyse critically and reorganise information using a range of thinking processes and to discriminate between important and less important relationships;
•To move from concrete to abstract ideas towards the formation and application of generalisations and the transfer of understanding from one situation to another;
•To envisage different viewpoints, be aware of uncertainty, ambiguity and the limitations of evidence, to avoid uncritical, assertive responses and conclusions;
•To develop a line of reasoning that is ordered and logical. As children are increasingly able to demonstrate this ability, they will show evidence of greater sophistication in the selection and balance of points they make; their arguments and discussions will show greater consistency; they will support and justify contentions with evidence and notions of cause and effect;
•To work independently and responsibly, making decisions and drawing conclusions after the careful consideration of all the available evidence or alternatives. Once conclusions are drawn, they are defended and not changed simply to be in line with others.

Progression and differentiation can only be achieved through rigorous planning. A process is described in Chapter 2 which gives criteria for three planning levels to ensure such rigour.

## Coherence

Curriculum planning should incorporate the whole curriculum through careful analysis and clear learning objectives, which give sufficient time to each component, either as an integral part of a project or as a discrete area of learning with one curriculum area in focus, and where skills and conceptual development are built upon as the child develops. It is possible to identify two continua as shown in Figure 1.

How schools organise their curriculum with regard to these two continua will determine the degree of coherence. In making decisions regarding the first continuum, a number of factors relating to the coherence of the curriculum must be recognised.
•The greatest coherence will be obtained within a project where no particular curriculum focus is selected, though this is often difficult to achieve unless the design of projects and project targets becomes artificial and contrived. There may be a tension between greater coherence within a project and a lack of progression of conceptual understanding or in-depth learning due to the range of curriculum areas involved. However, if breadth and balance are obtained over a year, part of a key stage or an entire key stage, then coherence will be obtained, albeit on a longer basis.
•It can be argued that there is an enquiry/investigative/ problem-solving process with common elements in most or all curriculum areas. This process may be developed in all projects through whatever curriculum area is under study, thus increasing the coherence of experience to teachers and children alike.
•While the work within a project may focus on an activity from one curriculum area, knowledge, understanding and skills from other areas are needed to complete a piece of learning successfully. For example, children carrying out an investigation of forces applied to a car might have to design and make an artefact to produce quantifiable units of force on a reliable, regular basis, record their results in a graph and communicate them to their peers. Here, children's

**Figure 1**

| 1. Curriculum area in focus | | |
| --- | --- | --- |
| ▪*Curriculum area specific – only the concepts, skills and knowledge of one particular curriculum area are intentionally included;* | ▪*Curriculum area focused – most emphasis is on the concepts, skills and knowledge of one curriculum area but others are also intentionally included;* | ▪*No specific focus – the concepts, skills and knowledge of a number of curriculum areas are intentionally included.* |

| 2. Regularity | |
| --- | --- |
| ▪*Daily/weekly revisiting, for example, maths, English, the weather – one term;* | ▪*Annual or biennial revisiting of themes or attainment targets – half-term or mini-project.* |

developmental levels in technology, mathematics and English need to be considered, as much as levels of development in science. Transferable skills, concepts and attitudes help to ensure coherence of experience and further children's ability to tackle 'problems' with an open repertoire of 'solutions'. Transferable concepts (e.g. cause and effect, continuity and change, similarity and difference, evidence) and attitudes (for example, reliability, resourcefulness, self-discipline, co-operation) should be developed in all projects and within each curriculum area to increase coherence. The development of cross-curricular skills such as literacy, numeracy and information technology in, for example, a history survey using a database, should be encouraged, as well as their development through the National Curriculum subjects of English, mathematics, science and technology.

•The inclusion of cross-curricular themes, dimensions and skills in the whole curriculum dictates that the teaching of all projects (and hence curriculum areas within projects) considers opportunities for their inclusion on a planned basis.

•Learning contexts provide in themselves opportunities to develop a number of curriculum areas. For example, a local study such as that detailed in Chapter 3, involves the inclusion of activities with a science, geography and history emphasis.

•There is an overlap in content between certain National Curriculum areas. For instance, both the science and geography documents involve work on soils, rocks, water, the seasons, weather and weathering, so that it is both logical and prudent to consider the closely related areas of learning as a coherent whole.

•It may be decided that as the depth of understanding of concepts and curriculum areas develops, there will be an increased use of one curriculum area as a focus for projects. This may occur towards the end of the primary phase, compared with the beginning when there is greater use of projects with little or no emphasis on any one curriculum area. It is important to retain the integrity of a group of activities developing a concept in a particular curriculum area, so that if a reasonable time cannot be allocated for that area, it should not be taught in that particular project. But it is also important to maintain the integrity of a particular project by involving activities relevant to the overall project theme. Thus the degree of integration of curriculum areas affects continuity and progression. It might be decided that certain aspects of certain curriculum areas can only be taught in a subject-focused project or that it is easier to ensure progression through a subject-focused approach, and this would outweigh considerations of coherence.

Decisions regarding the second continuum depend upon the mode of teaching and learning, organisation of the projects and the organisation of the whole curriculum. The way in which projects are chosen and organised will be different in each school and will depend on the aims of the school, on the children, the teachers' interests, the ability to plan collectively and the school's location. Whatever the chosen organisation, the taught curriculum should not be a sequence of fragmented and isolated experiences, but a coherent whole where the individual learning elements support and reinforce one another. Thus, learning experiences should be planned such that there are clear objectives in terms of concepts, knowledge, understanding, skills and attitudes which contribute to the development of each curriculum area. In this way, coherence, as well as progression and the integrity of individual curriculum areas, will be maintained.

# CHAPTER 2

# Cross-curricular planning - implementation

This chapter describes how rigorous, systematic school planning may be organised and implemented at three different levels. It gives detailed examples of these planning levels which have been devised and used in infant, junior and primary schools. These examples will not suit every school; however, they may easily be modified.

Before beginning whole-school curriculum planning it is necessary for teachers in a school to be clear about their aims and general philosophy. Based upon agreed principles such as those described in Chapter 1, a planning process should be devised to ensure a curriculum which meets statutory requirements, fulfils the needs of the children and relates to the locality. Here is a broad description of the planning process as identified by one LEA:

1. The school should consider the elements to be included in a broad curriculum and how these will be taught and learned. As a minimum, the legal requirements of the Education Reform Act must be met.

2. An appropriate time allocation should be made for each curriculum area, allowing also for cross-curricular themes.

3. Decisions need to be made about how the subject areas are to be taught, taking into account the degree of integration and amount of specialist input required.

4. Through an audit, the existing provision should be examined to identify current time allocations and to challenge inappropriate ones, so that adjustments can be made. This would be related to 1. and 2. above.

5. Planning should follow at three levels – long term, medium term and short term. The criteria on which planning at each of these three levels might be based are outlined on the following page.

# BACKGROUND

## Long-term planning

Long-term planning should:
• address the general organisation of all work to be undertaken in the school;
• relate to annual, biennial or whole key stage cycles
• identify the subject or subjects to be focused upon for major projects which provide a coherent curriculum;
• ensure a broad, balanced, relevant curriculum which provides continuity throughout and between schools and meets the assessed needs of children;
• give autonomy to teachers within a year group to devise medium-term plans within the agreed framework. This will recognise such factors as, for

example, the importance of teachers' and children's interests, the locality and current events;
• address the development of concepts, knowledge and understanding, skills and attitudes (mostly corresponding to National Curriculum), cross-curricular elements and religious education;
• address the requirements of the National Curriculum subjects and religious education.

## Medium-term planning

Medium-term planning should:
• derive from the long-term plan;
• address all the work to be undertaken by a group of children (class/year group, etc.) during a particular project;
• describe the organisation of projects, in terms of subject

inclusion and organisation and the main learning experiences at an undifferentiated level;
• identify parts of the programme of study and attainment targets of National Curriculum subjects to be covered, along with religious education and cross-curricular elements;
• identify the range of levels of attainment and understanding within a class or year group;
• take account of the knowledge, concepts, skills and attitudes to be covered (mostly corresponding to National Curriculum), cross-curricular themes and religious education.

## Short-term planning

Short-term planning should:
• derive from the medium-term plan;
• address all the work to be undertaken by children (class/year group, etc.) in specific terms over a short period such as two weeks, one week or a day;
• use the results of ongoing teacher assessment to address the needs of individual children;
• describe activities to be undertaken, including the following:
    – timing (approximate length/ongoing, day, time of day, and so on);
    – class organisation (activities occurring simultaneously);
    – resources;
    – teaching focus (which activities need most

teaching time/are more self-supporting);
– how the activity addresses National Curriculum programmes of study (if relevant);
– principal (and other) learning objectives (concepts, skills, knowledge) and attitudes usually associated with National Curriculum statements of attainment;
– organisation for differentiation (by task, outcome, pace, support);
– assessment.
• allow for evaluation and inform the next short-term plan;
• ensure that over the long term, a balance of the activities (in terms of principal learning objectives) and of subjects (identified in the long-term plan) is achieved;
• where appropriate, involve children in discussions about activities so that they begin to have some ownership of their own learning.

These three levels of planning will now be explored in more detail, with reference to examples currently implemented in schools.

## Long-term planning in practice

It is important for the headteacher and staff to recognise that more is accomplished when all staff are working together. Whole-curriculum planning requires a whole-school approach.

The process of designing a long-term plan must, by its very nature, be evolutionary. As they become more familiar with core and foundation subjects, schools will develop

**Teaching time per week** = 23 hrs 20 mins or 20 sessions (4 sessions per day at 1 hr 10 mins per session)

**5%** = 1 hrs 10 mins or 1 session

Percentage of time allocated per subject, i.e. learning focused on concepts, skills and knowledge of that subject:

| | | | |
|---|---|---|---|
| English | 17.5% | Maths | 15% |
| Science* | 15% | Technology | 7.5% |
| History | 7.5% | Geography | 7.5% |
| Music | 7.5% | Art | 7.5% |
| PE | 7.5% | RE | 5% |
| Other | 2.5% | | |

* up to 5% of science may be ongoing

**N.B.** This time allocation operates over the long term, rather than on a weekly or monthly basis. Thus, for example, music is allocated 7.5% of the time or 1.5 sessions per week, on average.

**Figure 1**

and refine their thinking and practice in the light of experience. Whole-curriculum planning must be a cyclical process which includes teaching and learning, assessment, recording and evaluation, as well as planning. Both the intended and the actual outcomes must inform the detailed planning. Initially, decisions need to be made regarding curriculum balance. Each school must make its own decisions concerning time allocation for particular subjects. The example given in Figure 1 illustrates the process.

Decisions then need to be made about criteria for integration of subjects into projects and the order in which those projects will be taught, bearing in mind the principle of coherence (see Chapter 1). These criteria include the following:
• Projects should not be contrived.
• Subjects or parts of subjects

which do not fit should be organised into mini-projects, stand alone or be ongoing over time.
• Subject content should derive from children's previous experiences and learning when appropriate, so that new teaching is relevant to the children and leads to more effective learning.
• Commonality is an important criterion in building up a project. It could be knowledge or skills common to more than one subject or similarity of context and content, as in a study of Tudors and Stuarts and Exploration.
• Projects which include history should be planned sequentially to give children a sense of chronology. Schools must decide whether to start from the distant past and gradually move to the present or vice versa.
• In planning geography, children should learn about the local, before the distant, environment. In all subjects,

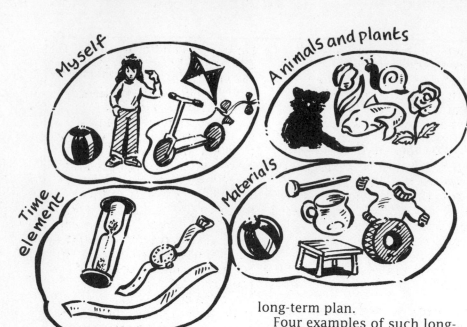

Myself

Animals and plants

Time element

Materials

children should, where possible, study the known before the unknown and move from concrete to abstract.
• Subject balance must be maintained in each project, term, year or key stage.
• Which parts of each subject or which projects could best be used to develop cross-curricular themes.
• Some projects will be ongoing, e.g. Weather and Climate and Sound and Music.

Such a long-term model allows for maximum interpretation by class teachers at the medium-term planning stage, if that is what is required. Teachers must adhere to the allocated time for each subject and agree to teach the concepts, knowledge and skills identified. Beyond this, teachers could decide whether to teach some subjects separately or to teach them all in an integrated, cross-curricular project. They might also decide the order of work and whether to include particular current events, as long as these fit in with the

long-term plan.

Four examples of such long-term plans are given at the end of this chapter. Example A (page 24) and Example B1 (page 25) are from schools which have taken a cross-curricular approach to most projects; projects in Example C (page 33) are totally cross-curricular but subject headings are identified within each project. Example D (page 34) incorporates the projects detailed in Chapters 3 to 9 of this book in the 6 years of Key Stages 1 and 2.

Example A (page 24) is from a primary school with a nursery and reception class and indicates much cross-curricular planning. A grid showing the projects over the 7/8 year groups is accompanied by attainment targets for various subject areas. These projects have been grouped under the major headings of 'Myself', 'Time element', 'Movement', 'Materials', 'Animals and plants', and 'Place', each corresponding to approximately half a term's work. Projects reflecting these headings are taught from the nursery class to year 6. Projects such as 'Vehicles' in

Year 2 include work from the programmes of study in science, geography and technology and 'How we live' in Year 3 incorporates the subjects of science, history and geography. Other projects such as 'Food we eat' consider work in science only. Likewise, the projects entitled 'Children and families in the past' and 'Ships and sea-faring' concentrate exclusively on history.

Example B1 (page 25) illustrates a long-term planning project grid from an infant school. Each project involves the integration of all curriculum subjects, though only science, geography historyand technology attainment targets are included on the grid. These are accompanied by two planning sheets which show the opportunities for cross-curricular themes and dimensions (Example B2, page 26) and attainment targets to be covered in each subject area. An example of the latter sheet for technology is shown in Example B3 on page 27.

Example C (page 33) illustrates cross-curricular project planning in a junior school from year 3 to 6 but identifies subject-focused headings within each project.

Example D (page 34) shows how the projects in this book could be incorporated into a school's curriculum planning. A cross-curricular planning approach has been used and this is indicated on the grid by references to subjects and attainment targets. 'Earth, seasons and weather' has been considered as an ongoing project at Key Stage 1 and as a discrete project at Key Stage 2. Similarly, 'Sound and music' could be approached in this way, but is presented here as a project in its own right. The projects do not exactly correspond to half-terms, which are in reality of unequal length.

The detailed discussions which have taken place to produce the four models are likely to acknowledge the place of some teaching and learning which focuses exclusively on one subject, some which puts an emphasis on one subject and some which clusters subjects within a project, to enhance children's learning.

It is unlikely that *all* relevant learning could be encompassed in a cross-curricular framework. Those omitted elements need to be covered in whatever way seems appropriate, through mini-projects, individual 'concept' inputs or ongoing studies. Where careful short-term planning follows that at medium and long term, the curriculum which results may contain the best elements of 'subject' and 'project' teaching.

Together, the activities which children carry out will be organised within a curriculum which is not a sequence of fragmented and isolated experiences but rather a coherent whole, where the learning elements support and reinforce one another. Rigorous planning is necessary in the short term to identify clear learning objectives which relate to National Curriculum programmes of study and therefore statements of attainment, and ensure progression in children's learning.

## Long-term planning process involved in Example A

Long-term planning may be illustrated in a little more detail by looking at one primary school. As more and more subjects were introduced into the National Curriculum there was a need to reappraise curriculum planning. Many of the original projects were modified to allow for the integration of geography and history, but which allowed scope for music, physical education and art in addition to cross-curricular themes and religious education.

The staff valued children's first-hand experience as an essential part of learning. The history skills, for example, would make reference to similarities and differences and would be an extension of the child's immediate environment and experiences to help retain relevance.

The school has a nursery and reception class in addition to nine other classes. These nine classes are organised into three groups, with each class following two years of the National Curriculum (i.e. 1/2; 3/4; 5/6). A two-year cycle has been designed to ensure that all subjects and attainment targets are met. A detailed time audit of curricular areas has been carried out, indicating the time allowances covered within a project and those which will stand alone. The projects are not rigid in length or of equal time allocation. Planning was carried out according to the following programme.
• Broad philosophy of long-term plan agreed.
• Infant and Junior teachers separately consider suggestions for projects and make comments to curriculum leaders.
• Proposed planning submitted.
• Staff selected to work in one of the core curriculum groups of English, mathematics and science, chaired by the teacher with responsibility for that subject. Each group has at least one member of staff from each two-year teaching group. Relevant programmes of study are identified for each project.
• Staff selected to work in one of the history, geography and technology groups. Relevant programmes of study are identified for each project.
• Staff agree school curriculum plan.
• Teachers from each two-year group work together to produce a medium-term plan. This defines quality tasks

within the programmes of study and ensures coverage of attainment targets.

• The school's long-term and medium-term planning files from nursery to year 6 are made available to staff.

Teachers accept that all the work required by the National Curriculum could not be done within the previously selected projects. A time audit is carried out to identify the percentage of each existing project which:
• could be met within the new projects;
• needed to stand alone or could be considered in a mini-project outside the main project.

Check lists from subject areas designed to help ensure that work believed to be going on 'all the time', e.g. Science AT1, is in reality being implemented.

Staff recognise that projects need to be reappraised following teaching and evaluation. Thus the planning is not finished, but, as the headteacher commented, 'I

hope it never will be, because if teachers ever felt it were, we might stop questioning, reasoning and justifying, and I think we need to make sure we never do that.'

## Medium-term planning

Using the agreed long-term plan, school policy, LEA guidance and programmes of study, year-group teachers may then develop the medium-term plan. This process is illustrated by work produced by an infant school:
1. Project web: staff fill in a project web 'blank' which identifies the content of National Curriculum subjects to be covered (see Example B4, page 28, project on Clothes) by relating them to the programmes of study. Religious education, visits and visitors may also be identified on the web.
2. Knowledge: knowledge statements for each week of a project are included on a proforma (see Example B5, page 29). These statements are based on the programmes of study.

3. Resources: a list of resources for the project is also identified on this proforma (see Example B5, page 29) and any details of contacts to be made.
4. Checklist: checklists of knowledge and understanding and skills directly relating to levels of attainment in the National Curriculum, as well as skills, attitudes and key concepts identified by the school as also being important, are filled in for each subject involved in a project. An example of the history, knowledge and understanding and skills for the projects entitled 'Homes', 'Light' and 'Clothes' are included in Example B6, page 30.

These checklists are for planning purposes only and can be used to identify learning not covered. Such gaps can then be included in a mini project or as a 'stand alone' input.

## Short-term planning

Short-term planning in the same infant school is organised on a weekly and daily basis.

### Weekly short-term planning (in year groups)

An example of a week's planning proforma is given on page 31 (Example B7) and this includes headings of the knowledge statements for the week, key attitudes and concepts to be developed and National Curriculum subjects. Assessment tasks which form an integral part of the planning process are also identified. This weekly part of the short-term plan, which is derived from the medium-term plan,

| Name | AT1 | AT3/1a | AT3/2a |
|---|---|---|---|
| | 1a, 2a, 2b, 2c | ✔ ✔ | ✔ |
| | 1a, 2b | ✔ | colour only | colour only |
| | 1a, 2a, 2b | ✔ | ✔ |
| | 1a,2a,2b,2c,3a | ✔ | ✔ |

**Figure 1**

establishes activities to be carried out, relating them to National Curriculum subjects and to specific statements of attainment which are to be addressed. Religious Education and cross-curricular issues are also identified. This weekly plan may be backed up by the production of a 'Planning Target' sheet for each subject area. One such sheet relating to science and the knowledge statement, 'Clothes can tell us what job people do' is shown at the end of this chapter (see Example B8, page 32).

The school also produces weekly tick-list assessment sheets, one of which has been adapted to fit the 'Clothes' project (see Figure 1 above).

## Daily short-term planning (individual)

Teachers use a 'Daily book' to show the organisation of the class for each planned activity. This plan also identifies activities in which specific groups or individuals will be involved and how tasks are differentiated. Particular children's difficulties are documented alongside progress task lists which may be used for assessment purposes. This information is transferred regularly to the children's individual records which are part of their Records of Achievement.

Assessment is mainly ongoing and continuous. However, science knowledge and understanding is assessed half-termly on a 1:1 basis, using questions and tasks derived by year-group teachers. This process, while giving valuable assessment information, also reinforces learning. History and geography tasks are being developed by a working party involving staff from a pyramid group of schools.

## Evaluation

This is carried out at the end of each project by individual teachers, who further discuss their thoughts and findings with year-group colleagues. Projects are evaluated in terms of whether the medium-term plans have been addressed successfully. Statements of attainment, skills, attitudes and knowledge not covered, or not fully covered, are noted, to be included again in a later project or as discrete inputs. Other questions which are addressed include the following:
• Was there interest, enjoyment and learning?
• Was the time allocation/ subject emphasis as anticipated?
• Was there a good balance in all subjects?
• Was a particular part of the project more successful than another?
• Were the first-hand experiences or visits of value in enhancing learning?

## Using or modifying the sheets

Teachers reading this chapter may consider some of the examples used to clarify medium and short-term planning too prescriptive and/ or too detailed for their own purposes. The plans presented here were worked out collectively by an industrious staff, willing to accept a curriculum which ensured total coverage at the expense of individual preferences for project titles. However, teachers, curriculum co-ordinators and headteachers must ensure that the individual preferences and expertise of staff are not given a higher priority than the need for a whole-curriculum plan which is adhered to and which ensures continuity between classes and coverage of National Curriculum skills and knowledge. In chapters 3–8 we have included science, geography and history activities, as well as activities involving other curriculum areas, in illustrative projects. Teachers and schools could keep the same or similar project titles, but reduce the amount of integration to say, two of science, geography and history. The remaining curriculum area could then be integrated into another project, taught as a mini-project or as a separate subject completely.

# Example A

| CLASS (YEAR) | ONGOING PROJECTS | AUTUMN TERM | | SPRING TERM | | SUMMER TERM | |
|---|---|---|---|---|---|---|---|
| | Atmosphere, earth and space | Myself | Time element | Movement | Materials | Animals and plants | Place |
| Nursery | Night and day G1 | Myself Sc (ii) Sc (i) | Families H3 H1 | Moving toys G1 S 4(iii) T1 | Materials Sc 3(i) Sc 3(iii) T3 | Pets Sc 2(i) Sc 2(ii) | Water H Sc 2(i) |
| Reception | Night and day Sc 4(iv) Sc 4(v) | Senses S 2(i) Sc 4(i) G5 | Homes H1 H3 Sc 4(i) Sc 4(iv) | Wheels Sc 4(iii) T3 | Properties of materials Sc 3(i), (ii) Sc 4(iv) G5 | In the garden Sc 2(i) Sc 2(ii) G1 T2 | Seaside Sc 2(i) H1 G3 G2 T1 |
| 1 | Day length Sc 4(v) G3 | Caring for ourselves Sc 2(i) G2 Sc 4(i) Sc 2(iv) | Children and families in the past H CSU 3 & 4 H 1, 2, 3 | Playgrounds and fairs Sc 4(i) Sc 4(i) Sc 4(iv) T 1, 2, 3, 4 | Building sites Sc 3(i), (iii) T 1, 2 | Farms Sc 2(i), (ii), (iv) G 2 T 1 | Local environment Sc 2(iii) G 1, 2, 3, 4, 5 H 1 |
| 2 | Seasonal change Sc 4(v) G 2 G 3 | Food we eat Sc 2(i) Sc 2(iv) | People we know H 1, 2, 3 G 1, 2 | Vehicles Sc 4(iii) G 1, 4 T 2, 3, 4 | Building materials Sc 3(i), (iii) T 3, 4 | Animals Sc 2(i), (ii), (iii), (iv) SATs | Egyptians Sc 3 H 1, 2, 3 G 1, 2, 3, 4, 5 H SSU C |
| 3 | Seasonal change Sc 4(ii) | How we live Sc 2(i), 2(iv) H 1 G 2 | Ancient Greece H CSU 5 H 1 H 2 T 3 | Transport Sc 4(iii), (iv), (ii) H 1 T 4 | Invaders; Romans, Anglo-Saxons, Vikings H CSU 1 H 2 T 2 | Habitats Sc 2(ii), (iii), (iv) | Local environment Sc 3(iv) G 1, 5 |
| 4 | Water cycle Sc 3(iv) G 3 | Ourselves and our bodies Sc 2(i) | Food Sc 2(i) Sc 2(iv) H CSU 2 H 3 G 5 T4 | Domestic machines Sc 4(i), (ii) H 1 T 2 | Tudors and Stuarts H CSU 2 H 1, 2, 3 T 4 | Habitats revisited G 2 Sc 2 | Local environment Sc 3(iv) G 5 |
| 5 | Sundials Sc 4(v) Sc 4(iv) G 1 G 3 | Docks G 1 T 4 | Ships and seafaring through history H CSU 1, 2, 6 H 1 | Caring for our bodies Sc 2(i) | Victorian Britain H CSU, 3 H 2, 3 T 2, 4 | Local history unit History unit G 1 T 4 | Agriculture Sc 2(i), (iii) Sc 3(iv) |
| 6 | World weather G 2, 3 Astronomy Sc 4(v) | Airports Sc 4(i) Sc 4(iv) T 4 | Exploration and encounters H CSU 6 H 2 H 3 Sc 4(v) | Changes as we grow Sc 2(i) Sc 2(ii) | Life in Britain H CSU 4 H 2, 3 T 2, 3, 4 | SATs | Coastal areas G 3 |

## Example B1

| Long term plan | | | | | | |
|---|---|---|---|---|---|---|
| **TERM** | **SUMMER TERM** | | **AUTUMN TERM** | | **SPRING TERM** | |
| **YEAR** | *April* | *June* | *September* | *November* | *January* | *February* |
| **Reception and Year 1** | **OURSELVES** | **SUMMER (Plants and animals)** | **HOMES (People and how they live)** | **LIGHT (Earth, atmosphere and space)** | **CLOTHES (Materials)** | **FLIGHT, AIR AND WIND (Energy, forces and movement)** |
| | *Sc 2(i)*<br>*G 1, 2*<br>*H 1, 3* | *Sc 2(i), (ii), (iii),*<br>*4(ii)*<br>*G 3* | *Sc 2(iv)*<br>*4(i)*<br>*G 1, 3, 4, 5*<br>*H 1, 3* | *Sc 4(iv), (v)*<br>*H 1, 3* | *Sc 3(i), (iii)*<br>*G 2, 4, 5*<br>*H 1, 2, 3* | *Sc 4(iii)*<br>*G 1, 3, 5*<br>*H 2* |
| **Year 1 and Year 2** | **WATER** | | **SCHOOL AND SURROUNDING ENVIRONMENT** | **FOOD** | **PEOPLE AROUND THE WORLD** | **NIGHT AND DAY** |
| | *Shadows*<br>*Sounds and music*<br>*Water power*<br>*Forces and sinking and floating*<br>*Plants/animals and water*<br>*Sc 2(i), (ii), (iii)*<br>*3 (iii)*<br>*4 (iii), (iv)*<br>*Maps, rivers and landscapes*<br>*Rainwater and drainage*<br>*Water as fog, rain*<br>*Ice as hail, frost and snow*<br>*Reservoirs and dams*<br>*G 1, 2, 3, 5*<br>*H 2, 3* | | *Electricity*<br>*Materials in buildings*<br>*Sc 3(i), (iii)*<br>*4(i)*<br>*Maps, routes, services/ amenities in area*<br>*G 1, 3, 4, 5*<br>*H 1, 2, 3* | *Food and feeding*<br>*Decay*<br>*Baking/ ice-cream/ jellies*<br>*Food and energy*<br>*Sc 2(i), (ii), (iv)*<br>*3(iii)*<br>*4(i)*<br>*Transportation*<br>*Sources of food*<br>*G 2, 4*<br>*H 1, 2, 3* | *How people differ*<br>*Sc 2(i) PoS*<br>*Places beyond UK*<br>*European awareness and developing countries*<br>*Map of the world*<br>*Occupations*<br>*World weather*<br>*Different kinds of homes and landscapes*<br>*G 1, 2, 3, 4*<br>*H 1, 2, 3* | *Daily patterns, rest, eating*<br>*Light sources*<br>*Earth, Sun, Moon*<br>*Sc 2(i) PoS*<br>*4(iv), (v)*<br>*Weather and seasonal patterns*<br>*Jobs, night and day*<br>*G 3*<br>*H 1, 3* |

# Example B2

## Cross-curricular themes and dimensions
## Multicultural, gender issues and safety

| Topic / Cross-curricular themes and dimensions | Homes | Light | Clothes | Flight and air | Summer |
|---|---|---|---|---|---|
| Education for economic and industrial understanding | Visit to building site | Visit to fire station | Clothing factory Visit by crafts-people | Visit to airport | Leisure services |
| Health Education | Balanced meals Dangers of medicines | Safety with fire and electricity | Seasonal clothes | Body functions Breathing/lungs | Sunburn Personal hygiene |
| Careers Education and Guidance | Building work Jobs in the home | Night/day workers | Uniforms to identify jobs | Airforce and airport careers | Leisure Jobs related to seasons |
| Environmental education | Care of streets/home | Air pollution | Use of natural materials | Air pollution | Water pollution - sea, rivers Litter - country-code |
| Education for citizenship | Caring for family and friends | Services to community | Clothes for the needy | Noise level, pollution Consideration for others | Behaviour, on school trips/out of school |
| Safety | Journey to school/home | | | Air safety | Water safety |
| Gender/equal opportunities | Jobs in the home | Access to all activities by all children (electricity) | Careers What we wear | Role-play in school Drama - relate to careers | Role-play in school Drama - relate to careers |
| Multicultural | Different materials for different climates | Festivals e.g., Diwali, Christmas | Clothes worn by ethnic minorities | Journeys to other countries | Hot lands |

# Example B3

| | Long-term plan | | | | | |
|---|---|---|---|---|---|---|
| | **Technology checklist** | | | | | |
| | **Autumn term** | | **Spring term** | | **Summer term** | |
| | *1* | *2* | *1* | *2* | *1* | *2* |
| **AT1 Identifying needs and opportunities** | ✓ | ✓ | ✓ | ✓ | | |
| Home | ✓ Homes of the past | | | | | |
| School | | | | | | |
| Recreation | | | ✓ Holidays | | | |
| Community | | ✓ Festivals Diwali/ Christmas | | | | |
| Business and industry | | | | ✓ How does an airport work? | | |
| **AT2 Generating a design** | ✓ | ✓ | ✓ | ✓ | | |
| **AT3 Planning and making** | ✓ | ✓ | ✓ | ✓ | | |
| Artefact | ✓ Models | ✓ Candle | ✓ Pegdolls | ✓ Hot-air balloons Aircraft | | |
| System | ✓ With bulbs | ✓ Circuit grid system | ✓ Shoe shop Transport of raw materials | ✓ Airport | | |
| Environment | ✓ Model furniture in home | | ✓ Wooden models in shop | ✓ Travel agents Airports | | |
| AT4 Evaluating | ✓ | ✓ | ✓ | ✓ | | |
| **AT5 Information technology capability** | ✓ Folio and games | | | | | |
| | HOMES | LIGHT | CLOTHES | FLIGHT | | |

# Example B4

## Medium-term planning

**Language**
- Reporting
  Imaginative
  letter/poetry  } writing
  descriptive
- Re-telling
- Use of tapes
- Speaking/listening
- Higher-order reading skills
- Stories/poems
- Role-play/drama simulation (home, shops, etc.)

**Science**
- Types and uses of materials
- Similarities and differences
- Materials for different weather/seasons
- Properties/uses/strengths of materials
- Use of man-made or natural materials
- What clothes are made of; reasons for
- Absorbency of materials; water proofing
- Which sort of materials dry the quickest
- Fire resistant materials – dangers

**Mathematics**
- Shopping; money, exchange, 1p to £1 recognition and change
- Graph work; letter home to involve parents
- Measurement – comparative language; use of cms; size of shoes, etc.
- Size of shoes/feet – difference
- Counting in 2s, 5s and 10s (multiplication)
- Problem solving activities
- Patterns – repeating, rotating, tesselations
- Sort/classify types of clothes
- Computation
- Number games
- Logic (Carroll/Venn/tree)
- Probability

**Physical Education**
- Small apparatus skills
- Exploring body movements
- Rhythm
- Gross motor skills

## CLOTHES
### Key concepts *

**Technology**
- Design and select materials for school uniform/ occasion
- Design/make a hat to keep the head dry
- Design for weather/seasons
- Computer games and folio

**Religious Education (social/moral)**
- Values and beliefs
- Clothes in different cultures/ jobs
- Story of Joseph and his coat
- Role-play

**History**
- Cause/consequence
- Looking at traditional clothes
- Victorians. Compare clothes worn by grandparents
- Real/imaginary stories, e.g., The Elves and the Shoemaker, Cinderella, The Emperor's New Clothes, Florence Nightingale

**Geography**
- Communication
- Special clothes for jobs
- Where clothes are made (UK locations)
- Transportation of clothes and raw materials
- Where raw materials come from i.e., cotton, wool, silk, nylon
- Clothes worn by people in different countries
- Use of maps/globes to locate places

**Creative**
- Fabric painting
- Sewing, weaving
- Colour mixing; tie/dye
- Material collage
- Music/movement
- Pencil/ink work
- Spinning/weaving demonstrations
- Lace-making (visitor)
- Costume/period dolls

# Example B5

| Medium-term planning | |
| --- | --- |
| **Topic - clothes** | |
| **Date:** 7 January - 21 February | |

| | **Knowledge statements** | **Resources** |
| --- | --- | --- |
| **Week 1** | We wear clothes to keep us warm, cool, dry, safe. | Books:<br>History of Clothes<br>Cinderella<br>Alex's New Clothes<br>Emperor's New Clothes<br>Joseph and the Amazing Technicolour Dreamcoat |
| **Week 2** | Clothes are made of different materials which have different properties. | |
| **Week 3** | Some materials are natural. Some are man-made. | Photographs/posters:<br>Ethnic costumes<br>Victorian wear<br>Grandparents' clothes<br>Clothes from the 1950s |
| **Week 4** | We need new clothes as we grow. We are all different in size. | Costume dolls |
| **Week 5** | Clothes can tell others what jobs people do (uniforms). | Uniforms<br><br>Ethnic costumes |
| **Week 6** | We wear different clothes for different functions. | Different materials |
| **Week 7** | Clothes can tell others where we come from; traditional clothes/costumes. | Thread, wool for sewing/weaving<br><br>Contact visitor |

# Example B6

| Medium-term planning | | | | | | | |
|---|---|---|---|---|---|---|---|
| **Checklist - History** | | | | | | | |
| | Autumn term | | | Spring term | | Summer term | |
| | *1* | *2* | | *1* | *2* | *1* | *2* |
| | Homes | Light | | Clothes | | | |
| **AT1 Knowledge and understanding** | | | | | | | |
| *1a Place events in sequence in a story about the past.* | ✓ | ✓ | | ✓ | | | |
| *1b Give reasons for their own actions.* | ✓ | | | ✓ | | | |
| *2a Place objects in chronological order.* | | | | ✓ | | | |
| *2b Suggest reasons why in the past people acted as they did.* | ✓ | ✓ | | ✓ | | | |
| *2c Identify differences between past/present.* | ✓ | ✓ | | ✓ | | | |
| *3a Describe changes over time.* | ✓ | ✓ | | ✓ | | | |
| *3b Give reasons for an historical event.* | ✓ | ✓ | | | | | |
| *3c Identify difference between times in the past.* | | | | | | | |
| **AT2 Interpretation of history** | | | | | | | |
| *1a Understand stories, may be real/fiction.* | ✓ | ✓ | | ✓ | | | |
| *2a Different stories have different versions.* | | ✓ | | ✓ | | | |
| *3a Distinguish between fact/fiction point of view.* | | ✓ | | | | | |
| **AT3 Use of historical sources** | | | | | | | |
| *1a Communicate information acquired from an historical source.* | ✓ | ✓ | | ✓ | | | |
| *2a Recognise historical sources. Stimulate questions about the past.* | ✓ | | | ✓ | | | |
| *3a Make deductions from historical sources.* | ✓ | | | ✓ | | | |
| | | | | | | | |
| | | | | | | | |

# Example B7

## Short-term plan - weekly short-term planning proforma

### Knowledge statement(s) - Clothes can tell us what job people do

Week commencing: 3 February

Key concepts: Similarities and differences (also Family and Friends theme for class assembly)

| Area of curriculum | Maths | English (language) | Science | Technology | History/ Geography | Art | Music | Cross- curricular themes/ issues |
|---|---|---|---|---|---|---|---|---|
| A C T I V I T I E S | Shopping for clothes - money 1p - £1 change. Logic (clothes and not clothes). Carroll diagram. Multiplication. Place value. Data handing (red group only). Computation (green group only). | 1. For assembly write 'Mum/Dad' and a friend - talk about families. 2. Phonic work - initial sounds and blends. 3. Write about a person who wears a uniform (guess who). 4. Spelling test. 5. Handwriting - word families. | 1. Investigation with sandpaper - how strong/ hardwearing, etc., are certain materials? 2. Sort materials into groups using own criteria. 3. Continue care of hamster and class plants. | School uniform designs Role-play in costume corner Folio - Grannie's garden Construction toys | Geography: Origin of shoes Class graph Monitor weather (temperature)<br><br>History: Family tree for assembly Story of the Elves and the shoemaker | Clay shoes - continue as last week. Pencil drawing of shoes. Paint picture of Mum/Dad for assembly.<br><br>**PE**<br>Large apparatus (Monday) Theme of curling and stretching Assembly practice | What the clothes factory sounded like - design music. Shoemaker's song.<br><br>**RE**<br>Joseph as last week (NO TIME) and long term plan | Uniforms Compare clothes worn by people in other countries - why?<br><br>Care of family and friends (assembly theme) |
| ATs | AT1/1a, 1b, 1c; 2a, 2b<br>AT2/1a, 1b; 2a, 2b<br>AT5/1a (2a, 3b red group) | AT1/1a, 1b, 1c; 2a, 2b, 2c, 2d, 2e<br>AT2/1a, 1b, 1c, 1d; 2a, 2b, 2c, 2d<br>AT3/1a; 2a, 2b, 2c, 2d; 3a<br>AT4/1a, 1b, 1c; 2a, 2b, 2c, 2d; 3a<br>AT5/1a, 2a, 2b | AT1<br>AT2/2a<br>AT3/1a, 2a | AT2/1a, 2a<br>AT3/1a, 2c<br>AT4/1a, 1b<br>AT5 Levels 1 and 2 | Geography: AT2/1b AT3/2a, 3a AT5/1a<br>History: AT1, 2, 3 | Art: AT1/1a, 1b, 1c, 1d<br><br>PE: Key Stage 1, a, b | Music: AT1/1b, 1c, 1d | |
| | **Attitudes:** Tolerance Empathy | | | | **Assessment:**<br>- Reading - assess strategies (SAT level)<br>- Shopping - money continued - add coins, 1p - £1<br>- Using dictionary<br>- Computation levels<br>- Ability to measure in cm<br>- Logic work (Carroll diagrams) | | | |

# Example B8

| Weekly, short-term planning target sheet |
|---|
| **Science** |
| **Knowledge statement: 'Clothes can tell us what job people do'** |

**Attainment target 1  Scientific investigation**

Strands (i), (ii) and (iii) as appropriate.

**Attainment target 3  Materials and their properties**

Programme of Study (Key Stage 1) Strand (i) The properties, classification and structure of materials.

'Pupils should collect and find similarities and differences between a variety of everyday materials.... They should explore the properties of these materials referring for example, to their *shape, colour and texture...*

1a  be able to describe the simple properties of familiar materials

2a  be able to group materials according to observable features'

*Children should describe materials as rough, smooth, soft, light, and group them on the basis of these properties and colour.*

# Example C

| Long-term plan | | | |
| --- | --- | --- | --- |
| **Term**<br><br>**Year** | **Autumn term** | **Spring term** | **Summer term** |
| **3** | OURSELVES<br>Human health Sc 2(i)<br>Electricity and safe usage Sc 4(i)<br>Own environment<br>Home/school G 1, 2, 4, 5 | MOVEMENT<br>Materials - floating and sinking Sc 3(i), 4(iii)<br>Settlements G 4<br>Invaders and settlers H CSU 1 H 1, 2, 3 | FORCES<br>Forces and energy Sc 4(ii), 4(iii)<br>Volcanoes and earthquakes G 3<br>Ancient Greece H CSU 5 H 1, 2, 3 |
| **4** | GROWTH<br>Life processes (plants/animals) Sc 2(i)<br>Soil/landuse (farming) G 3, 4 | WEATHER<br>Weather and weathering Sc 3(iv) G 3<br>Atmosphere, earth and planets Sc 4(v) | CHANGE<br>Melting and cooling Sc 3(iii)<br>Rivers G 1, 2, 3, 5<br>Tudors and Stuarts H CSU 2 H 1, 2, 3<br>Contrast area - Ilam, Derbys. |
| **5** | BUILDINGS<br>Materials and structures Sc 3(i), 3(iii), 2(iii)<br>Using the Earth's resources G 1, 4<br>Egyptians H 1, 2, 3 | COMMUNICATION<br>Movement Sc 2(i)<br>Human communication Sc 2(i)<br>Electricity, light and sound Sc 4(i), (iv), (v)<br>Transport networks G 1, 4<br>Victorians H CSU 3 H 1, 2, 3 | LOCAL<br>Local geography G 1, 2, 3, 4, 5<br><br>Mini-projects:<br>Acids/alkalis Sc 3(i)<br>Separating mixtures Sc 3(i)<br>Chemical reactions Sc 3(iii) |
| **6** | OUR WORLD<br>Energy; environmental issues Sc 2(iii), (iv)<br>EC country: Greece G 1, 2<br>Britain since 1930 H CSU 4 H 1, 2, 3 | EXPLORATION<br>Earth, atmosphere<br>Weather station Sc 3(iv), 4(v)<br>Home region G 1-5<br>Exploration and encounters H CSU 6, H 1, 2, 3 | ENVIRONMENTS<br>Life processes (animal, human and plant) Sc 2(i)<br>Improving the environment G 4<br>Contrast Fairbourne Sc 2(iii) G 1, 2, 3, 4, 5 |

# Example D

## Long-term plan

| TERM / YEAR | Autumn term | | Spring term | | Summer term | |
|---|---|---|---|---|---|---|
| **1** | Me, my home and my journey to school Sc 1, 2, 3, 4; G 1, 2, 3, 4 | Materials and packaging Sc 1, 3; G 4, 5 H 1 | Toys, old and new Sc 1, 4 H 1, 2, 3 | Water Sc 1, 2, 3 G 3; H 1, 3 | Local study Sc 1, 2, 3; G 1, 2, 3, 4, 5 H 1, 3 | Holidays Sc 1, 4; G 1, 2 H 1 |
| | **Earth, weather and seasons Sc 1, 3, 4; G 3** | | | | **Earth, weather and seasons Sc 1, 3, 4; G 3** | |
| **2** | Autumn and harvest Sc 1, 2; G 4, 5 H 1, 3 | Sound and music Sc 1, 4 H 1, 3 | Energy past and present Sc 1, 4; G 4, 5 H 1, 3 | Keeping healthy Sc 1, 2 H 1, 3 | SATs | Local study Sc 1, 2, 3; G 1, 2, 3, 4, 5 H 1, 3 |
| | | | **Earth, weather and seasons Sc 1, 3, 4; G 3** | | **Earth, weather and seasons Sc 1, 3, 4; G 3** | |
| **3** | Energy and forces Sc 1, 3, 4 | Light and sound (festivals) Sc 1, 4 | How people live Sc 1, 2, 3, 4, 5 G 1, 2, 3, 4, 5 T 1, 2, 3, 4 | Living things and growth Sc 1, 2 | Buildings through the ages H SSU C Ancient Egypt H CSU 5 Ancient Greece H SSU A Houses and places of worship Sc 1, 3, 4; H 1, 2, 3 T 1, 2, 3, 4 | Local study Sc 1, 2, 3 G 1, 2, 3, 4, 5 H 1, 3 |
| **4** | Invaders and settlers; Romans, Anglo-Saxons and Vikings H CSU 1 Invaders and settlers Sc 1, 3, 4; G 1, 2, 4 H 1, 3; T 2, 3 | Materials around us Sc 1, 3 | Earth, weather and seasons Sc 1, 3 G 3 | Ourselves and our bodies Sc 1, 2 | Tudors and Stuarts H CSU 2 Tudors and Stuarts Sc 1, 4; H 1, 2, 3 T 2, 3, 4 | Improving the environment Sc 1, 2 G 1, 2, 5 H 1, 3 |
| **5** | Food and farming H SSU A Food and farming Sc 1, 2, 3 G 1, 2, 3, 4, 5 H 1, 2, 3 | Exploring H CSU 6 Exploration and encounters 1450-1550 H SSU A Ships and seafarers Sc 1, 4; G 1, 2, 4 H 1, 2, 3 | Change Sc 1, 3 G 1, 2, 3, 4, 5 H 1, 2, 3 | Our home region G 1, 2, 3, 4, 5 | Victorian Britain H CSU 3 Victorian Britain SSU A Domestic life Sc 1, 4 G 4 H 1, 2, 3 | Local study Sc 1, 2, 3 G 1, 2, 3, 4, 5 H 1, 3 |
| **6** | Britain then and now H CSU 4 Britain since 1930; H SSU B; G 1, 4, 5; H 1, 3 | On the move Sc 1, 2, 4; T 2, 3, 4 G 1, 2, 3, 4, 5 | Earth, sky and space Sc 1, 3, 4 G 3 | My body and health Sc 1, 2 | SATs | Airports, docks and roads Sc 1, 4; G 1, 2, 3, 4, 5 H 1 |
| | | | **Earth, weather and seasons Sc 1, 3, 4; G 3** | | | |

# CHAPTER 3

# Local study

The study of the local environment should be an essential part of every child's experience. It is appropriate, therefore, that the first project in this book focuses on children's familiar surroundings. This chapter describes a study of the local environment at Key Stages 1 and 2. There is a real opportunity within the project to develop knowledge and understanding, as well as intellectual and practical skills. Children could begin by investigating their own school and school grounds. They can then build on this experience by examining a range of other local habitats, for example, a nearby pond or river. The Science National Curriculum states clearly that children should be introduced to important ideas such as 'plants are the ultimate source of all food in the living world'. Aspects of the local environment which have been affected by human activity such as farming or industry can be considered.

The Geography National Curriculum states that opportunities should be created to compare the children's local environment with one in an economically developing country. Examples included in this chapter are drawn from the Indian subcontinent. Children can identify similarities and differences between these localities, for example, their own school and a school in India, their own leisure pursuits and related resources and leisure pursuits of Indian children. Historical perspectives include the concept of change and an awareness and understanding of the characteristics of past societies. These will be developed through learning about the history of the children's own school and a study of a Victorian school day.

# BACKGROUND

Work should be linked to children's own experiences and interests and should lead to investigations based on both fieldwork and classroom activities. Skills will include questioning, making observations, hypothesising, collecting and analysing data and drawing conclusions. The use of maps and fieldwork techniques are all important in a study of this kind.

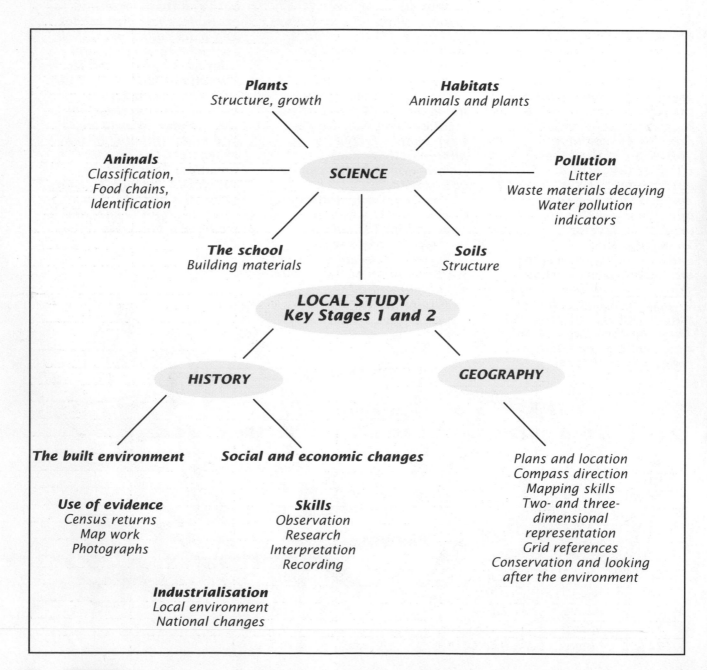

**Plants**
*Structure, growth*

**Habitats**
*Animals and plants*

**Animals**
*Classification,*
*Food chains,*
*Identification*

**SCIENCE**

**Pollution**
*Litter*
*Waste materials decaying*
*Water pollution*
*indicators*

**The school**
*Building materials*

**Soils**
*Structure*

**LOCAL STUDY**
**Key Stages 1 and 2**

**HISTORY**

**GEOGRAPHY**

**The built environment**

**Social and economic changes**

**Use of evidence**
*Census returns*
*Map work*
*Photographs*

**Skills**
*Observation*
*Research*
*Interpretation*
*Recording*

*Plans and location*
*Compass direction*
*Mapping skills*
*Two- and three-*
*dimensional*
*representation*
*Grid references*
*Conservation and looking*
*after the environment*

**Industrialisation**
*Local environment*
*National changes*

| Activity | Curriculum area | ATTAINMENT TARGET AND LEVEL | | | | |
|---|---|---|---|---|---|---|
| | | AT1 | AT2 | AT3 | AT4 | AT5 |
| 1 | Science | | | 3b | | |
| 2 | Science | | PoS(iv) | | | |
| 3 | Science | 2a, 2b | 2a | | | |
| 4 | Science | | 1a, 2b | | | |
| 5 | Science | | 1b, 2c | | | |
| 6 | Science | | 2d | | | |
| 7 | Science | | | 4e | | |
| 8 | Science | | 2c, 3b | | | |
| 9 | Science | | 2a, 3a | | | |
| 10 | Science | | 2b, 4b | | | |
| 11 | Science | | | 5b | | |
| 12 | Science | | 2c, 3b, 5c | | | |
| 13 | Science | 3a,4a,4b,5a,5b,5c | 5d | | | |
| 14 | Science | | 2b, 4b | | | |
| 15 | Geography | 1b, 2b | | | | |
| 16 | Geography | 1a, 1b, 2b | | | | |
| 17 | Geography | 1a,1b,2c,2e,3b | 1a, 1b, 2b | | 1a, 1c, 2c | |
| 18 | Geography | 1b, 2a | | | | 1a,1b,2b,2c,3b |
| 19 | Geography | 1a, 2a, 2b, 2c | 1d | 1a, 2b | 1b, 2b | 1a, 2a, 2b |
| 20 | Geography | 2a, 2e | 1d, 2c, 2d | 3a | 1a, 2a, 4a | 1b, 2a |
| 21 | Geography | 2a, 2e | 1d,2c,2d,3a,3b | | | 1b |
| 22 | Geography | 2a | 1d, 2c, 2d | 3a | | 1b |
| 23 | Geography | 1b, 2e | 1b, 1d, 1e, 2c, 3a, 3d | 3a | 1c, 2c | |
| 24 | Geography | | 2c, 4b, 4e | 1a, 2a, 2b, 3a, 3b, 4b, 4c | 3d, 4e | 2a, 2b, 2c, 3a, 4b, 4c |
| 25 | Geography | 3b, 3c, 3d, 4c, 5a, 5c | 3b, 3c | | 4a, 4b | |
| 26 | Geography | 4b, 5a, 5c | | 3c | | |
| 27 | Geography | 4c, 5a, 5c | 3c, 3e, 3f, 4b | | 3d, 4e, 5c, 5e | |
| 28 | Geography | 5a, 5b, 5c | 4c, 5b | | 4c, 4e, 5d | 4b |
| 29 | History | 2a, 2c | | 1, 2, 3 | | |
| 30 | History | 2a, 2c | | 1, 2, 3 | | |
| 31 | History | 2c | | 1, 2, 3 | | |
| 32 | History | 2c | | 1, 2 | | |
| 33 | History | 2c, 3a, 3c | | 1, 2, 3 | | |
| 34 | History | 2c,3a,3b,3c,4a | | | | |
| 35 | History | 2a,2c,3a,3c,4a | | 1, 2, 3 | | |
| 36 | History | 2c, 3a, 3c, 4a | | 2, 3 | | |
| 37 | History | 2b, 2c, 3a, 3b. 3c, 4a, 4b | | 3, 4 | | |
| 38 | History | 2c,3a,3c,4a,4b | | 2, 3, 4 | | |
| 39 | History | 3a, 3c, 4a | | | | |
| 40 | History | 3a, 3c, 4a, 4c | | 5 | | |
| 41 | History | 3b,3c,4a,4b,5c | | 3, 4, 5 | | |
| 42 | History | 3a,3b,3c,4a,5b | | 3, 4, 5 | | |

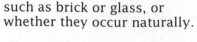
# Science: Key Stage 1

## 1. My school – what is it made of?

### Group size
Pairs, small groups, the whole class.

### What you need
Paper, pencils, crayons, clipboards.

### What to do
A study of different building materials can begin usefully with an investigation of the children's own environment – their school building. Ask the children to examine the building materials used in their school. Discuss what sort of materials they might find. They can begin with a survey of their own classroom and then go outside the school looking for brickwork, wood, plaster, concrete, tiles, slates, glass, metal and so on. The children could record the results in a number of ways. They could draw simple pictures of the outside of their school showing the different materials used, for example, roof – tiles; walls – bricks; windows – glass and so on. Alternatively, they could make a list of the types of materials they have seen and where they were used in the buildings.

Encourage the children to look for parts of the building which are painted. Why do we paint these parts?

Ask the children to consider whether the various types of materials are manufactured such as brick or glass, or whether they occur naturally.

### Content
A wide range of building materials will be evident in the school. Wood and slate are naturally occurring materials but glass and plastic are manufactured. Wood is painted to protect it from the weather.

*Sc AT3/3b*

## 2. Plants, the source of all food

### Group size
Individuals and the whole class.

### What you need
Pictures of different plant foods, pictures of animals eating plants – e.g animals such as rabbit, cow, gorilla, panda, giraffe, elephant.

### What to do
Talk to the children about what they eat and their favourite foods. Discuss the feeding habits of other animals and show the children the pictures. Explain that some animals eat plants while others eat animals. Select an animal such as a lion and establish that it eats other animals, for instance, antelopes. Try to get the children to understand, perhaps through a series of drawings, that the antelopes

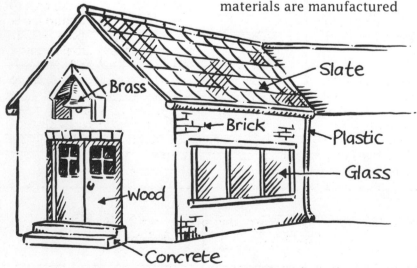

Brass
Slate
Brick
Plastic
Glass
Wood
Concrete

eat plants and that therefore the lion gets its food from plants. This is a very difficult concept but it might be made more interesting and concrete by challenging the children to name a foodstuff that does not ultimately come from a plant. For example, if they said 'chicken', you would point out that chickens eat grain and that grain comes from wheat or barley.

## Content

Plants are the ultimate source of all food in the living world. Without them, there would be no animals and no life. However, the children might need to be reassured that this is not an immediate danger, but that everyone on Earth should play their part in planting and looking after plants.

The concept of all food being derived from plants is a difficult one, and, having been introduced here, should be considered again in Key Stage 2 at level 4.

## Further activity

Children showing an interest in the feeding relationships of animals could be introduced to food chains at this stage, although this concept does not appear in the statements of attainment until Key Stage Two. Ask the children to observe a rosebush or similar plant that is being attacked by aphids, ladybirds, ants and so on. They should see birds visiting the plant and feeding on the insects. Introduce

children to the accepted way of representing food chains, as in Figure 1.

*Sc AT2/PoS (iv)*

# 3. What do they need?

## Group size
Small groups.

## What you need
Fifteen yoghurt pots, plastic teacups or purchased plant pots, soil or compost, germinated cress, pea or cereal seeds grown in a seed tray.

## What to do
Ask the children if they have grown any plants at home. Ask them how they grew them and raise the question of what conditions the young plants

might need to grow well. The children might suggest that soil or compost, light, warmth and water are needed for growth.

Show the children the young germinated plants growing in a seed tray. Inform the children that you are going to continue to grow them with one of the special ingredients/conditions missing. Ask how you can prevent the plants getting a) water, b)soil, c)warmth and d) light. Divide the yoghurt pots into five groups (three pots in each group) and label them a)no water, b)no soil, etc. Ensure that groups a)–d) have the other three conditions (see next page*) and that a further group of pots is given all the conditions; this is the 'control' group.

rose bush ⟶ greenfly (aphid) ⟶ ladybird ⟶ blue tit
        **fed on by**             **fed on by**        **fed on by**

*Figure 1*

Transplant the seedlings from the tray. Place the pots that are getting no warmth in a fridge and place all the other pots, separated and clearly labelled in a light, warm environment in the classroom. Ensure that they are not too hot and that those requiring water do not dry out through a lack of it. Ask the children to predict which seeds will grow (germinate) and which plants will continue to grow in a healthy manner. Leave the plants for a few days and then ask the children to record and talk about their findings. Look at the pots again a few days later.

## Content

Plants need certain conditions to sustain life. Most plants require water, warmth and light to grow, though soil is not required in the short term.

The children might ask questions, suggest ideas and make predictions. They might also use their observations to support conclusions and compare what they have observed with what they expected.

*The teacher should be aware that the pots in the fridge are actually deprived of warmth and light, and so the test is not strictly fair. This could be avoided by leaving the fridge door ajar.

## Safety

The children should wash their hands after handling soil and compost.

*Sc AT1/2a,2b*
*AT2/2a*

# 4. Looking at plants 1

## Group size

Pairs, small groups.

## What you need

Large sheets of paper (A3 size), pencils, crayons, trowels, absorbent paper.

## What to do

Accompany the children into the school grounds. Let one child from each group dig up one common plant – a weed or a small bedding plant grown for the purpose. Emphasise

care for the environment and for less common plants. Bring the plants back into the classroom and wash the roots carefully. Lay the plants out individually on absorbent paper.

Ask the children to choose a plant to draw – one plant for each group or pair. Discuss with the children what they have noticed about the plants, for example, colour, scent, shape, stem, leaves, roots, flower, petals, hairy or non-hairy. The children should draw large pictures of the plants. Observations can be discussed as they draw. Identify common features of stem, roots and leaves. Discuss differences among plants, colour of flowers, shape of petals, non-hairy or hairy stem. The children should label the plant parts such as stem, roots, flower, leaves.

## Content

A typical flowering plant is divided into two main parts – the root system and the shoot system. There is usually a main root which grows straight downwards into the soil. Lateral roots branch from the main root. The shoot system consists of a stem (sometimes branched), leaves, buds and flowers. Leaves may be simple (a single blade) or compound (divided into leaflets). Petals of the flowers are usually brightly coloured to attract insects for the purpose of pollination.

## Note

Wild plants should not be dug up in situations where damage to the habitat may result. It is an offence to dig up plants without permission from the landowner.

*Sc AT2/1a,2b*

# 5. Minibeast search

### Group size
The whole class, small groups.

### What you need
Paper, pencils, clipboards, plastic teaspoons, pooters, collecting jars, trowels.

### What to do
Discuss with the children where in the school grounds they might find minibeasts. Talk about different minibeasts, for example, snails, slugs, woodlice, aphids (greenflies), caterpillars, spiders, ants and earthworms. Do the children know where these animals live? Take the children into the school grounds to search for some of these. They could look under stones, near vegetation, in damp places such as under rotting wood, in the soil, on the grass, near a hedge or a wall, in leaf litter. Using a grid similar to the one shown in the illustration, the children can record their findings.

Back in the classroom, discuss with the children the minibeasts they saw and the places where they found them. The children could study some of the minibeasts further, either by observing the animals in their natural habitats or by collecting specimens using pooters, teaspoons and collecting jars. Great care should be taken with the animals, which must be returned to their natural habitat after the study.

### Content
The children will learn to recognise different animals in their natural habitats. They will associate certain types of

animals with particular habitats, for example, woodlice under stones, aphids feeding off the green parts of plants. The children will also gain experience of recording their observations.

*Sc AT2/1b,2c*

# 6. Throwing rubbish away

### Group size
Small groups.

### What you need
A collection of waste items of different types such as soft drink cans, sweet wrappers, plastic and glass bottles, different sorts of paper, polystyrene packaging, vegetable peelings, disposable gloves, a diary or recording sheet, a pencil, a trowel, flags for marking the position of the buried rubbish.

### What to do
Ask the children to think about the sorts of rubbish which they throw away in a day. They could talk to their families to find out what rubbish is thrown away at home everyday. What happens to it? Is it all put in the dustbin or is

some of it saved and put in special collection bins such as bottle banks?

Ask the children to help collect samples of rubbish. They could bring into school items which would have been thrown away at home. Stress the importance of hygiene – items such as soft drinks cans or fruit juice cartons should be rinsed thoroughly and vegetable peelings should be wrapped carefully. Explain to the children that they are going to bury some of the rubbish in the school grounds, in order to see what happens to it over a period of time. They will keep a diary to record their findings.

Wearing disposable gloves, the children should bury some of the rubbish in a suitable place in the school grounds and mark the position and name of each item with a flag. Ask them what they think will happen to each item after it is buried. They can keep digging the rubbish up over a period of time, once a week for several months to see whether any changes have taken place. They should record their findings in a diary.

### Content

Some waste materials decay naturally over a period of time. These items are biodegradable – they can be broken down by biological means, by bacterial action. Plastics are made from oil and are not biodegradable.

### Safety

Great care must be taken when handling rubbish. Children must wear disposable gloves and wash their hands thoroughly afterwards. Items made of glass must be handled especially carefully.

*Sc AT2/2d*

# Science: Key Stage 2

## 7. Looking at soil

### Group size

Small groups or pairs.

### What you need

Samples of soil of different types or from different locations, old newspapers, sieves (fine and wide mesh), magnifiers, scales, jam-jars with lids, rulers.

### What to do

The children will make observations of the soil samples. Tell the children to find out as much as they can about the soil by looking at and feeling the soil samples. Each soil sample should be tipped on to an old newspaper (separate papers for each sample). Ask the children to examine each soil sample carefully.

- What colour is it?
- Does it feel wet or dry?
- Are there any stones in the soil?
- Are they large or small stones?
- Are there any plants or animals? If so, are these alive or dead?

Tell the children to use a magnifier to look more closely at the soils. Are the particles of the soil stuck together? Can the children see what shape these particles are? Give the children the following instructions:

Spread the soil sample out on the newspaper and break up any large lumps. Pick out all the large stones and weigh them. Shake the soil through the wide-mesh sieve on to the newspaper. Weigh the soil which is still in the sieve. This is called coarse soil. Collect the soil which came through the wide-mesh sieve and shake it through the fine-mesh sieve on to a newspaper. The soil that remains in this sieve is called medium soil. Weigh this soil. Weigh the fine soil that has passed through both sieves. Are there equal weights of each type of soil particles?

### Content

Soil is the outermost layer of the planet on which we live. It is the solid substance in which plants grow. Soil has been formed by the weathering of rocks over many thousands of years. The type of underlying rock influences the type of soil produced. Soil is composed of soil particles of different sizes, water, air, minerals, living organisms and decayed plant and animal material called humus.

### Further activity

The children could investigate types of soil particles in different samples of soil (e.g. clay soil, sandy soil) by putting soil samples into jam jars, adding water, shaking and making observations as the soil settles. How many different layers are there? Where are the largest/smallest particles? What is the depth/colour of each layer? Are any particles floating?

### Safety

Children must wash their hands thoroughly after handling soil. Make sure that they do not put their fingers in their mouths during this activity.

*Sc AT3/4e*

# 8. Looking at plants 2

## Group size
Small groups.

## What you need
A hoop from PE store, paper, pencils, rulers, clipboards.

## What to do
Tell the children to investigate two areas of the school playing field, for instance, a well-used, trampled area around the goalpost and a lesser-used area nearer the edge of the field or by a hedge. Tell the children to place the hoop on the grass in each chosen area and to make a survey of the plants (excluding grasses) within the hoop. Ask the following questions:
• How many plants are there which are not grasses?
• Is there a big difference in the number of plants found in the two areas?
• Are there plants growing in shady areas?
• Are there plants of different heights?
• Did you find some plants in one area but not in the other?
• Does the presence of one type of plant indicate trampling (a trampling indicator)?

Ask the children to record the presence or absence of the most common plants, such as dandelions, daisies, buttercups, groundsel, plantains or mosses, using a grid like the one shown in the illustration. Encourage the children to discuss their findings. Each group could make a small presentation to the whole class.

## Content
Plants adapt to different environmental conditions. Some plants such as plantain have tough leaves which lie flat on the ground and can tolerate being trampled upon. Other plants, like buttercups, have leaves raised above the ground and are susceptible to trampling.

## Further activity
Using a plan of the study area, the children could mark where the trampling indicator plant is found. What does this tell them about the intensity of use of the playing field?

Sc AT2/2c,3b

# 9. Going down

## Group size
Small groups, the whole class.

## What you need
A large jar or clear-sided aquarium, coarse soil and fine soil, sand, leaf litter, gravel, a trowel or a spade, plastic containers with lids, hand lenses.

## What to do
Discuss with the children how important earthworms are in maintaining a healthy soil. Take the children outside into the school grounds and in an appropriate location dig up some earthworms. Place a number of the worms with a quantity of soil in a container and return to the classroom to examine the animals in more detail.

The children should work in small groups to study the worms. They should observe external features of the worms, noting the segments and the slimy bodies. Hand lenses can be used to observe the animals more closely.

It is a good idea to make a wormery to demonstrate how important worms are in moving soil around. This is easily made by filling a large jar or aquarium with layers of soil and sand of different-sized particles, and different colour and consistency. Do not pack the soil and sand down too tightly as aeration is important. Introduce approximately six worms to the wormery. Once the worms have burrowed into the wormery, cover the surface with a light layer of leaf litter, for example, grass cuttings. Keep the wormery moist but do not overwater. The children should observe the wormery over a period of about a month to see any changes that have taken place due to the activity of the worms. They could make drawings of the wormery and should discuss the process which they observe. Make sure the worms are returned to their natural habitat after the observation is completed.

## Content
The worms 'eat' the soil which passes through their digestive system. This serves to mix and aerate the soil, while the worms' digestive process breaks down organic material and helps to release nutrients into the soil. Worms pull freshly cut leaves down into the soil and eat them. The burrowing motion of the worms also helps aeration and mixing of the soil.

*Sc AT2/2a,3a*

# 10. Grouping animals

## Group size
Pairs or small groups.

## What you need
Pond animals on a white tray, plastic teaspoons, small transparent containers or Petri dish lids, hand lenses, magnifiers or a stereoscope microscope, pond animal books, simple keys of plants and animals such as photocopiable page 180.

## What to do
Present the children with the tray of pond animals, asking them to transfer the animals carefully using plastic teaspoons. Ask the children to identify the animals using observable features and to assign them to the major groups, with the help of photocopiable page 180.

## Content
The children will be able to identify numerous pond

animals and assign snails to the group of animals called the molluscs, dragonfly larvae to the group called the arthropods (jointed-legged animals) and to the subgroup called insects. They would also be able to allocate the freshwater shrimp and the water louse to the group called the arthropods and to the subgroup called the crustaceans.

## Safety
Children should be reminded to treat all living organisms with care and respect. They should wash their hands after being in contact with pond water and should not put their fingers in their mouths.

*Sc. AT2/2b,4b*

# 11. Cleaning up the water

## Group size
Pairs.

## What you need
Water from a stream or river which is obviously dirty. a filter funnel, filter or blotting paper, a yoghurt pot or a clear plastic container, gravel of different sizes, sand, cotton wool.

## What to do
Talk to the children about tap water, where it comes from and what happens to it before it is safe to drink. Show them the dirty water collected from a local stream and ask how it might be cleaned. This investigation could be approached at three levels of difficulty. First, and least demanding, the equipment could be given to the children; second, the equipment could

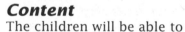

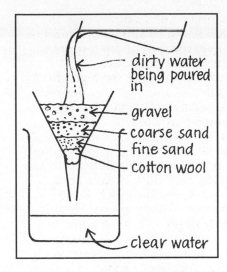

dirty water being poured in

gravel
coarse sand
fine sand
cotton wool

clear water

be shown to the children who will then decide how best to use it, or third, and most demanding, the children themselves devise how they might clean the water.

## Content

Liquids containing solid particles in suspension (dirty water) may be cleaned by using the technique of filtering. This is a technique for separating solids from liquids. Two methods may be usefully employed – a filter funnel containing filter or blotting paper, or a filter funnel containing sand at the base and progressively larger particles of gravel at the top. In the first method the relatively larger particles cannot get through the filter and are therefore separated and collected in the filter paper. In the second method, the larger particles are filtered out by the large pieces of gravel and the smaller particles are collected in the sand.

## Safety

It must be emphasised that, though the filtered water looks clear, it is unfit to drink as it has not been treated with

chemicals to kill bacteria. Children should wash their hands after the investigation and should not place their fingers in their mouth or taste the water they are using.

*Sc AT3/5b*

# 12. Pollution indicators

## Group size
Pairs.

## What you need
Recording sheets, pencils, lichens from another locality or data on the type and numbers of lichen found in another locality. It would be helpful if the specimens or secondary source material (pictures and/or data) came from a location with different pollution characteristics.

## What to do
Let the children walk around the school grounds, churchyard, woods or other suitable location where lichens might be found. Lichens grow

on paving stones, roof tiles, the tops of walls or on the branches or trunks of trees. Ask the children to identify the lichens as the crusty, leafy or shrubby type. Which type of lichen did they find most frequently? Did they fail to find certain types of lichen? Inform them of the relative air pollution in the two localities and ask them what air pollution might do to the lichens.

## Content
Lichens are good indicators of air pollution in a locality. They are made up of two plants, an alga and a fungus which live together for mutual benefit. The alga provides the food by photosynthesis and the fungus provides moisture and minerals. Some lichens are very sensitive to the amount of sulphur dioxide in the air.
• Crusty lichens look like grey-

green crazy paving and are found on walls, stones, roofs and trees. If the children find *only* crusty lichens it means that the air is fairly polluted.
• Leafy lichens look like flat rosettes of thin leaves and are found on walls, stones, roofs and trees. They can tolerate some air pollution.
• Shrubby lichens look like greenish-grey branches and are found on the branches and trunks of trees. These lichens will usually only grow where there is no air pollution.

*Sc AT2/2c,3b,5c*

# 13. Why do things decay?

## Group size
The whole class and small groups.

## What you need
Pieces of apple and potato, apple and potato peelings, lettuce leaves, bread, clear plastic containers, clear food wrapping, a fridge.

## What to do
Talk to the children about the process of decay. Do they know what factors might be responsible for decay? They might suggest that a high temperature is necessary for decay or predict that the higher the temperature the quicker the decay, or the greater the extent of decay. Other variables might be suggested such as 'moisture' and 'air'(compactness); some children may already know about the role of microbes in decay.

Show the children the vegetable matter to be investigated. Divide the class into groups of three or four and ask them to plan an investigation to discover the effect of one of the variables on decay. Ensure that the children write down how they are going to carry out the investigation bearing in mind the following points:
• What they are trying to find out?;
• What they must keep the same (control);
• What they must vary/change?

The children will need to set up a minimum of two pots, each containing vegetable matter. If they are looking at the effect of temperature, it would be useful to have one container in the fridge at 4°C and another at room temperature (18–20°C). For safety reasons (transfer of fungal spores), cover the containers with clear food wrapping. Ask the children to record the results over a period of ten days, using a table such as the one below:

|  | In the fridge (4°C) | At room temperature (18–20°C) |
|---|---|---|
| Day 1 |  |  |
| Day 2 |  |  |
| Day 3 |  |  |
|  |  |  |

Discuss the results with the children on a regular basis and at the end of the investigation.

## Content
A relatively warm temperature, air (little compactness), moisture and microbes are required for living matter to decay. The first three conditions are necessary for microbes to live, reproduce and to break down materials.

Children will be encouraged to ask questions, suggest ideas and make predictions/hypotheses in a form which can be investigated. Their prior knowledge and scientific understanding will determine the level of achievement. They will also have the opportunity to carry out a fair test. Children will evaluate the validity of their conclusions by considering different interpretations of their experimental evidence. For instance, if they were considering the variable of temperature they might come to the conclusion that vegetable matter decays well at 20°C but poorly on the radiator (say, 40°C). Some children may realise, particularly if they did not cover the container, that moisture has reduced and a fair test has not been achieved. The variable of moisture may be easily tested but that of air (compactness) is more difficult. However, it may be achieved by compressing vegetable matter with a 1kg weight. The effect of microbes is difficult to investigate unless sterile conditions are achieved. Cutting fruit and immediately putting the pieces in a clean, covered container may achieve the 'required' result but there are so many microbes naturally in the air and on the surface of fruit that the obtained results may be difficult to interpret. However, this will lead to an interesting discussion on 'microbes all around us'.

## Safety
The containers should be covered with clear food wrapping or another suitable covering to prevent unnecessary escape of fungal spores which may be harmful to asthmatics. Do not let the children uncover the containers while recording the results.

*Sc AT1/3a,4a,4b,5a,5b,5c*
*Sc AT2/5d*

# 14. Leafy differences

## Group size
Small groups.

## What you need
A collection of different types of leaves, pencils, paper.

## What to do
Tell the children to lay the leaves out on the table and to look at them carefully. Ask them to sort the leaves into two different groups – such as leaves with leaflets and leaves which are entire (without leaflets). Through discussion, introduce the idea of an identification key. The children can experiment with their own groupings.

Help the children to sub-divide each group on the basis of another characteristic such as hairiness; nature of leaf edge, for example, wavy, spiky, straight; pattern of veins. Ask them to draw and fill in the chart below, identifying the leaves of each tree.

## Content
Unknown specimens can be identified with the help of a simple key. Pairs of questions can be asked and identification made by a process of elimination.

*Sc AT2/2b,4b*

# Geography: Key Stage 1

| Hazel | Horse chestnut | Elder | Sycamore | Ash | Holly |
|-------|----------------|-------|----------|-----|-------|
|       |                |       |          |     |       |

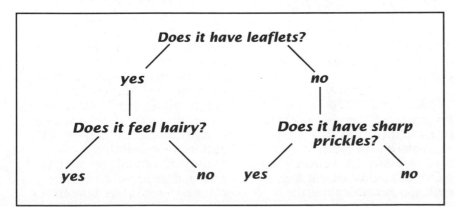

# 15. My bedroom

## Group size
Individuals.

## What you need
Old shoeboxes, cereal packets and so on, matchboxes of various sizes, an assortment of different quality paper, plain and patterned, scissors, pencils, wax crayons, adhesive, rulers.

## What to do

Spend about twenty minutes with the children talking about various rooms in their houses. Make sure everyone understands the concepts of upstairs and downstairs. Focus the discussion on bedrooms, and bedroom furniture and fittings. Encourage the children to talk about their own bedrooms. The children will need to think about proportion – How big? How much room? On which wall is the window? – as well as 'next to', 'behind', 'in front' and so on. Explain how they will create models of their own rooms using the materials available. The larger boxes will represent the floor and walls of their bedrooms, but they will make the furniture and fittings from the other materials.

Leave the children to get on with the task. Avoid directing them, except in matters of construction, because the results of this activity can be used for assessing each child's understanding of proportion, 'bird's eye' view and eye for detail.

Allow the children time to explain the layout of their bedroom to others. You must decide whether that will be the whole class or to a partner, but you should endeavour to monitor carefully the language being used.

## Content

Children are introduced to the notion of different viewpoints while engaging in a purposeful exploration of their own environment. They will also learn about proportion and change of shape in objects viewed from different perspectives.

## Safety

Care should be taken when using scissors.

**Gg AT1/1b,2b**

# 16. My classroom

## Group size

Groups of six to eight children, pairs.

## What you need

A large, card-backed, laminated plan of the classroom with all the 'fixed' furniture and fittings drawn in (walls should be marked in with spaces indicating the position of windows and doors; laminated cardboard templates of all the furniture in the classroom drawn to scale; a large side elevation drawing of the classroom as seen looking through a window would be useful; A4 and A3-sized paper; pencils.

## What to do

Ask the children to undertake a classroom audit, counting the number of desks, chairs, bookcases, trolleys, and so on. They need to draw each item they have listed. This can be done by sitting at the side and drawing what they see. Then they need to draw a 'bird's-eye view' of each item. Allow them to get into a position to see what it looks like, particularly if the first attempt to draw it is inaccurate. This part of the activity can be carried out by the whole table of six to eight children.

You will need to spend ten to fifteen minutes with the children talking about what they have drawn, comparing results where necessary. Discuss with the group where the various items are in relation to each other. Children will have a tendency to point, so you must give them some reference point. Use the large plan and ask the children to place the cardboard templates in the correct position on the plan. Decide how much the group is capable of understanding and place on the plan only as many items as the children can locate easily at any one time.

Finally, ask the group to copy a plan on to their own pieces of paper. The accuracy of their plans will help you to monitor the children's understanding of this activity and to decide whether they can move on to the task of placing all the tables and chairs in the correct position.

## Content
Children will see their classroom from at least two viewpoints. They will consider the relationship between the plan and the side view. They will discuss the role of the plan or map as a guide to a place looks like, a tool to help locate a place and a way of storing and displaying information.

*Gg AT1/1a,1b,2b*

# 17. The corner shop

## Group size
Individuals or groups.

## What you need
A large-scale simplified map of the locality, pictures of the outside and the inside of a typical mini-supermarket or a newsagent's, a camera, paper, pencils, crayons.

## What to do
Check if there is a local shop that the children call at on their way to and from school. If there is, ask the owner if you could photograph both the outside and the inside of the shop, as well as the people who normally serve behind the counter. If this is not possible, use pictures of small shops.

Talk to the children about the types of goods they normally buy for themselves. Encourage them to bring into school the empty wrappers and packaging, and to mount a display. Ask them to read the wrappers to find out where the goods are made and to make a shopping list showing the name of the product and the

town and/or country where it was made.

Ask the children to draw from memory, in pencil only, the outside of the local corner shop. Encourage them to visit the shop after school and to look more closely at it with a view to updating their drawings the following day.

Introduce the local area map and ask each child to identify on it the position of their own local corner shop. A display can be created linking the drawings to the correct position on the map. The children should be encouraged to draw or write down the route they take from home to the shop.

If possible, arrange for someone who works at the local corner shop to come along to school and talk about their work. Ask them to bring out the variety of activities, including ordering, serving customers, stocking the shelves, and so on. They could also mention the type and range of goods in the shop and where the shop gets its goods from.

## Content
This activity allows the children to compare the reality of their locality with a street

plan or a large-scale map. They will use a map to determine a route in their own area and check the accuracy of their route as they walk to and from school. The children's own plan will also provide an elementary land use map of their locality.

*Gg AT1/1a,1b,2c,2e,3b; AT2/1a,1b,2b; AT4/1a,1c,2c.*

# 18. Litter

## Group size
The whole class and small groups.

## What you need
A large-scale plan of the school, showing the different classrooms, corridors, cloakrooms, tarmac and grassy playing areas; tally charts for each group, clipboards, pencils, protective gloves, a plastic bag for the litter.

## What to do
Talk to the children about the sorts of food they eat at break times, for example, sweets,

crisps, fruit. Make a list on the chalkboard, categorising items under two headings: 'Wrapped in disposable packaging' and 'Unwrapped'.

Show the children a plan of the school and divide the whole area into zones. Allocate groups of children to each zone. Before the groups go off to collect the litter, ask the class to predict which area will have the most.

Ask the children to tally all the results and to complete a histogram, showing the number of items of litter in each area in the school grounds. Ask the children why some areas have more litter than others and steps they could take to reduce the litter. You could also ask them to compare the histogram with their earlier predictions.

## Content

This activity will involve the children in developing, implementing and evaluating a plan for dealing with environmental problems. It will encourage the attitude of

actively caring for a shared environment.

### Safety

The collection of litter should be supervised so as to ensure there is order. The children should wear protective gloves and wash their hands thoroughly afterwards.

**Gg AT1/1b,2a; AT5/1a,1b, 2b,2c,3b**

# 19. Treasure island

## Group size

Pairs or groups of three.

## What you need

Pictures and photographs of tropical islands, showing deserted beaches and tropical inland vegetation; a small box to represent a treasure chest, full of chocolate coins and costume jewellery; a copy of R.L. Stevenson's *Treasure Island* (R. Steadman [1985] Harrap Publications is recommended) and *Jenny's Buried Treasure* by B. and G. Tomalin (1986) Fun to Read Picture Books; a variety of

workcards giving clues to different places where the treasure can be found; photocopiable page 181.

## What to do

The children will need an introduction to the idea that pirates hid their treasure. This can be done by reading selected passages from 'Treasure Island' or telling them stories about Blackbeard's Treasure or Captain Kidd's Treasure, or making up one of your own. The point to make is that once they buried the treasure, the pirates made a map marking the spot, so that later they could return and find it. A game of 'hide the thimble' might be a good way to introduce this activity.

Using the same principle, the children need to be shown how to hide an item within the classroom and then devise clear instructions for the person waiting outside the door. A useful book to read at this point is *Jenny's Buried Treasure* by B. and G. Tomalin.

Introduce the Treasure Island Map on photocopiable page 181. (If you are introducing this to the whole class, enlarge the map). Explain that you know where the treasure is hidden and that you will give the children directions to find it. When they have discovered the treasure, show the children the treasure chest of chocolate coins and jewellery.

Give out copies of page 181 and ask the children to work in pairs or groups of three. Give each group a prepared workcard. Explain that each workcard has the treasure buried on a different part of the island.

As the children become more confident following the

directions, introduce the notion that the pirates did not want other people to find their treasure so they wrote the directions in riddles, codes or series of clues.

## Content
This activity develops the children's sense of orientation and their ability to locate places using grid reference systems. The emphasis is on encouraging accuracy in giving and finding locations.

*Gg AT1/1a,2a,2b,2c; AT2/ 1d; AT3/1a,2b; AT4/1b,2b; AT5/1a,2a,2b*

# Geography: Key Stages 1 and 2

## 20. My house

### Group size
Individuals or pairs.

### What you need
Pictures and descriptions of typical Indian houses, rural or urban, depending on your school's catchment area; a weather chart for the appropriate region of India; pictures of typical British houses, showing detached, semis, terraced and blocks of flats; paper, pencils and crayons.

### What to do
Talk to the children about their own houses. The buildings will need to be classified in two ways, by construction materials and type (semi, flat and so on). You will need some knowledge of

the catchment area in order to help the children.

Then ask them to draw from memory a picture of the outside of their house. They should then take their pictures home, check them against what they actually see and make alterations where necessary. A further development would be to ask the children to count the number of rooms in their house and make a list of them. A 'finished' picture would also specify the following:
• type (flat, bungalow, and so on);
• construction material (brick, stone and so on);
• number of rooms;
• number of inhabitants.

You might like to display the children's pictures around a map of the school's catchment area, marking the exact location of each house on the map.

Now show the children a comparable type of an Indian house – rural or urban, to match your school's catchment area. Challenge the children to think about why the houses are different. The climate, the family's wealth, availability of building materials, location, are all important factors in determining the architecture,

size, design and comfort of the houses.

### Content
The National Curriculum requires that children compare their own locality with others, including those in economically developing countries. This activity, together with the following four activities (21–24), focuses on the localities in the Indian subcontinent. The aim of all these activities is to develop children's understanding of the idea that the environment is the central determinant of human activity, affecting housing, food, work and resources available. People are also constantly trying to modify their environment in order to improve their standard of living. Children's understanding of these issues develops as they identify similarities and differences between locations and explain their causes and effects.

### Further activity
India is a land of greater contrasts than England and children should be encouraged to research the different types

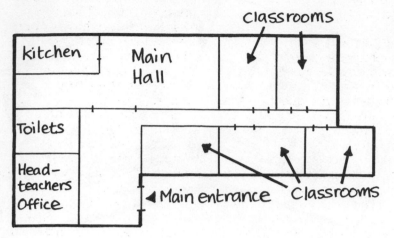

of houses, both rural and urban, in order to avoid stereotyping. Parents born in India could be invited to talk about their childhood.

*AT1/2a,2e; AT2/1d,2c,2d; AT3/3a; AT4/1a,2a,4a; AT5/1b,2a*

# 21. Our school

## Group size
Small groups.

## What you need
An atlas, photographs, pictures and descriptions of urban and rural schools in India, photographs and a large floor plan of your own school, a list of facts about the school, for example, the number of children, number of teaching and non-teaching staff. This information can be gathered by the children beforehand.

## What to do
Begin with a class discussion about why children come to school generally, but to this one in particular. Find out if anyone has been to another

school; if so, can they compare the two schools? Talk about class sizes and why the school is organised into classes, the ratio of teachers to children, rules and who decides on them and so on. Refer to the plan of the school while you are talking; try to involve the children in thinking about the design of the building, particularly about the siting of the hall, the headteacher's office, the kitchens and the lavatories.

Ask the children to write down what they like and what they dislike about school. Use categories to help the children think in a structured way. For example, the classroom, the whole building, the location, the school rules.

Provide the groups with photographs of Indian schools which show both buildings and teachers and children working. Find India on the atlas and identify the cities and regions where the photographs were taken. Ask the children to scrutinise the photographs. You can help to focus their attention with the following types of questions:
• observational – What can you see?
• reasoning – What do you think is happening?

• empathetic – What might the children be thinking?
• evaluative – Why has the teacher organised the class in rows?

The children should be encouraged to look for similarities and differences with their own school based on the categories outlined above (classroom, architecture, location, school rules).

## Content
See Content in Activity 20, page 51.

*AT1/2a,2e; AT2/1d,2c, 2d,3a,3b; AT5/1b*

# 22. At play – outdoors

## Group size
Small groups.

## What you need
A large-scale map of the locality on which the children can mark the areas where they play, pictures of both rural and urban Indian children playing outdoors, photocopies of a map of India (enough for the whole class), paper pencils.

## What to do
Ask the children what games they play outdoors, in the evening or at weekends. Make a list of the games and where they are played. Are there any games played specifically by boys or girls only?

Ask the children about hobbies in which they participate themselves, but which require specialist facilities, for example, swimming, skating, riding. What do they do? Where can these special facilities be found? How do they get to them? How much does it cost per lesson or per session? Now ask the children to study the pictures of Indian children playing. Ask them to think why most of the photographs show boys. Talk about the most popular sports and games in India, including cricket, hockey, football and a type of wrestling called Kabaddi. In Kabaddi, one player runs into the opponents' area holding his breath and tries to touch as many of the other side as possible before taking another breath. The opposing team try to grab the attacker and prevent his return. Anyone touched by the attacker before his successful return to his own team is out.

Ask the children to list some of the reasons why children from rural areas of India tend to play games such as catch, dare, goodies and baddies, skipping or Kabaddi.

## Content
See Content in Activity 20, page 51.

*Gg AT1/2a; AT2/1d,2c,2d; AT3/3a; AT5/1b*

# Geography: Key Stage 2

## 23. The market

### Group size
Individuals and small groups.

### What you need
Photographs of typical British open-air markets, photographs of Indian markets, weather maps of the UK and India, cameras, cassette recorders, audio tapes, paper, pencils, crayons.

### What to do
If possible, arrange for the children to visit a market in order to take their own photographs and question the stall holders. They could record their interviews on tape. Here are some of the questions they might ask:
• Which other markets do you go to during the week and why? (The group should make a map of the towns where the different stall holders go to sell their goods.)
• Do you always hire the same stall and, if so, why? (Some will be prime stalls because of their position near the entrance.)
• From where do you get your goods? (The group should draw a map showing their sources.)
• What are the problems and difficulties of being a stall holder?

Ask the children to make a plan of all the stalls in the market. The plan should show what is sold on each stall. There are normally a number of ethnic minority stall holders. Ask the children to consider what goods they sell and why.

If it is impossible to visit a market, you will have to discover through questioning the children what knowledge they possess and then create a 'typical' market plan from their combined observations and experiences.

The children should be encouraged to draw a stall with its goods displayed. This will help you to assess whether they have understood the discussion.

Now show the photographs of Indian markets and ask them to look for similarities and differences. Here are some questions they might consider:
• What are the main commodities sold in the Indian markets?
• Where do the goods originate and how are they brought to market?
• Are the same commodities available in all the regions of India?

## Content
See Content in Activity 20, page 51.

*Gg AT1/1b,2e; AT2/1b, 1d,1e,2c,3a,3d; AT3/3a; AT4/1c,2c*

## 24. Deforestation

### Group size
Pairs and/or small groups.

### What you need
Atlases that show the provinces of India and Bangladesh in detail, blank maps of the world and India, pictures of eroded landscapes and hillsides covered in trees (in the United Kingdom, India and Bangladesh), reference books on trees.

### What to do
Talk to the children about the differences between coniferous and deciduous trees. They should identify the names of the most common trees growing in the UK and decide whether they are deciduous or coniferous. They should identify on a graph or class display chart the main uses which industry makes of both coniferous and deciduous trees.

Ask the children to colour in the areas of equatorial rain forest on a blank map of the world. They could then make a list of the main varieties of trees growing in the rain forest and research what happens to them once they have been felled. A display chart could also be used to present this information.

Using the blank map of India, the children should colour in the rain forest areas and draw or trace the course of the river Ganges. Ask them to imagine they live in Bangladesh in the Ganges delta. They have to write a letter to the Indian Government complaining about the silting up in the region. They should explain why they think this is happening and make suggestions as to what the government should do to help them.

### Content
There are a number of concepts of which the children must have some understanding: erosion/deposition (cause and effect), the water cycle, a delta, different types of trees – fast-growing conifers and slow-growing hardwoods.

The foothills of the Himalayas were thickly wooded in the early 19th century. Expanding towns and the need for cheap fuel both for industrial and domestic use, development of the railways, land clearance for crops, all contributed to deforestation. The effect of deforestation has been the silting up of the Ganges delta, particularly in Bangladesh, so that during the monsoon season the winds blowing in rain from the Bay of Bengal lead to flooding on a major scale. Houses in the region are built from concrete on two-metre stilts in order to withstand the winds and floods that come with the monsoons. The main delta channels need to be constantly dredged. However, the delta soil is very fertile, so people do not want to leave the area. Therefore the government need monsoon early warning systems so that people can get to safety.

*Gg AT2/2c,4b,4e;*
*AT3/1a,2a,2b,3a,3b,4b,4c;*
*AT4/3d,4e;*
*AT5/2a,2b,2c,3a,4b,4c*

## 25. My school's catchment area

### Group size
Groups of three or four.

### What you need
1:50,000, 1:25,000 or 1:10,000 Ordnance Survey maps of the local area; if available, a print-out from the school's computer of all the pupil addresses, by class; aerial photographs of the catchment area; a clipboard, graph paper, pencils, pens.

### What to do
Talk to the children about the concept of a catchment area.

Display an OS map showing the catchment boundary. Use the questions below to stimulate the children's curiosity.
• On which street do most children live?
• How many children live outside inside the catchment area?
• Which child lives nearest to school?
• Who has the longest journey to school on foot and by vehicle?
• How many children walk to school? How many come on the bus? How many come in their parents' car?

Divide the classes in the school among the groups. If there is no computer print-out available, each group must obtain class registers and photocopy the lists. The groups will need to make a list of all the street names mentioned on each register and do a tally count, by class and for the whole school. They will then need to produce a distribution pattern showing where all the children in each class live, and, if possible, another one for the whole school.

## Content
In this activity children will be adding information to prepared maps, using a key and colour codes to emphasise the detail. They will thus develop and build on their existing map-reading skills.

## Further activity
Give a number of children a stop-watch and ask them on their way home to note down the name of the street they find themselves on at 5, 10 and 15 minute intervals. Ensure that the children take different routes.

On a laminated OS map draw concentric rings from the school indicating:
• 5 minutes' walking time;
• 10 minutes' walking time;
• 15 minutes' walking time.

*Gg AT1/3b,3c,3d,4c,5a,5c; AT2/3b,3c; AT4/4a,4b*

# 26. The country park

## Group size
Small groups.

## What you need
An outline map of a country park (such as Shipley Country Park in Derbyshire), 1:50,000 and 1:25,000 Ordnance Survey maps on which the country park is shown; aerial photographs of the area, visitors' leaflets provided by the park, camaras, paper, pencils, crayons.

## What to do
Ask the children to plan a route through the park for each of the following people:
• an ornithologist interested in water birds. Mark the best places for bird-watching (give six-figure map references);
• an arboriculturalist;
• a jogger who runs at 6mph

and only has 45 minutes available (plan a route of approximately 4.5 miles); an equestrian.

Remind the children that the directions should be written down giving exact distances, and six-figure map references at intersections where a change in direction is required.

The children will need the following information:
• good walking speed (brisk walking, no stopping) – 4mph;
• moderate walking speed (e.g. walking the dog) – 3mph;
• ambling (stopping to look at interesting sights) – 2mph;
• walking with a small child or pushing a wheelchair – 1mph.

## Content
This activity will develop children's ability to relate their map-reading skills to the specific needs of a particular map-user. This is quite an advanced skill and children will need help in developing it as they compare maps with the actual area and its pictures or photographs. Field experience is therefore essential if children are to visualise a locality from a map effectively. Route-finding is also crucial to

good map reading since it gives children the opportunity to practise orientation, interpretation of scale and symbols, and the giving and following of instructions.

*Gg AT1/4b,5a,5c; AT3/3c*

# 27. The supermarket

## Group size
The whole class, then individuals.

## What you need
1:50,000 and 1:25,000 Ordnance Survey maps of the local region, and a 1:10,000 OS map showing the area around the supermarkets; if possible, aerial photographs of various areas where supermarkets are located.

## What to do
Talk to the children about the local supermarkets, showing their location on the map. Ask them where their parents usually shop. Mark the positions of the supermarkets on the map. Ask the children to look carefully at their location and to speculate as to why they have been built in those specific places. (Supermarkets need large plots of land. Land becomes more expensive the nearer one gets to the city centre.) Discuss the reasons why supermarkets have grown in popularity with shoppers. (They are cheaper than smaller local shops and carry a wider range of goods.)
Ask the children the following questions:
• Which supermarket do your parents use and why do you think they prefer this particular one?

• How frequently do they shop? On what day? Why?
• Who actually does the shopping? (Mum, Dad, or both?) How do they get there?
Ask the children to trace the route from home to the supermarket and calculate the mileage. They could estimate how much money this adds to the cost of the shopping. (They will need to find out the various makes of cars, engine sizes, miles per gallon, petrol prices for leaded/unleaded, distances to supermarkets and calculate costs.)

## Content
Children will have the opportunity to study the regional distribution of a familiar feature of their environment – the supermarket, gaining some insight into the complex links between rural and urban areas, between residential and industrial areas, and between population, employment, goods, services and leisure.?

*Gg AT1/4c,5a,5c; AT2/3c, 3e,3f,4b; AT4/3d,4e,5c,5e*

# 28. The by-pass

## Group size
Small groups.

## What you need
Written and graphical information relating to a road-building proposal that is (or was) an issue for local debate – for example, a map showing the existing situation, a brief description and a map showing the proposed alternative route(s), and a brief outline of comparative advantages/disadvantages of alternatives.

## What to do
This is a role-play activity that involves children in examining information and gathering evidence to present a case for/against why a road should take a particular route.
Divide the class into four or five, each to represent an 'interested party' – for example, the residents who

# History: Key Stage 1

live along the existing and new route(s), the Department of Transport, The Green Party, and so on.

Each group needs to examine the information and put together evidence to support its case. Once all the parties have presented their case, a final decision on the specific route should be decided by a majority vote.

## Content
In this activity, children will discuss vital environmental issues, gaining awareness of the conflicting interests within the society. They will gather, interpret and present evidence to support their particular point of view.

*Gg AT1/5a,5b,5c; AT2/4c, 5b; AT4/4c,4e,5d; AT5/4b*

## 29. Houses – old and new

### Group size
Small groups.

### What you need
Three photographs of local houses of different ages – e.g. one modern, one Victorian, one Georgian; boxes, glue, paint, collage material, newspaper.

### What to do
Show the children the three photographs and discuss with them how they are alike and different. Introduce relevant vocabulary – e.g. new, old, older, more recent, modern. Help the children relate the similarities and differences to the age of the houses and encourage them to make

comparisons between the photographs and their own houses.

Divide the children into small groups or pairs and ask them to make a model of one of the houses. Help them to make labels to describe the houses they have made.

### Content
You will need to draw the children's attention to the historical significance of these changes:
• Technological developments in building illustrate the ways in which people are constantly finding new ways of doing things – e.g. the absence of chimneys in modern housing shows advances in heating methods; brick replacing local stone illustrates use of new materials and improved transportation.
• Changes in style and decorative features can be explained in terms of people's taste changing through time.

*H AT1/2a,2c; AT3/1,2,3.*

## 30. School – then and now

### Group size
Small groups.

### What you need
A photograph of your school as it is now, a photograph of your school in the past or of another older school – e.g. Victorian, drawing paper, pencils, crayons.

### What to do
Ask the children to compare the photographs. What has changed? What has stayed the same? Help them to make a group list of these features and to illustrate it.

Talk about the age of the school or schools. When were they built? How old are they? Is the date on the school?

Ask the children to draw a picture of the school as it is now (this can be done outside, weather permitting). Display these pictures with suitable captions – e.g. 'Our school is ____ years old. It was built in ____.' Features of the school can also be labelled.

### Content
If your school is fairly modern then it will be more effective to compare it to an older building, preferably Victorian, as contrasts will be more evident. The kind of features which will probably be most readily noticed are likely to include:
• the position of windows (these were higher in Victorian times to prevent children looking out and being distracted);
• girls' and boys' entrances (sexes were segregated);
• outside toilets;
• school grounds.
It is more important to encourage the children to

speculate on the reasons for these differences.

Attitudes and values are reflected in building style. Modern schools reflect a gentler approach to children and learning. Children are no longer cut off from the world by high walls and windows but are able to look out on the world from which they learn. Their comfort is considered (inside toilets), they are given more freedom and stimulation (pleasanter school grounds) and both sexes are considered to be equal (same entrances).

*H AT1/2a,2c; AT3/1,2,3.*

# 31. Churches and chapels

### Group size
Whole class.

### What you need
Paper, clipboards, pencils.

### What to do
Arrange a visit to an old church or chapel in your area. If you are having a guided tour, explain to the guide that the focus of the visit is the architecture. Make sure the children notice the main features of the building –

spire, door, windows, roof – as well as its shape. Explain to the children that these features are part of an architectural style and can help us know how old a building is. Ask the children to record their observations by drawing the shapes of the key features. Discuss the reasons why the building has certain characteristics.

Stress the importance of the church's role in community life as a place of worship and as a symbol of continuity.

### Content
There are many old churches in the United Kingdom and it is worth researching the particular one you choose. Some general points might be helpful:
• The church was often the largest and most important building in the community. The size emphasised the power and glory of God and provided room for a large congregation.
• Churches were often designed to reflect the glory and mystery of God, e.g. stained glass windows, religious paintings and frescoes, spires and towers pointing heavenwards.
• Many churches have clocks or bells to remind people of the time for worship.
• Gargoyles frightened away evil spirits.
Some internal features to consider are:
• the altar where the priest leads worship;
•t he nave for seating the congregation;
• the chancel where the choir is seated;
• the porch is the main entrance;
• the aisle for processions;
• the font for baptisms;
• the graveyard for burials.

Also note that different parts of the church would date from different periods.

*H AT1/2c; AT3/1,2,3*

# 32. Hard at work

## Group size
The whole class.

## What you need
An elderly person who has worked locally over a number of years, a tape recorder.

## What to do
Brief the visitor about the purpose of the activity, stressing the need to bring out the difference between past and present, to describe the job they did and aspects of working life.

Brief the children by explaining that their visitor started work a long time ago. Try to make this meaningful to the children in terms of time, e.g. 'When your grandmas and grandads were young'. Tell them their job is to find out from the visitor as much as possible about the work they did and what it was like.

The visitor can talk to the children and they can then ask questions. This can be recorded on tape.

## Content
The kind of information which the visitor needs to give should include a variety of aspects of their working life, explaining what they made or did and illustrating factors of change. Key questions could include the age of starting work, the length of the working day, holidays or days off, wages and what these would buy, meal breaks and canteens, aspects of safety and sick pay regulations, the relationship between worker and boss, changes in the nature of the job brought about by technology. As well as obtaining information, children need to explore attitudes and feelings. Their questions should therefore focus on how the person felt about these experiences.

*H AT1/2c; AT3/1,2*

# 33. At the library

## Group size
Small groups.

## What you need
A photograph of the local library, a selection of local history books from the library, paper, pencils.

## What to do
Talk to the children about the library picture. Do they recognise it? Do they go there themselves?

Focus on how a library stores information which can help us find out about the past of our locality – maps, books, photographs, and so on. Show the children the books and explain that they are from the library. Encourage them to look through the books and discuss the pictures. Can they recognise any places? What changes can they see? Encourage them to express opinions about these changes.

Each child can then choose a picture from the book and list the differences they can see and try to explain them.

## Content
Many children will have visited the local library either from home or school. The building itself may be old and worth discussing, but the focus of the activity should be the importance of books and libraries as sources of information about the past. We can find written accounts and stories (fact/fiction) and pictures (drawings and photographs) which tell us about what has changed.

*H AT1/2c,3a,3c; AT3/1,2,3*

# History: Key Stage 2

## 34. Dig that style!

### Group size
Whole class.

### What you need
Three houses from different periods which you can visit in the locality – e.g. Georgian, Victorian, modern. If it is not possible to get out, photos could be used; photocopiable page 182, clipboards, papers, pencils.

### What to do
Explain to the children that houses built at different times have particular styles and that they will be looking at three different houses in the local area.

Take the children to look at the houses and tell them when they were built, pointing out the key features that give the house its style – roof, tiling, brick patterns, building material, windows, and so on. The children can then complete the worksheet on photocopiable page 182 in as much detail as possible (diagrams can be used to show architectural detail).

Encourage the children to think of reasons for the particular differences they have noticed.

### Content
It is important that children observe closely and make their own comparisons. Help will need to be given in terms of knowledge of building materials, but encourage the children to describe shapes and features in their own language from their own observations. Also, when encouraging children to think of reasons for variation in style, bear in mind factors of function, new materials and decoration. These will include such things as the availability of local raw materials, difficulties in transporting materials from other areas, the need for small windows in exposed locations, the larger size of window in some newer homes (central heating/double glazing). Bring in the question of taste – people in different times liked different styles; they often copied styles from earlier periods. Some modern houses have copied styles, for example, mock Georgian. Abstract notions of fashion and taste need to be explored. Encourage the children to express own preferences.

*H AT1/2c,3a,3b,3c,4a*

## 35. A school through time

### Group size
Small groups.

### What you need
A selection of items illustrating the history of the school – e.g. old photographs, photocopied extracts from the school log, class photographs, newspaper articles; a prepared time-line on a display board (this can be marked off in decades or single years depending on the age of the school).

### What to do
Give each group a few of the items to discuss – e.g. a class photo, a school photo and a school log entry. What do they tell us about the school?

Ask the children to put their items in chronological order and discuss in their group the reason for the choices they have made. When each group has finished they can be put on the time-line in the appropriate place. The display can be added to throughout the topic or year. As children find out about national or local issues in other historical periods these can be added.

## Content
Some of the items may be clearly dated; otherwise estimations will need to be made. If a range of formal class photos is available over a period, this would be ideal for children to identify changes in class size, clothes, hairstyles, and so on. Less formal photos may identify activities such as school fairs, visits and PE. Extracts from the school log may show a range of aspects of school life – class size, illnesses, special events, building work. Key historical events can also be presented on the time-line to give children additional reference points. Children's birth dates can also be added.

*H AT1/2a,2c,3a,3c,4a; AT3/1,2,3*

# 36. A place to pray

## Group size
Whole class.

## What you need
A local place of worship, photocopiable page 183, clipboards, pencils, cameras.

## What to do
Make arrangements to visit a local place of worship. Prepare the children for the visit and focus on the historical importance of the building in the community – its role in recording the past and providing continuity between past and present. Remind the children to look carefully at

the building for clues about the past.

When you are at the place of worship, give each child a copy of photocopiable page 183. Help them to fill in the worksheet and to photograph the features they identify. Encourage them to identify and photograph any features which give us clues to the way the church has developed and the lifestyle of the people using it.

When you are back in the classroom display the photographs and ask the children to make appropriate labels naming the features and explaining what it tells of the past.

## Content
Features which give clues or provide evidence of the past will probably include:
• war memorials linking local experience to national events;
• tombs, effigies, brasses giving evidence of dress, headstones giving evidence of life-span, causes of death, family size, family history;
• dedicated seats/windows showing evidence of local families and dignataries;
• renovations and alterations

showing the development of the building through time;
• personal memorials and inscriptions – do these tell us what the people were really like or are they a matter of opinion?

*H AT1/2c,3a,3c,4a; AT3/2,3*

# 37. The world of work

## Group size
Whole class.

## What you need
Information books about jobs and work which include historical aspects and jobs and work which are related to your area, pencils, paper, crayons.

## What to do
Talk to the children about work done by people in the area today – include work done by their parents and grandparents. Make a class list of these jobs. You will need to

show sensitivity to the problem of unemployment.

Discuss the changing nature of work in the local area over the past 100 years:
• some jobs have stayed the same;
• some new jobs have been created;
• some jobs have disappeared or changed.
Classify the jobs on the class list according to these categories.

In pairs or small groups the children can then select one job and use the information books to research its background and identify reasons for changes. Their findings can be recorded in writing and drawing – for example, a picture of a farmer with a scythe in 1890; a picture of a farmer with a combine harvester in 1990; a written comment on the reasons for and the effects of the change.

## Content
Most jobs will have remained but aspects will have changed. For example, a shopkeeper now has electronic tills, prepackaged goods and refrigeration. Dentists have much more sophisticated equipment and can deal with pain more effectively due to new drugs. Some new jobs have been created, e.g. in supermarket management, due to changes in social and economic organisation – improved transport, working women, population growth and mass production. Other jobs may have disappeared from the area, e.g. blacksmith.

*H AT1/2b,2c,3a,3b,3c,4a,4c; AT3/3,4*

# 38. Then and now

## Group size
Whole class.

## What you need
Two large-scale maps of the local area, one showing it in the present and one in the past; paper, pencils or pens.

## What to do
Make sure all the children have an opportunity to study the maps, comparing them. Make a chalkboard list of changes the children have identified from the maps. Ask the children to close their eyes and listen. Describe the local area as it was in the past. Make the description as detailed as possible – describe clothes, transport, games, countryside, houses, factories and so on. Then ask the children to write and illustrate an account of the area in the past, expressing their views and opinions about the changes which have occurred. Ask them to think about reasons for the changes.

## Content
It may be possible to find a description of the area in the works of a local writer – e.g. Hardy in Dorset, Alan Sillitoe in Nottingham. Photographs may also be used. Help children explore reasons for the change such as growth of towns, depopulation of countryside, invention of machinery, industrialisation, new forms of transport.

*H AT1/2c,3a,3c,4a,4b; AT3/2,3,4*

# 39. A Victorian school-day

## Group size
The whole class.

## What you need
Costumes for teacher and children, a cane, a dunce's cap, small chalkboards or slates and squares of black paper, chalks/dip-pens/ink, a globe, prepared proverbs for handwriting practice, prepared sums to write on chalkboard, a

copy of John Bunyan's *Pilgrim's Progress*, hoops, an adult to role-play school inspector (optional).

### What to do

Prepare the classroom as authentically as possible to look like a Victorian classroom, e.g. seats in rows separating boys and girls; lower parts of windows covered if necessary, the globe, dunce's cap and cane in prominent positions.

Work through several Victorian school activities such as chanting tables, spelling (each child standing up to spell out a word), handwriting (copying from board on to chalkboards or sugar paper), maths (copying sums from board). Learn English counties by rote. Read an extract from John Bunyan's *Pilgrim's Progress*, each child in turn. Children can play with hoops at playtime.

### Content

The degree of authenticity in terms of discipline, use of dunce's cap and so on, will depend on the relationship between teacher and class. The room can be made as grim as possible by removing much of the furniture and equipment for the day. The school inspector can come in and check attendance records and quiz children on their work.

*H AT1/3a,3c,4a*

# 40. A grave affair

### Group size

Whole class.

### What you need

A local churchyard or cemetery with Victorian graves, clipboards, paper, pencils.

### What to do

Explain to the children that graveyards can tell us about the local people who lived in the area, and that the purpose of the visit is to collect some of that evidence. Talk about the kind of information recorded on headstones, for example, name of deceased, dates of birth and death, age at death, symbols, other information.

At the graveyard make sure the children spread out to look at as wide a variety of graves as possible. Stress that information should only be recorded for people whose birth or death is later than 1837. Help the children to record this information when they get back to school.

### Content

Aspects which should relate to Victorian values and experiences may include:
• attitudes to death – romanticised symbols and inscriptions;
• differences between rich and poor – paupers' graves and monuments;
• events – death in war, at sea, epidemics;
• health – epidemics, child mortality, bodysnatching for medical research (railings around graves dissuaded this practice);
• occupations – inscriptions often give this;
• family relationships and history;
• position of women.

*H AT1/3a,3c,4a,4c; AT3/5*

# 41. Civic pride

### Group size

Small groups.

### What you need

Pictures of local Victorian public buildings – e.g. station, town hall, library, museum, school, church, swimming baths; information books on aspects of the Victorian Age.

### What to do

Make sure the children understand the concept of a public building. Ask the children to look at the pictures

and discuss the purpose for which the building was intended.

Discuss the value of the building as evidence – for example:
• station – importance of railways;
• town hall – social reform and town planning;
• schools/libraries – importance of education;
• museums – classification of knowledge.

Ask the children to select one of the buildings and research the aspect of Victorian life which it reflects.

### Content

In some areas there may be no local examples. In this case use examples from the nearest possible locality and discuss the reasons why there is no such evidence in your area. The reasons for this could be:
• it was not a centre for industrialisation;

• it was not a centre of expanding population;
• buildings were destroyed in World War II.

**H AT1/3b,3c,4a,4b,5c; AT3/3,4,5**

# 42. Counting heads

### Group size
The whole class.

### What you need
A population table showing ten-yearly figures 1801–1891 for your area, paper, pencils, crayons, graph paper.

### What to do
Ask the children to study the table carefully and make sure they can read the figures accurately. Ask them to draw a line graph to show the population trend for their area

for 1801–1891, and to write an account explaining the reasons for the particular population trend. They should try to discover whether it was typical of the national trend. The figures are given in Figure 1 if you wish to provide them.

### Content
The population table for your area will be available from your local library or archive office. Reasons for population growth vary from area to area but may include:
• development of towns and cities during the process of industrialisation;
• improved health and hygiene;
• improved diet;
• greater prosperity.
Population decline could be due to:
• depopulation of the countryside caused by moves to towns;
• emigration due to famine (e.g. Ireland) and the search for new opportunities.

**H AT1/3a,3b,3c,4a,5b; AT3/3,4,5**

*Figure 1*

|  | *England and Wales* | *Scotland* | *Ireland* |
|---|---|---|---|
| *1801* | *8.9* | *1.6* | *5.2* |
| *1891* | *29.0* | *4.6* | *4.7* |

# CHAPTER 4

# Sound and music

Everyday sounds form an important part of our experience. From the moment we are woken up by the alarm clock, we need to be able to make sense of the world by interpreting the sounds we hear.

This project offers children at Key Stage 1 the opportunity to explore a wide variety of sounds in their immediate environment and to find out about their causes and uses. These range from bird song and rustling leaves to the sound of car engines or the washing machine. Not all of these sounds will be pleasing to the ear and the children should be aware that some sounds can be unpleasant and obtrusive in the environment.

Children will have an opportunity to experiment with sounds and music by making simple musical instruments from readily available materials. They will explore the world of rhythm and song and derive great enjoyment and satisfaction from creating music of their own.

# BACKGROUND

**Making sounds**
- speaking, striking, blowing, plucking, shaking, scraping
- musical instruments
- vibrations, sound waves

**Sound in the environment**
- at home, at school
- natural sounds and sound produced by machines

**SOUND AND MUSIC Key Stage 1**

**Listening and hearing sounds**
- making sounds louder
- unwanted noise
- sound reflection

**Music**
- playing instruments
- songs
- pitch and loudness
- musical scale
- weather sounds

| Activity | Curriculum area | ATTAINMENT TARGET AND LEVEL | | | | |
| --- | --- | --- | --- | --- | --- | --- |
| | | AT1 | AT2 | AT3 | AT4 | AT5 |
| 1 | Science | 1a | | | 1c | |
| 2 | Science | 1a | | | 1c | |
| 3 | Science | 1a | | | 1c | |
| 4 | Science | | | | 1c | |
| 5 | Science | 1a | | | 1c | |
| 6 | Science | | | | 1c | |
| 7 | Science | | | | 1c | |
| 8 | Science | | | | 1c | |
| 9 | Science | | | | 1c | |
| 10 | Science | | | | 1c | |
| 11 | Science | | | | 3d | |
| 12 | Music | AT1 | AT2 | | | |
| 13 | Music | AT1 | AT2 | | | |
| 14 | Music | AT1 | AT2 | | | |
| 15 | Music Science | AT1 | AT2 | | 1c | |
| 16 | Music Science | AT1 | AT2 | | 1c | |

# ACTIVITIES

## 1. 'I can hear a pin drop!'

### Group size
The whole class at first, then pairs and small groups.

### What you need
Paper, pencils.

### What to do
First, talk to the children about the sounds that can be heard in the school. In the classroom, ask the whole class to sit very still and listen to the sounds that they can hear. They need to be very quiet. Discuss with the children some of the sounds they heard and what caused those sounds to be made.

In pairs or small groups, the children could walk around different areas of the school to listen to the everyday sounds of a busy school. They should go to the playground, the school kitchen, the hall during a PE lesson, outside different classrooms, the offices, the library. When the groups return to the classroom, they could talk to the rest of the class about the sounds they heard and who or what they think was making those sounds. They could make a chart recording their findings.

### Content
Sounds are made in a variety of ways. The children have heard a range of sounds of different intensities, from voices in classrooms, to saucepans clattering in the kitchen, to the keys of a

typewriter or a computer clicking in the office. Anything which vibrates produces a sound.

### Further activity
The children could carry out this activity at different times of the day, e.g., playtime or dinner time, to see if the range of school sounds varies throughout the day.

*Sc AT1/1a; AT4/1c*

## 2. Sounds at home

### Group size
The whole class, individuals, small groups.

### What you need
Paper, pencils, catalogues, magazines, scissors, adhesive.

### What to do
Discuss with the children the sounds that they hear at home everyday. What makes these sounds? Ask them to spend some time at home listening to everyday sounds: e.g. doors closing, toilets flushing, water dripping from a tap, the vacuum cleaner, and so on. Can they decide which room the sounds are coming from and what is making them? How loud or quiet are these sounds? Ask the children to list on a large sheet of paper all the different machines and objects in their home that make sounds, for example, television, washing machine, food mixer. Ask them to group

**What to do**
Discuss with the children the range of sounds that they would hear outside the school, for example, traffic, birds, leaves rustling in the wind. Ask the children to listen to the traffic sounds on their way to school. What sort of sounds did they hear? Tell the children to divide up into small groups, go out into the playground and make a list of the sounds they hear. They could divide their sounds into types, for example, traffic sounds and sounds made naturally (birds, wind, etc.). One child in each group could be responsible for writing down the traffic sounds and another for the natural sounds. Do sounds travel better when it is windy?

The children could carry out this activity at different times of the day. Back in the classroom, show the children how to make a poster displaying their results. Where possible, they should draw pictures showing the sources of the sounds, for example, birds, cars and trees.

the sounds according to which room they come from, for example, sounds from the kitchen, sounds from the living room.

In the classroom, discuss the findings with the children. Working in small groups the children should look through catalogues and magazines and cut out pictures of everyday machines and household objects that make sounds. They can make a chart sticking their pictures together in groups, if possible according to the room in the house in which these machines can be found. Next to each machine or object the children could write a word which describes the sound the machine makes, for example, a food mixer *whirrs*. The children could put

their charts up on the wall and compare results from different groups.

**Content**
A range of sounds can be heard in the home. These are made in a variety of ways. Anything which vibrates produces a sound. Sounds vary in pitch and loudness. The loudness of a sound is measured in decibels.

**Safety**
Care should be taken when using scissors.

*Sc AT1/1a; AT4/1c*

# 3. Out and about

**Group size**
The whole class or small groups.

**Content**
A range of sounds can be heard outside the school and these can originate from many sources and be made in a variety of ways.
Anything which vibrates produces a sound which can vary in pitch and loudness. The intensity of sound is measured in decibels.

**Further activity**
The activity could be carried out at different times and in different environments, for example, in the local shopping precinct or in the park.

Discuss different types of sounds with the children, for example, road sounds – pelican crossing; warning sounds – siren on a police vehicle or ambulance; a car horn; a fire alarm bell.

*Sc AT1/1a; AT4/1c*

# 4. Quiz your friends

## Group size
Small groups.

## What you need
A cassette recorder, an audio tape, paper, pencils.

## What to do
How easy is it to recognise sounds in a familiar environment? Tell the children they are going to make a tape of everyday sounds in the school and school grounds. They could follow a route through the school, recording familiar sounds such as the headteacher's voice, the school secretary typing, children eating their lunch (clatter of plates, knives and forks), a squeaky door and so on. Back in the classroom, the children should play their tape and ask the rest of the class to guess what each sound is. If they had taken an easily recognisable route, they could ask the other children in the class to guess the sound route travelled.

Was it easy to identify each sound? How many children were able to recognise all of the sounds?

## Content
Sounds are caused by vibrations. Sounds travel in waves to the ear.

*Sc AT4/1c*

# 5. Making music – 1

## Group size
Small groups.

## What you need
A collection of simple musical instruments, for example, a drum, a recorder, a xylophone, a triangle, a tambourine, shakers, a guitar, a scraping instrument. Include some from other countries, for example, castanets, a kazoo.

## What to do
How many different sounds can be made with the instruments available? Discuss with the children what sort of music they enjoy. What are their favourite songs? Ask them to use the instruments to make sounds. Do they like the sounds that they are making? How are they making sounds with the instruments? Ask the children to pluck the guitar string to make a sound. Ask them to try putting their fingers on the string to feel the string vibrating. Discuss words such as shake, strike, pluck, blow. Ask the children to sort the instruments into groups, i.e. all the instruments that produce sounds by plucking, blowing and so on. The children could make a chart to show what they have found.

## Content
Sounds can be made in a variety of ways such as plucking, shaking, scraping and blowing.

*Sc AT1/1a; AT4/1c*

## 6. Making music – 2

### Group size
Groups of eight to ten children.

### What you need
A collection of scrap materials that can be used to make sounds by striking, blowing, plucking, scraping – for example, cardboard tubes, metal spoons, wooden sticks, tins, wooden beads, bottle tops, elastic bands of different thicknesses, straws, dried beans, plastic containers.

### What to do
Ask the children to use the materials provided to make sounds in different ways. The children can shake a tin containing dried peas, blow down the cardboard tubes, twang the elastic bands and scrape the side of a plastic bottle with a stick. Then ask them to describe the sounds they are making. Can they make the sounds soft or loud? Can they group their 'instruments' into sets according to how the sound is produced? Help the children to make a chart grouping the 'instruments', and describing the sound each one makes. Using their musical 'instruments', the children could compose a simple tune with different sounds and simple rhythms.

### Content
Sounds can be made in a number of different ways, for example, by striking, blowing, plucking and scraping. Different materials and objects can be used to produce these sounds.

### Further activity
The children could investigate the sounds using only one group of their 'instruments' such as the 'blowers'. They could test out 'blowers' of different lengths to see if they make different sounds or put some holes in the 'blowers' and see what effect this has on the sound produced.

*Sc AT4/1c*

## 7. How many sounds can you make?

### Group size
Individuals, small groups.

### What you need
Paper, pencils, crayons.

### What to do
Discuss with the children the sounds that they can make with their voices – speaking, singing, laughing, shouting, whispering. Do they like singing? Can some of the sounds be too noisy, for example, a lot of people talking or shouting at the same time? Ask the children to make some different sounds with their voices such as whistling, or animal noises. Can they imitate a clock ticking or a dog barking? How many different sounds can they make? Are these sounds recognisable? Are they high sounds or low sounds? The children could draw pictures to represent some of the sounds they are making, for example, draw a clock and write 'tick-tock' next to it. Discuss with the children how they make sounds with their voices. If they hold their fingers gently against their throats while they speak, they will be able to feel the sound vibrations.

## Content

Voice sounds are made by air from the lungs moving over the vocal cords in the throat and making them vibrate. Controlling muscles can alter the tension in the cords and the distance between them. In this way they vary the pitch and quality of the sounds produced.

## Further activity

The children could investigate other sounds which they can make with their bodies such as clapping their hands and clicking their fingers.

*Sc AT4/1c*

# 8. Making our voices louder

## Group size

Pairs, small groups.

## What you need

Large sheets of strong paper or card, sticky tape, chalk, crayons.

## What to do

Discuss with the children how people can make their voices sound louder, for example, on stage in a theatre or outside in a crowd. Tell them they are going to make an instrument which will make their own voice louder so they will be able to talk more easily to their friends who are standing some distance away in the playground. Give the children the following instructions:

Roll a large sheet of paper or card into a cone shape. Try to make the cone as wide as possible. Secure the ends of the cone with tape.

They now have a 'megaphone'. Tell the children to test out their megaphone in the playground. Two children should stand some distance from each other. One child should shout a message to the other, who should walk towards his or her partner until the message is clearly audible. Mark this position with chalk. The children should now repeat the test, but tell them to use the megaphone to shout the message, speaking into the narrow end of the cone. Once again, they should mark the position where the message is clearly heard. Is the result the same if the children speak into the wide end of the megaphone? Suggest that they count the number of paces between the child holding the megaphone and the chalk marks. When they return to the classroom, ask the children to make a poster showing how well their megaphone worked. They could draw a picture of it and write down how many paces away they could hear the message.

The children could use the megaphone as an ear trumpet and see how effective it is for helping them hear sound more easily.

## Content

The megaphone helps to direct the sound-waves and the voice will travel further as a result. By turning the cone around and using the megaphone as an ear trumpet, sounds can be collected and directed to the ear.

*Sc AT4/1c*

# 9. Unwanted sounds

### Group size
Small groups.

### What you need
A cardboard box, a variety of packing materials such as newspapers, different fabrics, polystyrene chips or beans, cotton wool, a cushion, a collection of clocks including an alarm clock.

### What to do
Discuss with the children what time they wake up in the mornings. Do they sleep in at the weekends? How are they woken up in the morning? Some of the children may have an alarm clock in their bedroom. This may be a radio alarm or it may have a traditional alarm bell. Is the alarm bell a welcome or an unwelcome sound? Tell the children that they are going to carry out a test to see if they can make the alarm bell quieter or make the alarm sound disappear altogether. Each group could test out a different clock. They should first place the clock in the cardboard box. Can they hear the ticking? How loud is it? If it is an alarm clock, they should set the alarm and let it ring inside the box. How loud is the alarm bell? Can they easily hear both noises? The children could then try surrounding the clock with a single layer of packaging, for example,

newspaper. Does this make a difference to the loudness of the sound? More layers could be added until the sound becomes very faint or even disappears altogether. Is the ticking easier to eliminate than the alarm bell? Ask the children to repeat the activity using different packing materials. They could make a chart or collage to show the results of the tests.

This activity provides a good opportunity to talk to the children about fair tests. You could discuss the following variables:
• size of the box;
• number of layers of packaging;
• position of the listener in relation to the box.

Was it a fair test? How could they improve it?

### Content
Soft materials such as fabrics absorb the vibrations which create sound. Carpets in a room deaden the noise and reduce echoes.

### Further activity
Discuss with the children ways of reducing unwanted noise and where these might be needed, for instance, workers using noisy machinery wear ear protection.

*Sc AT4/1c*

# 10. Percussion instruments

### Group size
Pairs.

### What you need
A variety of containers made from plastic, cardboard and metal: small boxes, tins of different sizes, plastic bowls,

yoghurt pots, margarine tubs, plastic bottles, all with lids; a selection of different materials to fill the containers: dried peas and beans, lentils, bottle tops, pasta, salt, counters, nails, rice; clear food wrapping or a plastic bag, adhesive, sticky tape, some wooden sticks (for drumsticks).

## What to do

Talk to the children about different musical instruments, in particular about percussion instruments such as drums and maracas. Ask the children to make some percussion instruments of their own using the scrap materials available. They can make a variety of shakers with the pots and cartons. Two yoghurt pots filled with peas or salt, for example, and glued together will make an excellent shaker. Containers made of different materials can be used to make simple drums. Clear food wrapping or a plastic bag can be stretched tightly over empty containers to make drums. Drumsticks or the fingers can be used to produce the sound.

The children can experiment with different amounts of filling for the shakers. Can they make loud or soft sounds? Do different fillings make different sounds? Can they make up a simple rhythm?

They could make a tape recording of the sounds that they make. They could also make a display of their percussion instruments.

## Content

An instrument whose sound is produced by being struck or shaken may be classed as a percussion instrument.

*Sc AT4/1c*

# 11. Echoes or bouncing sounds

## Group size

The whole class.

## What you need

Locality which produces echoes such as a cliff, tunnel, well, building or courtyard.

## What to do

On a visit to a quarry, the seashore, tunnel, well or enclosed buildings, it might be possible to produce echoes. If practical, allow the children to experience the echo for themselves. Ask the children to suggest what is happening. If they have difficulty, help them by comparing the production of the echo to a light shining on a mirror.

## Content

Children will begin to appreciate that the sound bounces, or is reflected, off the walls of a building, cliff or tunnel to produce an echo. This can be compared with the reflection of light using a mirror.

*Sc AT4/3d*

# 12. Start or stop

## Group size

Small groups.

## What you need

A collection of percussion instruments, a conductor's baton or a drumstick.

### What to do

The children should work in groups. Each child should choose one of the percussion instruments and the group should then stand in a circle holding their instruments. A conductor is chosen and given a baton (or drumstick). The conductor should point at a child who then plays her instrument. The conductor should then point to another child to play. The first child should stop playing when the stick is no longer pointed at her. Once the group has become familiar with the idea of playing/not playing, i.e., starting and stopping, a short tune or series of sounds can be developed and repeated.

### Content

This activity introduces the children to the important idea of starting and stopping and following instructions from the conductor.

*Mu AT1, AT2*

# 13. Loud and soft

### Group size

Whole class/groups.

### What you need

A variety of instruments such as tambourines, triangles, maracas, shakers, (including percussion instruments which the children have made themselves), audio tapes of music which include loud and soft passages.

### What to do

Initiate a discussion about loud sounds and soft sounds. Play short pieces from the taped music and ask the children to identify loud and soft parts of the music. Which parts do they like best? Each child could try making a loud and soft sound with their chosen instrument. Using the start/stop idea (see the previous activity), the children can play loud and soft sounds when directed by the leader (conductor).

Ask the children to play very softly 'Baa, Baa Black Sheep' and loudly 'The Grand Old Duke of York', or other songs with which they are familiar. The children with bells, triangles and tambourines should play an appropriate song very softly and those with drums should play an appropriate song loudly. Ask the children to suggest 'loud' songs and 'quiet' songs. They could then sing these songs using their instruments to accompany them.

### Content

The children will learn to distinguish between loud and soft sounds through this activity. The activity will also develop listening skills.

*Mu AT1, AT2*

# 14. What instrument am I playing?

### Group size

The whole class.

### What you need

A collection of simple musical instruments, a screen.

## What to do

The children should carry out this activity after investigating the simple musical instruments in Activity 5. They should now be familiar with the sounds each instrument makes. A number of the instruments should be placed behind the screen before the children arrive. The children should take it in turns to go behind the screen and play one of the instruments. The rest of the class can try to identify which instrument has been played.

The activity can be repeated with the children playing a loud or soft sound. The rest of the class can then identify the instrument played and whether the sound is loud or soft.

## Content

This activity will help the children to understand that different sounds can be made using different instruments. They will also understand that sounds can be made in a variety of ways such as plucking, blowing, using different instruments. Listening skills will be developed through this activity.

*Mu AT1, AT2*

# 15. High and low

## Group size

Small groups, the whole class.

## What you need

A piano, a xylophone, chime bars, bottles, water, a soft beater.

## What to do

Play a 'scale' on the xylophone or piano to show how sound moves up and down. Ask the children to identify whether the sound is low or high, or moves up or comes down. Play high and low notes and ask the children to raise their arms in the air if the note is higher, or lower them to the ground if the note is low. Tell the children to sing a low note if you have your arm near to the ground, and to sing a high note if you raise your arm high.

Using a xylophone, chime bars, or a 'bottle organ' which they have made themselves (same-size bottles containing increasing amounts of water), the children can experiment with making their own high and low sounds. Can they make a musical 'scale'?

## Content

This activity introduces the children to the idea of pitch and a musical scale.

*Mu AT1, AT2*
*Sc AT4/1c*

# 16. Weather sounds

## Group size

Whole class, then groups of five or six.

## What you need

A variety of different musical instruments, including ones the children have made; weather story *Mixed-up weather*.

## What to do

Talk to the children about different weather sounds. Ask them what sounds rain makes on the windows; what about wind rattling a door? They could make rain or wind sounds with their voices. What sort of sound does thunder make? They could then select

instruments to play rain, wind, thunder and snow sounds. The snow will be a more muted sound than rain (perhaps a soft beater on a xylophone). Thunder may be represented by a loud drum beat.

The musical sounds the children make can then be used to illustrate a 'weather story' (see end of activity). It is important to read the story to the children a number of times so that they are familiar with it. The children could take turns being the narrator. The children should work in groups of five to six with selected instruments for each weather sound. The weather sound should be played after the relevant weather is mentioned in the story.

Give the children time to work together in their groups to practise making their weather sounds together.

## Content

This activity will help children to develop a response to visual images and experiences and sharpen auditory skills. It will deepen their understanding of weather conditions. Children will be encouraged to work co-operatively. They will also become more aware of the different sounds that instruments make and how they are produced.

*Mu AT1, AT2*
*Sc AT4/1c*

## Mixed-up weather

It was a cold winter's morning when David got out of bed. He looked out of the window and could not believe his eyes – it was *snowing*. The *snow* fell very softly and gently at first and everywhere was covered in a fresh, powdery-white blanket. David got out of bed, put on his clothes and ate some breakfast.

By the time he had gone outside, a *gentle wind* had started to blow. It blew the *snow* round and round making it very hard for David to see in front of him. Suddenly, the *wind* blew louder and the *snow* began to fall very heavily. David decided to build a lovely big fat snowman. Very soon he finished the snowman who had a big black bowler hat, a red and blue striped scarf and a small orange carrot for his nose.

Then David's dad called him in for lunch. As David sat eating his sandwiches, he noticed the *snow* had stopped and that big drops of water were dripping from the snowman's head. Just at that moment he realised it was *raining*. The *rain* began to fall so heavily that David's snowman began to melt away. Dad told him not to worry as the weather forecast said it would *snow* again that night. David finished his lunch and ran outside into the *rain*, just in time to rescue the hat and gloves from falling into the puddle made by the melting snowman. As he was walking back to the house, he noticed how the raindrops were sparkling in the sun. He thought how beautiful they looked, like hundreds of diamonds.

Later that afternoon when David was sitting in his *sun-filled* bedroom, he noticed a cloud crossing the sky which turned very dark. Soon he saw a flash of *lightning* which was followed by a crash of *thunder*. 'My goodness,' said David, 'I wish the weather would make up its mind today. First it was *snow*, then *wind*, then *rain*, then *sun* and now *thunder* and *lightning*.' He was so scared by the *thunder* and *lightning* that he hid under the table. 'I wish it could be *sunny* again,' he thought, 'then I could go out and play!'

# CHAPTER 5

# Earth, weather and seasons

The weather, seasons and climate affect our lives in a number of ways. They influence what we wear, what we do, affect our moods and lifestyles, determine the food that farmers grow and the food we eat.

The Science and Geography National Curriculum documents both make reference to rocks, soil, weather and seasons. The Science document also includes the position of the Sun relative to the Earth at different times of the day and during the different seasons and the physical processes involved in the water cycle. The geography document considers the concept of climate in various parts of the world, the different forms of water, and the passage of rainwater from hill to stream to river to sea. Clearly, the concepts, knowledge and understanding and skills associated with these two curriculum areas may be considered in a cross-curricular project. In this chapter an 'Earth, Weather and Seasons' project is considered at Key Stages 1 and 2, so that teachers may select the activities appropriate for the ages and abilities of their children.

At Key Stage 1 children may observe rocks, soil and water, consider the changes in day length, weather and seasons at different times of the year and in different parts of the world, record the weather over a period of time, investigate the different forms of water and explore weathering of buildings and rocks.

At Key Stage 2, children may study the different forms of water in the environment, how rainfall reaches lakes and the sea from the slopes of hills via streams, tributaries and rivers, and the physical processes involved in the water cycle. They may record temperature, rainfall, windspeed and wind direction, and study extremes of weather, the effects of weathering and erosion of rocks to form soil and the characteristics of soil.

While some aspects of 'Earth, weather and seasons' may be studied as a project, other aspects such as recording the weather or investigating the path of the Sun are more appropriately studied on an ongoing basis.

# BACKGROUND

**Weather**
- Seasonal patterns
- Different forms of water, e.g. ice
- Factors affecting temperature and wind
- Seasonal distribution in the UK

**Natural materials**
- Rock and soil characteristics
- Water in the environment
  - the water cycle
  - melting and freezing
  - drainage
  - parts of a river system
  - flooding and prevention
- Erosion and transport

**EARTH WEATHER AND SEASONS**

**Key Stages 1 and 2**

**Weather recording**
- Temperature
- Rainfall
- Wind speed and direction

**Weathering and erosion**
- Buildings
- Rocks
- Erosion and transport and deposition of materials
- Soil formation

| Activity | Curriculum area | ATTAINMENT TARGET AND LEVEL | | | | |
|---|---|---|---|---|---|---|
| | | AT1 | AT2 | AT3 | AT4 | AT5 |
| 1 | Science<br>Geography | 1a, 2a | | 1a<br>1a | | |
| 2 | Science | 1a, 2b | | | 1d, 2e | |
| 3 | Science<br>Geography | 1a, 2b | | 2a | | |
| 4 | Science<br>Geography | 1a, 2b, 3b | | 2a | | |
| 5 | Science<br>Geography | 1a, 2a, 2b | | 2b<br>2b | | |
| 6 | Geography | | | 3a | | |
| 7 | Science<br>Geography | 3a | | 3c<br>5d | | |
| 8 | Science | | | | 3e, 4e | |
| 9 | Science<br>Geography | (Sc)1a,2a,2b,2c,<br>(Sc)3a,3b,3c,3d | | 3b, 3c, 4c, 5c | | |
| 10 | Science | | | 4d | | |
| 11 | Science | | | 4d | | |
| 12 | Science | | | 4d | | |
| 13 | Science | 4a, 4c | | 4d | | |
| 14 | Science | | | 4e | | |
| 15 | Science | | | 4e | | |
| 16 | Science<br>Geography | | | 3b, 4e, PoS(iv),<br>4e | | |
| 17 | Geography | | | 5a | | |
| 18 | Science<br>Geography | | | 5d<br>3c, 4c | | |

# ACTIVITIES

## Key Stage 1

### 1. Rocks, soil, sand and water

**Group size**
The whole class or large groups.

**What you need**
Samples of rocks, sand, soil and water in appropriate containers, magnifying lens.

**What to do**
Show the children the four samples and play a naming game with them. Label each sample. Take one of the samples of rock and ask the children to suggest words to describe it. They might suggest that it is 'big', 'heavy', 'hard'. Encourage them to ask questions about the samples, for example, 'what will happen if we put the sand in water?' Ask the children to draw what they see and describe each item using simple words.

**Content**
All four samples are found in the natural environment. Rocks are large, heavy, hard and will scratch soft items. Sand is made up of tiny, sharp rock particles. Soil is soft and can be broken up and flattened out. Water is wet and runny. Rocks, sand and soil are solids while water is a liquid, but this will be difficult for most seven year-olds to understand. The children will be observing familiar materials and may ask questions, suggest ideas and predictions.

**Safety**
Rocks can cause a great deal of damage to little toes and care should be taken that sand is not blown into eyes. Hands should be washed after touching soil and reminders should be given to keep fingers away from the mouth.

*Sc AT1/1a,2a; AT3/1a*
*Gg AT3/1a*

### 2. Day length and the seasons

**Group size**
Small groups.

**What you need**
Window through which the sun may be observed for as much of the day as possible.

**What to do**
On a day when little or no (thick) cloud is expected, talk to the children about night and day. Why do we have night? What is always present during the day, even if sometimes we cannot see it because it is behind clouds? Ask the children if they have noticed any changes to the sun during the day. Is it at the same height in the sky? Does it appear to move in the sky? Ask the children to draw accurate pictures out of the window three or five times in the day to show the position of the sun (but see Safety below). Alternatively, you might like to provide them with a pre-drawn picture on which they add the Sun. Add times of the day

(e.g., early morning or 9 o'clock) to their pictures.

## Content
The children should be able to see from their pictures that the sun appears to move in the sky during the day. They should be able to describe how it is low in the sky in the morning, high at the middle of the day and low again in the afternoon and evening.

Teachers need to be aware that it is the Earth that moves around the Sun and not vice versa. The height of the Sun at any particular time varies with the seasons. For instance, in the winter the Sun has barely risen above the horizon at 9am but in the summer, is high in the sky by this time. Children could compare and contrast a typical day in each of the seasons, looking at such aspects as length of daylight, weather and visibility, and the way their daily routine is affected.

Children should be informed that the Sun, the Moon and the Earth are separate, round (spherical) structures. This could be reinforced by models or photographs taken in space. The children might be of the view that the Sun and the Moon belong with the background of the sky, rather than being separate bodies on their own.

## Safety
It is dangerous to look directly at the Sun and children must be reminded of this. For this reason it may be advisable to produce pre-drawn pictures of the view out of the school window to reduce the viewing time.

*Sc AT1/1a,2b;*
*AT4/1d,2e*

# 3. Changing weather and seasons

## Group size
The whole class.

## What you need
Pictures showing different weather conditions associated with particular seasons; paper, pencils and crayons or paints, paintbrushes.

## What to do
Talk to the children about the weather at different times of the year (seasons). Ask them whether they know any poems or songs about the weather and seasons. Introduce them to sayings such as 'March winds and April showers' in the spring or songs such as 'Frostie the Snowman' which we sing in winter. With the assistance of the pictures, help the children to identify the weather associated with these seasons and summer and autumn. Ask them to draw pictures and to use words to describe their observations and experiences of the weather and seasons.

## Content
This activity helps the children to recognise weather patterns and to associate these with the four seasons of the year.

*Sc AT1/1a,2b*
*Gg AT3/2a*

# 4. Recording the weather

## Group size
The whole class and pairs.

## What you need
A chart on which the weather can be recorded; cards showing the day of the week, date, month and weather type, cards with pictorial representations of the weather, Blu-Tack.

### What to do

Encourage the children to record the weather at the same time each day or to summarise the day's weather at the end of the day. While a daily or weekly weather chart could be made, possibly with help from the children, a monthly chart would be beneficial for more advanced children. Some children might see the benefits of using more than one symbol to describe the day's weather, particularly if it has changed substantially. The temperature and wind direction could be added to the chart if felt appropriate to the children's ability. The daily chart requires cards with the date, weather and related picture to be attached with Blu-Tack.

The children, working in pairs, could fill in a weekly chart with symbols they have produced together. Words could be added to this, while a monthly chart could record the number of days a particular type of weather was experienced.

### Content

There are many different types of weather. Weather changes frequently. Particular types of weather such as hot and sunny, and cold and snowy may be associated with particular seasons – summer and winter. The weather may be recorded over a period of time using a variety of methods of communication, for example, words, drawings, pictures and charts.

### Further activity

Collect weather sayings such as 'The North wind shall blow and we shall have snow' and 'Red sky at night – shepherd's delight'

**Sc AT1/1a,2b,3b
Gg AT3/2a**

# Key Stages 1 and 2

## 5. Ice and water – one and the same thing?

### Group size

Large groups or the whole class.

### What you need

Ice cubes or an ice balloon, made by filling a balloon with water and placing it in the freezer (remove the balloon after freezing); water, a kettle (optional), pictures of rain, fog, clouds, rivers, ponds, seas, hail, frost and snow.

### What to do

Show the ice and water to the children. Show them the pictures and ask whether, for instance, fog is like ice or water. Talk about the dampness on their faces and clothes, on the ground and on vehicles, on a foggy morning. Repeat this line of questioning for hail, snow and rain. Ask the children if there is a connection between ice and water. What would happen if we heated up ice? What would happen if we put water in the freezer? Tell the children to record the various forms of water in the environment under the headings of 'Water' (liquid) and 'Ice' (solid).

### Content

Water occurs in the environment in two main forms. It is found as a liquid in rain, fog, clouds, ponds, streams, rivers, seas and oceans and as a solid in ice, frost, hail and snow. Water is also found as a vapour or gas when it evaporates or is boiled, and while this may be demonstrated with a kettle, it is a difficult concept for young children to appreciate.

The children will have found out from experience and from the above activity that ice melts to form water. Collecting that water and putting it in a container in the freezer will reinforce the idea that the process is reversible on cooling.

*Sc AT1/1a,2a,2b; AT3/2b*
*Gg AT3/2b*

# 6. Weather and climate in different parts of the world

## Group size
The whole class.

## What you need
A videotape, slides or pictures of polar regions, temperate areas, deserts and tropical rainforests, paper, pencils.

## What to do
Show the children the video, slides or pictures. After some discussion ask them to record what it would be like from a weather point of view to live in a polar region, a temperate climate such as Great Britain, in a jungle and in a tropical rainforest. What are the advantages and disadvantages of each?

## Content
In the polar regions it is cold and the land is covered completely in snow and ice. Temperate climates such as

the British climate are characterised by cool winters and warm summers. Deserts have much sun and little rain and are hot and dry. It is hot and wet in a tropical forest due to the high temperatures and high rainfall.

All the climates except the temperate climate will involve a level of abstraction for the children. It is important therefore that the learning is made as concrete as possible through good secondary sources.

*Gg AT3/3a*

# 7. Weathering

## Group size
The whole class.

## What you need
Drawings showing examples of weathering (see photocopiable page 184), pictures showing examples of weathering, a camera (optional).

## What to do
Take the children for a walk, if possible, in the countryside. Look for evidence of weathering, bearing in mind that it is difficult to spot, except for rock falls, scree slopes and erosion of paths. This evidence might need to be supplemented by secondary source materials and photocopiable page 184. If you are taking the children for a walk in town, look at statues, gravestones, steps and old buildings for signs of weathering. Is it worse on one side of the statue or gravestone? Why might this be? Can the children read all the inscription on the

## 8. Position and height of the Sun

### Group size
Small groups and the whole class.

### What you need
A window through which the Sun may be observed for as much of the day as possible by sitting on a chair in a fixed postion near to the window; smoked glass (see Safety below); relatively large pictures (10–15cm in diameter) of the Sun with space for time of day and month/season of the year to be added. Alternatively, set up a shadow stick or sundial in the playground and mark the position and length of the shadows throughout a whole day in winter. Repeat in the spring and/or summer using different colours. The shadows could be painted on the playground for use in future years, but it is preferable to draw them on to a large piece of paper for ease of comparison and for the sake of a concrete experience for the children.

### What to do
Sit a child on the chair. Get another child to position a picture of the Sun in direct line between the child sitting down and the Sun itself. This may be carried out by a squinted, quick estimate or by using smoked glass (see Safety below). Allow the children to follow the path of the Sun by placing other pictures of the Sun throughout the day at half hourly or hourly intervals.

gravestones? Is one type of stone affected more than another? Are some of the buildings changing colour or crumbling?

The children may record evidence and the effects of weathering in the form of annotated pictures and compare these with the secondary source materials.

## Content
Children should start to understand some of the effects of weathering on buildings and on rocks. For example, they should be able to describe and recognise the signs of weathering on the stonework of older buildings and gravestones in their locality. This might include discoloration, crumbling and loss of detail. The very slow damage and subsequent breakdown of buildings and the landscape due to physical and/or chemical processes is called weathering.

Weathering takes place in a number of ways, but wind and rain are the most obvious causes. As well as the physical impact of wind and rain, the wind might carry small particles which speed up the weathering process when they make contact with buildings. Pollutants in the atmosphere such as carbon dioxide and sulphur dioxide combine with water to produce weak acids which further the weathering process on stone, rocks and cliffs. Heat from the sun or from fire and from cold in the form of frost cause expansion and contraction of rocks, which eventually causes them to crack, thus allowing more surfaces to be attacked by wind and rain. The roots of plants can also cause rocks and tarmac to crack as they grow.

The children might suggest that there is more damage on one of the gravestones due to the wind direction and proceed to investigate this idea.

## Safety
Careful supervision will be required in graveyards to ensure appropriate behaviour.

*Sc AT1/3a; AT3/3c*
*Gg AT3/5d*

When was the Sun at its lowest point? When was it at its highest point?

Leave the pictures of the Sun on the window and mark the path throughout the day, and repeat at least once three or six months later. Compare the paths.

## Content
Like the appearance (phases) of the Moon, the position and height of the Sun in the sky changes in a regular way. Children should be aware of the predictable pattern in which the Sun appears low in the sky in the mornings and evenings and highest in the sky during the middle of the day. They should also be aware that in winter the day is short and that the Sun does not reach a high altitude in the sky, whereas in the summer the day is long and the Sun is very high at midday.

## Further activity
The children should be introduced to the difficult concepts of day length, day and night, year length, the seasons, phases of the Moon and eclipses by first learning about the motions of the Earth, Moon and Sun.

## Safety
Children should only look at the Sun through smoked glass or a suitable alternative unless a speedy, squinted estimate of the position is made. The alternative of using a sundial is preferable from a safety

point of view but extrapolation of the results obtained is more abstract and removed from experience.

*Sc AT4/3e,4e*

# 9. Rainfall, drainage and rivers

## Group size
Small groups and the whole class.

## What you need
A watering can; trays containing sand, soil, grass, concrete, watching water collected off the school buildings in guttering, drainpipes and drains; maps, pictures or other secondary sources on hills, valleys, streams, a river and a sea; large sheets of paper. A trip to

a nearby stream or river (or a video viewing of a river) to show streams (tributaries) joining a river and eventually flowing into a lake or sea.

## What to do
Encourage the children to watch what happens to the rainfall around their school or house. If possible, visit a river system in an area joined by streams/tributaries/other rivers. Set up four trays (see Figure 1 below) containing sand, soil, grass and concrete. Inform the children that they are to investigate drainage using a watering can to simulate rainfall, and that they should do everything possible to ensure a fair test. Ask the children to predict and explain which surface will drain most quickly and which surface will produce the most run-off. Keep the trays flat for the first test but repeat at a later date by sloping the trays. Discuss the results qualitatively or quantitatively if the run-off water is measured.

**Figure 1**

SAND        SOIL        GRASS        CONCRETE

Give the children a large piece of paper and ask them to draw a hill and, on its side, a small house with drainpipes, surrounded by fields. Ask the children what happens to rainfall once it has fallen on the house and the fields. Where does it go? Get them to draw and label, in as much detail as possible, the route it takes (shown with arrows) between the house and the fields, and the river and/or sea.

## Content
The amount and speed with which water drains will depend on the surface on which the water falls and the angle or slope of that surface. Thus the more absorbent the surface (e.g., sand), the faster the drainage although there may be little run-off of excess water. The initial amount of water in the soil also makes some difference. A wet soil may allow water to drain less quickly than a drier soil, but the run-off will be greater in the former as little of the water will be absorbed. Clearly, concrete or tarmac will not allow water to drain through it but the run-off will be great. The steeper the slope, the greater will be the run-off of water and also the erosion of sand or soil particles.

The trays should be set up with the same volume of materials, of equal dampness, with the same amount of bare space in the tray and with the same amount of water, sprayed on the trays with the same distribution and speed. Setting up the experiment properly enables the teacher to assess whether the children can carry out a fair test.

The children will label hills, valleys, streams, rivers and the sea on their picture. More able children could be introduced to terminology such as the source of the river, channels, tributaries and mouth. They could also be encouraged to estimate the height at various points of the journey from the house at 100 metres above sea level to the sea at 0 metres.

### Further activity
More able children could use secondary sources to find out why rivers flood and the methods frequently used to prevent flooding. For example, the Clywedog dam in Powys helps to prevent major flooding in the Severn valley while the Aswan dam in Egypt prevents the Nile delta from uncontrolled flooding. The Thames Barrier is intended to prevent London flooding when the river is in spate and the tides are high. The children could also be introduced to the idea that many of these methods are expensive.

### Safety
The normal safety procedures of adequate staff supervision should be imperative on any field outing, as should adequate research of the area for potential hazards.

*Sc AT1/1a,2a,2b,2c,3a, 3b,3c,3d*
*Gg AT3/3b,3c,4c,5c*

# 10. What is the temperature today?

### Group size
Individuals or pairs.

### What you need
A maximum/minimum thermometer, or a spirit type thermometer, temperature charts, pencils.

### What to do
It would be beneficial if a maximum/minimum thermometer was located just

outside a classroom window out of direct sunshine, but positioned so that it can be read from inside the room. Ask the children to read and record the maximum and minimum temperature for the day or, alternatively, to take a number of readings, for example, minimum overnight temperature, temperature at 9am, 12 noon and 3pm hours. If the maximum and minimum readings are to be taken, the maximum and minimum markers will have to be moved back to the mercury stream on a daily basis.

Alternatively, a spirit thermometer could be taken out of the classroom on a daily basis and readings taken and recorded. If this is the case, then a period of equilibration will be needed to allow the thermometer to adjust to the outside temperature.

### Content
Through carrying out this activity the children will know how measurements of temperature describe the weather. They will also be able to relate the temperatures recorded to a feeling of 'cold', 'cool', 'warm' or 'hot'. Children will gain experience in recording temperatures over a long period of time and gradually the school will be able to build up a bank of data, possibly on the computer, which may be accessed and compared with current data.

### Further activities
Possible follow-up activities could include:
• comparing temperatures in different parts of Europe and the rest of the world;
• comparing temperature in the locality with temperature one, two, three or more years ago;

• comparing temperature with that predicted on the weather forecast.

### Safety
Children must be careful when carrying glass thermometers. Spirit thermometers are preferable to mercury thermometers, due to the toxicity of this metal at relatively high temperatures.

*Sc AT3/4d*

# 11. Raindrops keep falling on my head

### Group size
The whole class and pairs.

### What you need
A commercially produced rain gauge, for example, NES Arnold; NB1170/1 or NB11714.

### What to do
Discuss with the children the purposes for recording the weather and in particular the amount of rainfall. Relate this to information given about

holiday resorts and information farmers might require before sowing crops.

Show the children the rain gauge and explain its function. Talk about the scale and ensure that the children are able to measure the amount of rainfall accurately. Organise the recording on a rota basis. Discuss where the rain gauge should be sited (in an open space, away from trees and buildings). Locate the rain gauge according to the instructions and record on a daily basis at a regular time each day. Remember that Monday readings will be a combination of rainfall on Friday, Saturday and Sunday.

### Content
Children have the opportunity to make regular quantitative records of the rainfall and to relate these to the seasons of the year. As records build up, they will be able to compare the rainfall in one month with the rainfall in the same month the previous year.

A cloud contains millions and millions of tiny water droplets. When the cloud rises and cools down, the tiny droplets coalesce to form larger droplets which fall as rain. Snow falls when these droplets freeze.

Very accurate measurements of rainfall may be made with purchased rain gauges as these have been calibrated. With home-made versions, accurate measurements may only be made if the surface area for collection is the same as the surface area for storage and measurement of the rain, or if calibration were carried out which would be beyond the mathematical ability of most primary school children.

### Safety
The siting of rain gauges needs some thought so that children do not trip over them. Open sites are prone to vandalism and interference.

Sc AT3/4d

# 12. Speedy winds

### Group size
The whole class and pairs.

### What you need
A commercially produced anemometer or a model constructed from a shoe-box, a knitting needle or a piece of dowel, double thickness of foil or thin card; photocopiable page 185.

### What to do
Ask the children to construct an anemometer as shown in Figure 1. Alternatively, they could design and make their own. Ask them to record the wind speed by measuring the

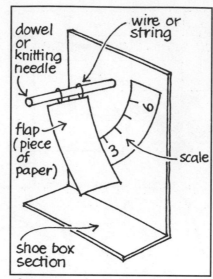

**Figure 1**

maximum deviation of the flap on the scale on the side of the box. Alternatively, look at the effects of the wind in the environment such as the leaves blowing and compare this evidence with the chart of the Beaufort scale (see photocopiable page 185). The speed of the wind may then be determined. Record the maximum wind speed at the same time or times each day.

### Content
An anemometer is a device to measure wind speed. The Beaufort scale was devised by Admiral Sir Francis Beaufort to estimate wind speed at sea but has since been adapted for use on land. He devised a 13-point scale (0–12) and at each point he gave the wind a number, a description, a range of speeds and a description of its effects. The Beaufort scale is shown on photocopiable page 185.

### Further activities
• Compare the different types of anemometers designed by the children.
• Compare this month's readings with last month's, or the same month last year.

• Ask the children to produce a pictorial Beaufort scale.
• Ask the children to research information about wind speeds in the *Guinness Book of Weather Facts and Feats* (Guinness Publications).

Sc AT3/4d

# 13. The North wind doth blow

### Group size
Pairs or small groups.

### What you need
Dowelling, a thin piece of balsa wood (30cm × 1.5cm) with a hole larger than the diameter of the dowel, a polystyrene tile, two beads, felt-tipped pens, a container full of soil, a compass. Alternatively, a commercially purchased weather-vane.

### What to do
Ask the children to make the weather-vane as shown in Figure 2 below. It is important that the force of friction between the balsa wood, dowel and beads is reduced to a

**Figure 2**

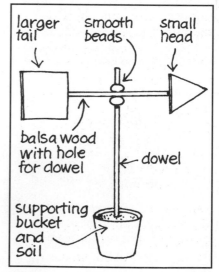

| Day | Date | Wind direction | | |
| --- | --- | --- | --- | --- |
| | | *at 9.00* | *at 12.00* | *at 3.00* |
| | | | | |
| | | | | |
| | | | | |

minimum. Ask them to mark North, East, South and West on the container. The children should set up the vane away from the buildings, ensuring that the North point on the vane faces the magnetic North on the compass.

Ask the children to record the wind direction at the same time or times each day, using an appropriate chart such as the one above.

Ask the children to compare the directions of the wind with the temperature on a number of days in the same week. From the data, the children could suggest a hypothesis which could be tested such as 'North and East winds give cold temperatures'.

## Content
Winds get their names from the direction from which they blow. Thus a North wind is generally cold and a South wind is usually warm. The most common winds in Great Britain are from the west, travelling across the Atlantic before reaching these shores.

The arrow on a weather-vane points in the direction from which the wind is blowing. The force of friction must be reduced if the vane is to move appropriately.

## Safety
Any form of construction has possible dangers, though the materials used to construct the weather-vane should not cause concern if used sensibly.

*Sc AT1/4a,4c; AT3/4d*

# 14. Soils: where do they come from?

## Group size
Pairs or small groups.

## What you need
Various rock samples such as chalk, granite, limestone, sandstone and slate; sandpaper, a file, a vice, safety glasses or goggles, a magnifier, hand lens or stereo microscope; containers.

## What to do
Talk to the children about rocks and soil and how the latter has been formed. Is there any connection between the two? Indicate the many ways in which rocks may weather. Ask the children to collect a rock and to rub it against a rock of the same type. Alternatively, they could file a piece of rock held in place in a vice, or rub it with sandpaper, though the latter will produce particles of its own. Collect the particles and ask the children to describe and draw what they observe. Relate the particles produced by rubbing the rock to the process of soil formation. It will be necessary to inform the children that they have gone some way to making soil in a few minutes but that the natural process of erosion takes much longer.

## Content

The weathering of rocks gradually leads to the formation of soil. The type of soil is indicative of the type of rock from which it was formed. In the south of England, the white-coloured soil reflects the chalk deposits below it. Elsewhere in Britain, soil can be a dark orange-red or yellow colour due to the underlying sandstone. In other cases, the link between the soil and rock is not so striking. Through this activity, children will be introduced to the idea that the weathering of rocks leads to the formation of soil. Rock particles mix with stone and humus (remains of plants and animals) to produce the soil in fields and gardens.

## Further activity

• Observe the composition of soil by mixing it with water in a deep, clear container, shaking it up and allowing it to settle.

• Compare the drainage speed of two different types of soils such as sandy and clay soils.

## Safety

Safety glasses are recommended to reduce the risk of small particles of dust getting into children's eyes.

*Sc AT3/4e*

# 15. A weather walk

## Group size

The whole class.

## What you need

Sheets of paper to record observations on the walk.

## What to do

Take the children on a 'weather walk', preferably after some extremes of weather conditions. A rural setting would be ideal and the walk could be repeated after different types of weather (though this may be difficult to organise). Discuss with the children how the weather affects the surroundings.

In the winter, they may witness frost, fog, ice and snow. The road sides might be dirty with melted snow and salted grit. The roads may be damaged by frost.

In the spring, heavy rains may have washed some of the soil from a ploughed field on to the path or road, or high winds might have broken twigs or branches off trees or even uprooted the tree itself.

In a dry, hot summer the vegetation may be dry and brown, with cracks appearing in the soil. The water level of rivers and pools may be low.

In the autumn, fogs may reduce visibility or heavy winds may lead to damage of trees, fences and buildings.

## Content

This activity will enable the children to understand better the effects of the weather and weathering, and erosion on their surroundings. Looking at the erosion of a ploughed field and the next activity will help them to understand that the weathering, erosion and transport lead to the formation of sediments and different types of soil.

## Safety

The normal safety precautions and staff supervision would be required on the walk.

*Sc AT3/4e*

# 16. The answer lies in the soil

## Group size

Small groups or individuals.

## What you need

A field trip to sites containing different soils or photographs of soil profiles; samples of a sandy soil, a clay soil and a loam soil; stereoscope microscopes, hand lenses; coarse, medium and fine sieves, tall plastic containers filled with water into which the children can pour the soil; universal indicator paper.

## What to do
On a field visit, identify characteristics of different soils by digging deep into the soil. Ask the children to record details about the depth of the soil and its colour. Pass some of the soil to the children so that they may comment on its texture and possibly on the appearance or absence of organic matter. These two characteristics may be looked at further in the classroom.

Alternatively, you can use secondary sources or bought specimens of soil profiles.

Back in the classroom, the children could find whether the soil was acidic, neutral or alkaline by mixing a small quantity of soil with water (preferably de-ionised water) and dipping a small piece of Universal indicator paper into the water once it has cleared. Water content of the three soils could be calculated by taking 100g of each and allowing it to dry over a radiator and then re-weighing. A fair test could be achieved by obtaining the soils from an open area on the same day and at the same depth.

## Content
The characteristics of soil such as colour, depth, presence of organic content and texture may be studied in the field and classroom. Clay soils contain very small, smooth particles, sandy soils have large, coarse particles, while a loam soil has characteristics of both, as well as a high organic

content. The occurrence of sandy soils close to riverbeds could be related to the weathering, erosion and transport of rock particles leading to sediment and soil formation.

## Further activity
Children could draw on a local map the position of certain natural materials such as sands, soils, deposits of coal and limestone and label the major rock types.

## Safety
The normal safety procedures of adequate staff supervision should be imperative on any field outing, as should adequate research of the area for potential hazards.

**Sc AT3/3b,4e, PoS(iv)**
**Gg AT3/4e**

# 17. The warmest and wettest places in the UK

## Group size
Individuals.

## What you need
Monthly, seasonal or annual rainfall and temperature records for the British Isles either on distribution maps or stored in, or transferred to, a database. For annual rainfall and summer average temperature of the British Isles see 'Bread – the staff of life', on page 132.

British Isles (see 'Food and Farming', activities 8–13, pages 131 to 136).

*Gg AT3/5a*

# 18. The water cycle

## Group size
The whole class and pairs.

## What you need
Photocopiable page 186.

## What to do
Discuss with the children where we get our water from. Follow up the likely answer 'the taps' with further questions about the origin of water, including the use of reservoirs or underground water reserves which are replenished via streams, rivers and ultimately rainfall. This could be drawn on a piece of paper, chalkboard or on an OHP transparency as ideas are raised and agreed upon.

Then ask the children to consider what happens to waste water in their homes and to the water in streams and rivers. Add this to the drawing and illustrate the water cycle by drawing arrows and naming the physical processes involved. Explain such processes as evaporation, condensation and precipitation.

The children may then work in pairs to further their understanding of the water cycle by cutting out the captions on photocopiable page 186 which illustrates the stages of the water cycle, and then sticking them on the relevant places on the picture.

## Content
Children should understand the water cycle in terms of the relevant physical processes. This will involve them in using their knowledge of heating, evaporation, condensation, movements in the atmosphere and flow of water on the Earth's surface, to explain the water cycle.

Water is usually found as a liquid but it can also be found as a solid (ice) and a gas (steam or water vapour). Nearly 98 per cent of the world's water is in liquid form, about 2 per cent is ice and very little (0.0005 per cent) is in the form of water vapour in the atmosphere.

Water evaporates at all temperatures above freezing. The water vapour so formed rises into the atmosphere where it cools and condenses. As a result, droplets of water are formed which become heavy as more water vapour condenses. These heavy droplets fall as rain (precipitation) or snow, sleet or hail if the temperature is cooler.

*Sc AT3/5d*
*Gg AT3/3c,4c*

## What to do
Ask the children to compare the monthly or seasonal rainfall and temperature data for their area. When is the highest and when is the lowest? Which other towns/counties/areas have similar records? The children could draw graphs to compare data from different areas or weather stations, using a database to store and retrieve information.

If maps showing seasonal and annual distribution of rainfall and temperature are available, as well as information on a database, these data could be described and compared.

## Content
Children will be introduced to the seasonal patterns of rainfall and temperature in the British Isles. This could be related to holiday locations and more importantly to the success of agriculture in the

# CHAPTER 6

# Tudors and Stuarts

This project concentrates on the Key Stage 2 study unit which is one of the in-depth studies of history. Following the recommendations of the National Curriculum documents, the project focuses on the way of life at all levels of society during the Tudor and Stuart period. There is a requirement that children become familiar with the factual content in order to understand the causes and effects of events of the time. In addition, there is the need to establish Tudor and Stuart times in the appropriate chronological slot. Such requirements might persuade teachers, especially those who are not historians by training, to teach in a formal way.

This project is designed to help teachers avoid such an approach, providing opportunities for children to be involved in a wide range of skill-based activities. Teachers are also encouraged to use diary extracts and other contemporary accounts as a basis for the development of the concept of evidence and its application.

A useful starting point for the project could be a classroom display of the Kings and Queens of England developed by both teacher and children. A television or video broadcast might help to focus on these particular dynasties, so that the main characters in the project come to life.

The project is extended into aspects of science and technology, including such activities as making a compass and investigating the many spices which were brought home to Europe by the early explorers.

# BACKGROUND

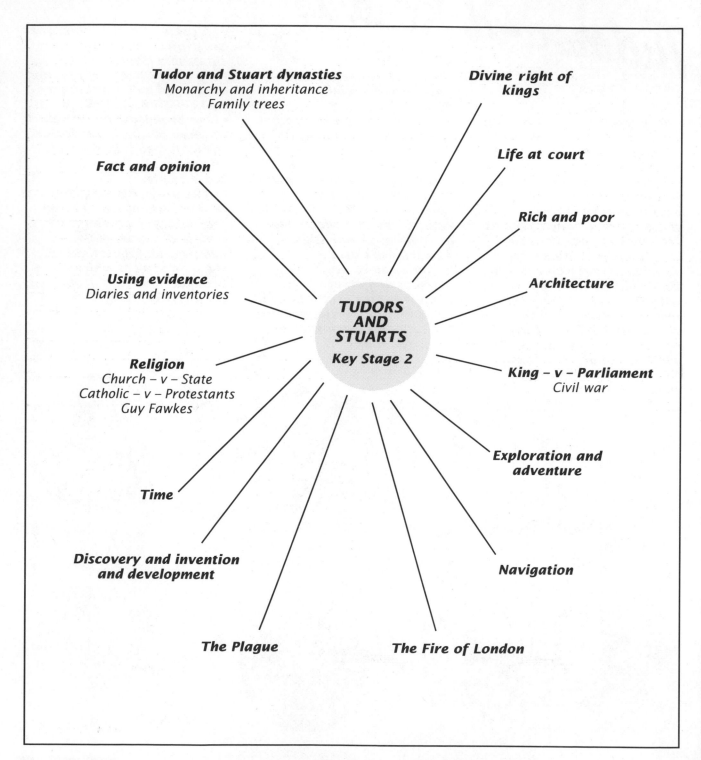

Tudor and Stuart dynasties
Monarchy and inheritance
Family trees

Divine right of
kings

Fact and opinion

Life at court

Rich and poor

Using evidence
Diaries and inventories

Architecture

TUDORS
AND
STUARTS
Key Stage 2

Religion
Church – v – State
Catholic – v – Protestants
Guy Fawkes

King – v – Parliament
Civil war

Exploration and
adventure

Time

Discovery and invention
and development

Navigation

The Plague

The Fire of London

| Activity | Curriculum area | ATTAINMENT TARGET AND LEVEL | | | | |
|---|---|---|---|---|---|---|
| | | AT1 | AT2 | AT3 | AT4 | AT5 |
| 1 | History | 2c, 3c, 4a | 2, 4 | 2, 3 | | |
| 2 | History | 3a, 4a | | 2 | | |
| 3 | History | | 3, 4 | 2 | | |
| 4 | History | 2b, 4c | | 2,3 | | |
| 5 | History | 2c, 3a, 4a, 4c | | 2,3 | | |
| 6 | History | 2b, 3b, 4b | 2, 3 | | | |
| 7 | History | 2b, 4a, 4b | 2, 3 | 2, 3 | | |
| 8 | History | 2b, 2c, 3b, 4a, 4b, 4c | 4 | 2, 4 | | |
| 9 | History | 2b,3b,4a,4b,4c | 2, 3 | 2 | | |
| 10 | History | 2b, 3a, 3b, 3c | 2, 3 | | | |
| 11 | History | 2b 2c 3b, 4b | | 2, 3, 4 | | |
| 12 | Science | | | | 2a | |
| 13 | Science | | | | 2a, PoS(i) | |
| 14 | Science Technology | | 3a, 3d, 4b, 4d | 3b,3c,3d,4b,4c | 4c 3b, 4a, 4b | |
| 15 | Science | | | | 2d, 3e | |
| 16 | Science | 2a,3a,3c,4a,4b | | | | |
| 17 | Science Technology | 2b,3a,3c,4a,4b | 3b, 3c, 3d | 3b, 3c, 3d | 3b, 4b, 4c | |

# ACTIVITIES

## 1. A Tudor and Stuart time-line

### Group size
Small groups.

### What you need
A prepared time-line on a display board marked off in decades from 1485 to 1702; Pictures of the monarchies who ruled during this time; A4 sized paper, pencils, crayons, felt-tipped pens.

### What to do
Explain the nature of the dynasties to the whole class. The Tudors and Stuarts were two related families who between them ruled Britain as kings and queens for over 200 years. Make sure the children understand the concept of hereditary monarchy and autocracy.

Working in groups of two to three, ask the children to look at a portrait of a monarch. Can they tell from the portrait what kind of a person they were? Would the artist paint them as they really were? Ask each group to design a poster which includes a portrait of a different monarch, dates of the reign and name. Make these into a time-line by placing them chronologically, by their dates of accession to the throne.

### Content
Children will be introduced to the following concepts;
• the principle of hereditary monarchy – when a monarch died, the crown passed to the eldest son, daughter, nearest male relative or nearest female relative (in that order of priority);
• royal authority was believed to be ordained by God;
• monarchs were very powerful and governed the country with the help of Parliament. This can be contrasted with modern democracies where governments are elected by the people.

### Further activity
Continue to add to the time-line throughout the topic, including political and cultural events as well as the lives of famous people.

**H AT1/2c,3c,4a; AT2/2,4; AT3/2,3; CSU 2**

## 2. A family tree

### Group size
Small groups.

### What you need
Photocopiable pages 187 and 188, pencils, crayons, a large sheet of paper.

### What to do
Ask the children to take turns at reading a card, working out the answer by looking at the family tree and turning the card over to check. Ask the children to place the cards on a large sheet of paper in such a way as to show the family relationships.

Paste the cards in place, draw in the lines of connection and illustrate to form a large poster.

## Content

Children need to talk through the relationships involved and emphasis should be put on the notion of inheritance, discussing such issues as why the crown went to the male heir, what might happen if there were no offspring and the divine right of kings to rule.

## Further activity

• Children can draw and illustrate their own family tree.
• Draw the family tree of the present royal family and discuss its role today and how it is different from the monarchy in Tudor and Stuart times. Should it be retained today?

*H AT1/3a,4a; AT3/2 CSU 2*

# 3. Fact or point of view?

## Group size
Small groups.

## What you need
Photocopiable page 189, a large piece of paper divided into two columns, headed 'Fact' and 'Point of view', a selection of sources on Henry VIII, a set of blank strips the same size as the statements on the photocopiable page.

## What to do
Explain the difference between a fact and a point of view. A fact is known to be true and cannot be disputed; a point of view is someone's opinion or own idea.
    Ask the children to categorise the statements by placing them in the appropriate columns. Encourage them to give reasons for their choices and

to discuss them in their groups.
    Ask the children to look at other sources and to list any information they can find about Henry VIII. Write these on blank slips and add to the appropriate column.

## Content
It will help if the children are reasonably familiar with the 'story' of Henry VIII. Focus on the importance of evidence. How do we know about what happens? How were the events recorded at the time? (diaries, letters, official reports, paintings, and so on). Some things may not be known because evidence is lacking. People who benefited from a particular event may have a different view from those who did not.

## Further activity
A similar exercise could be attempted using other Tudor and Stuart monarchs, or famous people from the period.

*H AT2/3,4; AT3/2 CSU 2*

# 4. Court life

## Group size
Small groups.

## What you need
Reference books showing aspects of court life, sixteenth- and seventeenth-century music, suitable costumes and props if desired, a large sheet of paper and felt-tipped pens.

## What to do
Make a class list of the people who would be present at a royal court, e.g, king or queen, royal family, ladies-in-waiting, courtiers, musicians, entertainers, ambassadors, a food-taster, servants, counsellors. Discuss the role of each person identified – why were they there? How would they be treated? How would they spend their time?
    Working in groups, the children can then develop a

role-play around a court scene and present it to the other groups.

## Content

The court was an assembly of counsellors, courtiers and servants who attended the monarch and their duty was to show allegiance and obedience. The court was the centre of government fashion and entertainment. The children will need to understand the role of those present:
• Counsellors – gave the monarch political and economic advice;
• Courtiers – companions to serve and amuse the monarch;
• Officials – responsible for the smooth running of the household;
• Servants – included clerks, cooks, butlers, serving maids.

It may be helpful to direct the role-play around a particular event such as the arrival of the Spanish Ambassador or a royal suitor.

*H AT1/2b,4c; AT3/2,3 CSU 2*

# 5. In the kitchen

## Group size
Small groups.

## What you need
Photocopiable page 190, paper, pencils.

## What to do
Ask the children to identify the kinds of evidence which tell us about life in Tudor and Stuart times, e.g. buildings, books, letters, paintings, diaries. Explain that inventories were made when a person died and can tell us a lot about their living conditions.
• Ask the children to read and compare the two inventories on photocopiable page 190.

• Ask them to make an inventory of their own kitchen equipment. What similarities and differences can they find between past and present? Focus on differences and similarities in terms of use, materials equipment is made from, the range of items and value.

## Content

Inventories tell us a lot about everyday life of people. John Herries was a poor man whose possessions were of little value and were made from simple materials – wood, earthenware, stone. Salt boxes were essential as much of the food was preserved in this way. William Hobby was a small farmer and craftsman. He was able to brew his own beer and his kitchen equipment was made of brass and pewter.

## Further activity

The children can look at further kinds of evidence relating to how people lived by visiting a Tudor or Stuart house to study building styles or furniture.

*H AT1/2c,3a,4a,4c; AT3/2,3 CSU 2*

# 6. Remember remember!

The children will need to be familiar with the story of the Gunpowder Plot.

## Group size
The whole class.

## What you need
Paper, pencils.

## What to do
Retell the story of the Gunpowder Plot and discuss

with the children how different people would have different views of the plot. How would Guy Fawkes justify his actions? How would a Protestant regard them? How would the King feel?

Ask the children to write a letter to a friend explaining the events surrounding the Gunpowder Plot as if they were one of the following:
• the King;
• Guy Fawkes;
• a Protestant soldier on duty at the Houses of Parliament.

The children can read their accounts to each other and discuss the different viewpoints.

## Content
The children will need to understand the significance of religion at the time. There were two main groups of Christians in the country, Catholics and Protestants. The Catholics believed the Pope to be head of the Church and the Protestants believed the King to be head of the Church. Catholics were not free to worship as they wished. James I was a Protestant who believed Catholics should be free to worship in their own churches but he was not supported in this by Parliament. Many Catholics who had hoped James would give them more freedom were bitterly disappointed, and the plotters were among those who sought revenge on the king.

## Further activity
• Hold a class debate on whether or not Guy Fawkes was justified in his action.
• Conduct a survey of the religions practised by members of the class today.
• Compare this with the religions practised in the seventeenth Century.

*H AT1/2b,3b,4b; AT2/2,3*

# 7. Cavaliers and Roundheads

## Group size
Small groups.

## What you need
Some background knowledge of the causes of the Civil war, books containing information about the Civil war, a cassette recorder and tape, photocopiable page 191, collage materials, card, paper, paint, scissors, glue, paintbrushes.

## What to do
Ask the children to compare and contrast the three illustrations on photocopiable page 191.

Discuss the importance of different aspects of their uniform and weaponry.

Ask the children to each make a particular part of the uniform or a weapon, e.g. a pikeman's helmet, a breastplate, a musketeer's bandolier, a cavalier's hat. When they have finished, ask one child to interview the others in costume. The interviewer needs to ask why they are supporting a particular side and how they will fight in the approaching battle.

## Content
Not many people wanted to fight in the Civil War, but most were forced to join one side or another. Their reasons may have been religious (Puritans favouring the Roundheads); political (decided by views about taxation, the role of the Parliament and the divine right of kings); social (depending on where you lived – people in towns were more likely to be Roundheads). Children need to

be aware that many soldiers, particularly in the Royalist army, would be ragged and poorly armed. Gentry on both sides would dress very much alike. The cavalry played an important part on both sides and although there were cannon and muskets, most fighting was still hand-to-hand.

### Further activity
• Write a letter from a soldier to his wife describing his life in the army.
• Make a plan or table top model of one of the Civil War battles.

**H AT1/2b,4a,4b; AT2/2,3 AT3/2,3**

## 8. Into The New World

Ensure that the childen are familiar with the story of Drake's expedition to the Isthmus of Panama in 1572–73.

### Group size
The whole class divided into four groups.

### What you need
Sixteenth-century and modern maps of the world/globe; books on ships and seafaring of the period.

### What to do
Give each group one of the following tasks.
• Research ships of the period and represent the information found through drawing or modelling.
• Draw a cartoon version of the story of Drake's expedition.
• Write a letter home as if you were Drake describing his first gimpse of the Pacific Ocean.
• Draw a map to show the journey of the *Swan*. Make sure the Isthmus of Panama, Peru (where the silver mines were) and Spain (where the treasure was taken) are marked on this map.
    The outcome of the group work can then be displayed.

### Content
European explorers had opened up the New World and much of the Americas was colonised by Spain in order to exploit its natural wealth. The Spanish would only allow foreigners to trade directly with the New World if they were Catholic and this led to disputes between England and Spain over trade. English adventurers such as Drake were Protestant and saw Catholic Spain as an enemy. They tried to plunder Spanish ships and towns overseas. Drake's motives were a mixture of dislike for Catholic Spaniards, revenge for earlier Spanish attacks and a desire to get rich. It is also important to stress how incomplete people's knowledge of the world then was.

### Further activity
• Trace Drake's journey round the world 1572–1580. Diary accounts could be written to illustrate particular aspects.
• Research the effect of European colonisation on the native populations.

**H AT1/2b,2c,3b,4a,4b,4c; AT2/4; AT3/2,4 CSU2**

## 9. Off with his head!

### Group size
Small groups.

### What you need
Some background knowledge of the causes of the Civil War, books and illustrations of the execution of Charles I, an eyewitness account (see following page), large sheets of paper, pencils, crayons, rulers.

### What to do
Read the eye eyewitness account of Charles I execution. Ask the children to discuss in

groups the reason for the execution and whether it was justified. Encourage them to consider different viewpoints – how would a Roundhead justify it? How would a Royalist feel?

Ask the children to work in groups to design the front page of a newspaper dated 31 January 1649. Encourage them to include a headline, an eyewitness report, background information, illustrations and interviews with a Roundhead and a Royalist.

### Eyewitness account
'On the day of his execution, which was Tues Jan 30th I stood amongst the crowd in the street before Whitehall gate, where the scaffold was erected ... the blow I saw given, and can truly say with a sad heart; at the instant whereof I remember well, there was such a groan by the thousands then present, as I never heard before and desire I may never hear again'.
(From *Diaries & Letters of Philip Henry,* (ed. MH Lee) 1682)

### Content
The causes of the Civil War were complex. The children need to understand that many people hated the king because of the high taxes he levied to pay for a lavish court, his army and warships. He punished people who did not belong to the Church of England and he had enemies in Parliament who would not make the laws he wanted. The Civil War was a conflict between King and Parliament to settle who should govern the country. Many people still believed the king ruled by divine right, so acting against the king was acting against the will of God.

### Further activity
• Research life in England during the Commonwealth. What difference did it make to people to have no king?
• Compare accounts of the execution of Charles I with accounts of the Restoration of Charles II.

**H AT1/2b,3b,4a,4b,4c; AT2/2,3 AT3/2 CSU 2**

# 10. Plague!

### Group size
Large groups.

### What you need
A clear space in which children can move freely, some background knowledge of the Great Plague.

### What to do
Tell the story of the Eyam Plague.

'In 1665 a widow named Mary Cooper and her two sons lived in the Derbyshire village of Eyam. Lodging with them was a tailor called George Viccars. According to tradition some cloth he had ordered from London, where the Plague was raging, arrived damp and was spread out to dry. This released plague-infected fleas. Just two days later he developed a fever. Swellings and a rose-red rash covered his body and on 7 September 1665 George died. The Plague had come to Eyam.

Within six weeks two more people from the same house died from the Plague and their neighbours became unwell. Fear spread through the village and a few people packed and fled. The rector, William Mompesson called the villagers together and persuaded them to stay inside the village boundary and so stop the disease from spreading to the rest of Derbyshire. In doing this, they knew that they would probably catch the Plague and die.

Mompesson arranged for supplies of food and other goods to be left at the boundary stone and well. Money payments for these provisions were 'disinfected' with running water and vinegar. The church was closed as people feared to gather closely and open-air services were held in a local valley, the Delf. As the disease spread people were buried in rough graves close to their homes in an attempt to stop the spread of infection. One women, Mrs Hancock, buried her husband and six children in eight days.

The Plague ended in October 1666. In 14 months it had claimed 259 lives out of a population of around 350.

*Ring a ring of roses,*
*A pocket full of poses,*
*Atishoo, atishoo,*
*We all fall down.'*

Ask the children to pretend they are villagers. The Plague has just taken its first victims and they are going to hold a meeting to decide what to do. Roles could include the rector, the schoolteacher, a girl whose sweetheart lives in the next village, the baker, the innkeeper, a mother with young children.

## Content
Bubonic plague had been a regular threat to life for centuries but in some years it would be particularly virulent and there were widespread epidemics. It was mainly a disease of overcrowded towns, originating from the fleas carried by black rats. People often fled to the countryside when the plague struck and villages were not likely to suffer unless they were situated on trade routes. Sometimes as in the case of Eyam, the disease was spread by goods being brought in from outside. Doctors had little idea of the causes of illness and disease and much of their treatment was guesswork.

## Further activity
• Visit Eyam village if possible.
• Study the account of the London Plague in the diary of Samuel Pepys.
• Compare his accounts of how people fled in panic to the reaction of the Eyam villagers.

*H AT1/2b,3a,3b,3c; AT2/2,3 CSU 2*

# 11. Fire!

## Group size
Small groups.

## What you need
Photocopiable page 192; pictures and maps of London at the time of the fire; paper, pencils.

## What to do
Read the extracts with the children and ask them how much trust we can put in the diary as evidence about the fire.

Ask the children to study the maps and pictures: how do these add to our knowledge? Encourage them to identify reasons why the fire spread so quickly.

Ask the children to pretend to be either a reporter writing an article describing the spread of the fire, or a child living in London at the time and writing a letter to a friend describing what happened to them.

## Content
Children need to understand the value of the diary as evidence – it is a first-hand eyewitness report. However, it is only one person's account – other things of significance may have happened that are not recorded here. It is not, therefore, the whole story and needs to be set alongside other evidence. The factors contributing to the spread of the fire include the wind, the building materials used for the houses, the closeness of the houses. Fire-fighting techniques were very simple.

## Further activity
• Make a model or collage of the Fire of London showing as many of the contributory

factors as possible.
• Research fire fighting through different historical periods.

*H AT1/2b,2c,3b,4b; AT3/2,3,4 CSU 2*

# 12. Poles apart

## Group size
Pairs.

## What you need
Bar magnets.

## What to do
The children are going to investigate magnets to see where they are strongest. Discuss with the children whether they think magnets always attract each other. Ask them to hold a bar magnet in each hand so that the ends of the magnets are pointing towards each other and slowly move the magnets together. What happens? Do the magnets attract each other or push each other apart? Repeat the experiment but turn one of the magnets round so that the opposite end is facing the other magnet. Again, do the magnets attract each other or push each other apart? Ask the children to try the activity using different parts of the magnet rather than the ends. Where are the magnets strongest?

## Content
The power of a magnet is strongest at two points called the poles. The poles are usually at the ends of the magnet. They are called the North pole and the South pole of the magnet. Magnets attract each other if a North pole is near a South pole. If two of the same poles are brought

together, the magnets will repel each other. Therefore, like poles repel, unlike poles attract.

## Further activity
There is a magnetic field in the area around a magnet which shows lines of force. The children could investigate magnetic fields and lines of force by placing a sheet of paper over a magnet and sprinkling iron filings over the paper. When they tap the paper gently they will see the patterns of the lines of force, showing the direction of the magnetic force near a magnet. Lines of force are closest together near the poles where the magnetic force is strong.

*Sc AT4/2a*

# 13. Which way?

## Group size
Pairs or small groups.

## What you need
Bar magnets, a reel of thick cotton, needles or pins, pieces

of cork, a shallow dishful of water, a 1.5V battery, a small compass, connecting wire.

## What to do
Early explorers used the natural magnet, 'lodestone', to find their way at sea. Pieces of lodestone were suspended in leather cradles on board ships to help navigation. The lodestone came to rest in a North–South direction.
  Explain to the children that they are going to make their own compasses using a magnetised needle. They can magnetise a needle or a pin by stroking it several times in one direction with a magnet. They should then put the needle on a piece of cork and float it in a dish of water. The needle will turn to point in a North–South direction.

## Content
Lodestone is a magnetic rock containing the iron ore magnetite. The earth behaves like a giant magnet with a

magnetic field surrounding it. The field is like the field of a bar magnet with the North magnetic field pole in northern Canada and the South magnetic pole in the Antarctic. A compass needle points to the North and South magnetic poles.

## Further activity
The children can investigate the magnetic effects of an electric current by making a simple electric circuit and bringing a small compass close to the wire. The needle will swing round to point at right angles to the wire. This is because the electric current flowing in the wire produces a magnetic field that affects the compass needle.

*Sc AT4/2a, PoS(i)*

# 14. Floating and sinking – the Mary Rose

## Group size
Small groups.

## What you need
Blocks of different types of wood (e.g., balsa, oak, pine, ash, beech, mahogany) of uniform size – convenient size is 10cm by 5cm by 5cm (these can be usually obtained from a local timber merchant or DIY shop); washing-up bowls containing water; margarine tubs, marbles, beads and similar materials to represent ship's stores, aluminium foil, strips of balsa wood, salt.

## What to do
Talk to the children about the sailing ships in Tudor and Stuart times and in particular about Henry VIII's ship the

*Mary Rose.* Explain that these ships were made of wood. The children can carry out an investigation to see whether some woods float better than others. Ask them to consider why they need to use pieces of wood that are the same size and shape. If necessary, discuss the idea of a fair test. The children could mark on each piece of wood the level at which it is submerged in the water.

After a discussion of the weight that ships needed to carry, ask the children to investigate distribution and amount of weight which floating objects can hold before they sink. Using empty, clean margarine tubs as ships, the children can design a fair test. They will need to consider the variables involved in the investigation. What will they need to keep the same? What will change? The 'ships' could be divided into compartments using pieces of foil or strips of balsa wood. How well do the 'ships' float when different compartments are loaded with cargo? Relate this activity to the sinking of Tudor ship the *Mary Rose.*

## Content
The density and shape of an object determines whether it floats or sinks. The forces that act on a floating body are the weight acting downwards and the upward push (upthrust) of the water. When an object floats in the water, the weight of the object equals the weight of the water displaced. If the object is denser than the water, it will sink.

A ship is shaped so that it displaces a lot of water and there is a large upthrust as a result.

## Further activity
The children could repeat the above activities using salt water. Salt water is denser than ordinary tap water and gives a much stronger upthrust. The more concentrated the salt water, the higher the wood will float.

*Sc AT4/4c*
*T AT2/3a,3d,4b,4d; AT3/ 3b,3c,3d,4b,4c; AT4/3b,4a, 4b*

# 15. Dial a clock

## Group size
Small groups.

## What you need
Bucket full of sand, large stick (a broom handle is ideal), chalk.

## What to do
Introduce the activity by discussing how people in Tudor and Stuart times were able to tell the time using shadows created when the sun shone on an object. Discuss sundials and use reference books to look at various types of sundial. The children can then work in small groups to make their own shadow clocks or sundials. On a sunny day they can set up their shadow clock in the playground by pushing a large stick into a bucket full of sand. They should mark off the shadows created by the stick on the playground at hourly intervals throughout the day. When was the longest shadow created? At what times were the shadows shorter? Why? In which direction does the shadow point?

## Content
The position and size of a shadow will change throughout the day because the Earth is orbiting the Sun and also spinning on its own axis once every twenty-four hours.

## Further activity
The children could mark the shadows of the stick on a large piece of white paper positioned under and around the bucket. They should label each shadow with the correct time. They could then replace the shadow clock and paper in the same spot on another sunny day. The clock can now be used to tell the time. Compare the shadow clock times with the time indicated by the children's own watches.

*Sc AT4/2d,3e*

# 16. The spice islands

## Group size
Small groups.

## What you need
Samples of ground and whole spices such as nutmeg, ginger, cinnamon, cloves, mixed spice, allspice, pepper; plastic spoons, magnifiers, a microscope, test tubes, dropping pipettes, cold water, vinegar, paper, pencils.

## What to do
Introduce the activity with a discussion of the use of spices in Tudor and Stuart cooking and the role early explorers played in reaching the Spice Islands. Once the Turks had captured Constantinople in 1453 and conquered Egypt, the routes were cut to the islands in Asia where spices were grown. Columbus said that he could reach these islands by sailing westwards. Some of the first Europeans to reach the islands, however, were Magellan's men.

The children could carry out an investigation to find out as much as they can about the spices. They should discuss first the tests they are going to carry out and then how they are going to record their results. Detailed observations could be made of each spice using a magnifier and the microscope. Are all the spices the same colour and texture? Which of the spices do the children think will colour cold water or warm water? In order to carry out a fair test the relevant variables must be considered such as using the same amount of each spice in the same volume of water. Consider the number of times each is stirred with a spoon. The children could add vinegar to each of the spices. What do they observe?

The children could then make their own classification key using appropriate characteristics such as colour, shape and size of particle, smell, texture and whether or not warm water becomes coloured when mixed with the spice. Other groups in the class could then carry out tests to identify some of the spices.

## Content
The children have carried out an investigation during which they made observations, predicted outcomes, asked questions and drew their own conclusions. They have carried out a fair test.

*Sc AT1/2a,3a,3c,4a,4b*

# 17. Time runs out

## Group size
Pairs or small groups.

## What you need
Plastic lemonade bottles, dry fine sand, sticky tape, felt-tipped pens, rulers, a filter funnel, scales.

## What to do
Talk to the children about clocks used in Tudor and Stuart times. Introduce the idea of sand clocks. When do we use sand clocks nowadays? (e.g., kitchen timers). Ask the children to bring in egg-timers from home and to compare sizes, the amount of sand they contain and the intervals of time they measure. How many activities can the children carry out before the egg-timers

run out? Can they count to 100? How many times can they walk around the school hall?

Let the children design their own sand clocks using lemonade bottles. Working in groups, the children should draw a design before they make a clock. They could invert one bottle over another of the same size, tape the bottles together and experiment with the size of the hole between the two bottles – too large a hole will let too much sand through too quickly. If it is a straight-sided bottle, they could make graduations on the sides to divide it up into equal intervals. This needs to be discussed carefully beforehand – how do they calibrate their bottle accurately? Encourage them to consider putting equal weights of sand into the bottle. Other factors to take into account are the volume of sand, how compacted it is in the bottle and whether its surface level is flat. This is an opportunity to discuss fair testing and variables.

Suggest that the children test their sand clocks by timing various activities as with the kitchen timers.

Ask the children to discuss the success or otherwise of their clocks and the suitability of materials and methods they used to make the clock.

## Content
Time is a difficult concept for children to understand. This activity will help them to gain the understanding of the duration of time, the nature of time-keeping instruments and an awareness of different methods of measuring time.

The children will have made observations and predictions and will have had an opportunity to test out their hypotheses. They will have carried out a fair test and considered the variables involved.

The children have generated a design, planned and made it and evaluated the effectiveness of their design.

*Sc AT1/2b,3a,3c,4a,4b*
*T AT2/3b,3c,3d; AT3/3b,3c, 3d; AT4/3b,4b,4c*

# CHAPTER 7

# How people live

One of the most fundamental ideas that an integrated curriculum can develop and reinforce is that people are affected by the environment in which they live. Life in the Scottish highlands – the work people do, the houses they live in, the crops they grow, even the food they eat and the clothes they wear - will be different from life in Hampshire or in Central America. This is not because the Scots are peculiar in some way: it is just that their environment – the weather, soil, vegetation, physical features – is different.

The second important idea is that people are constantly changing their environment. Sometimes the changes have beneficial results – for example, insulation has made houses warmer. Sometimes the effects are harmful, as in the case with pollution caused by industry and transport. This project explores some of these issues within the context of geography and science, so that the two important generalisations, environmental effect and environmental control, are better understood. The activities are mainly intended for the earlier year groups in Key Stage 2 but could easily be adapted for older children.

Much of the work investigates these ideas through studies of the pupils' own locality and then moves to wider regions of the UK, the European community and economically developing countries.

A useful starting point for this project would be a classroom display of the appropriate maps, charts, diagrams and pictures of the school's locality. You might also like to organise a village, town or district trail so that the children encounter the main geographical features in the school vicinity.

# BACKGROUND

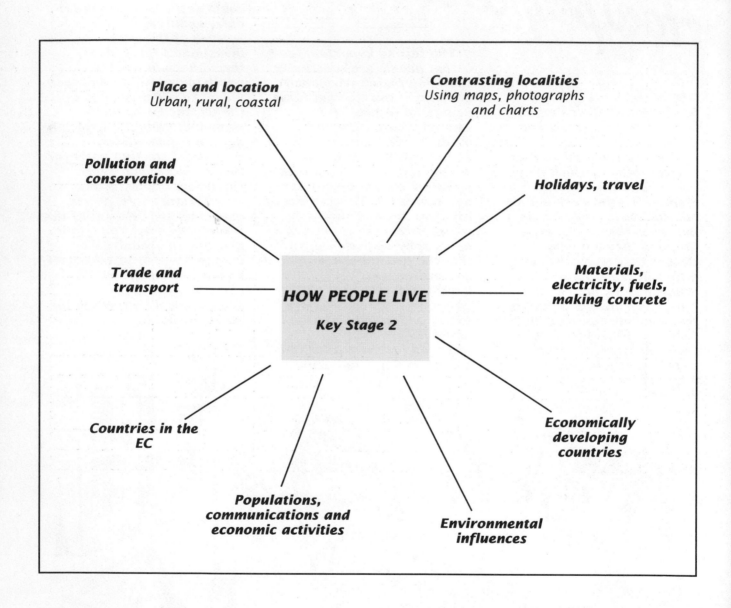

Place and location
Urban, rural, coastal

Contrasting localities
Using maps, photographs
and charts

Pollution and
conservation

Holidays, travel

Trade and
transport

HOW PEOPLE LIVE

Key Stage 2

Materials,
electricity, fuels,
making concrete

Countries in the
EC

Economically
developing
countries

Populations,
communications and
economic activities

Environmental
influences

| Activity | Curriculum area | ATTAINMENT TARGET AND LEVEL | | | | |
|---|---|---|---|---|---|---|
| | | AT1 | AT2 | AT3 | AT4 | AT5 |
| 1 | Geography | 2a, 4e | 2a, 2d, 3b, 3c, 3d, 3e, 4d | | 2a, 3b, 4a | |
| 2 | Geography | 2a, 2e, 4e, 5b | 2c, 2d, 3b, 4d | 3c | | |
| 3 | Geography | 2a, 2e | 2c,2d,3d,3e,3f | | 3b, 4a, 5c | 2a, 2b |
| 4 | Geography | 2a, 2e | 2b, 2c ,2d | | | 2a,2b,3a,4b,5a, |
| 5 | Geography | 2a, 4e, 5e | 5a | | | |
| 6 | Geography | 2a, 2e | 2c, 2d, 3c | 2b, 3c, 4c | | |
| 7 | Geography | 2a, 2d, 2e, 4e, 5b, 5d | 2c, 2d, 3d, 3e, | 2a, 3a, 3c, 5b | | |
| 8 | Geography | | | | 4a,4b,5a,5b,5c | |
| 9 | Geography | | 5a | | | |
| 10 | Geography | 2a,4e,5b,5d,5e | 4e, 5c | 3a | | |
| 11 | Geography | 4e, 5b | 2c, 2d, 3c, 3d, 4d, 4e | 3a | | |
| 12 | Geography | | 5c | | 2a, 2b, 2c, 3b, 3c, 4a, 4d, 5a, 5c, 5d, 5e | |
| 13 | Science | | | 2a, 3a | | |
| 14 | Science | | | 3b, 4b | | |
| 15 | Science Technology | 3a | 3b, 3d, 3e | 3b, 3c | 3a, 4a 3b | |
| 16 | Science | | | | 3b | |
| 17 | Science | | | 2b, 4c | | |

# ACTIVITIES

## 1. Where do you live?

### Group size
Pairs.

### What you need
A wall map and an atlas of the United Kingdom, a map of the UK showing county boundaries and the cities listed below referred to by their number only, a gazetteer, a dictionary, coloured pencils.

### What to do
Ask the children to look up in a dictionary the meaning of the following words: urban, rural, coastal, conurbation. Then ask them to find in the atlas a village, a town and a city nearest to the school that fit into these categories.

Give the children the map with numbered cities and the atlas. There are twelve areas shown on the map. These are the major conurbations within the UK. Ask the children to match up the number to the major cities and to identify the county within which each conurbation is situated (see Figure 1 below). The children should mark the location of their school by placing a dot on the map. Remind them to indicate in a key what the dot represents.

### Content
Where people live is likely to influence the kind of work they do – a city dweller is unlikely to be a farmer as his job will be a function of that particular environment. Children need to be clear as to the distinctions between urban and rural and associated types of work. Development of industry influenced the growth of settlements within a region to a point where town and city boundaries merged and a conurbation developed.

One of the difficulties today is identifying a particular industrial emphasis in an area. All the regions have had to diversify in order to maintain employment. However, all the areas developed a distinct identity during the 19th and the early 20th centuries.

*Gg AT1/2a,4e; AT2/2a,2d, 3b,3c,3d,3e,4d; AT4/2a,3b,4a*

## 2. What is it like where you live?

### Group size
Small groups.

### What you need
A wall map of the UK, atlases (showing the UK in some detail), blank maps of the UK, photographs or pictures of two contrasting locations from a tourist information centre, paper, pens.

### What to do
Discuss with the class the kind of landscape features that can be seen in the United Kingdom – hills, valleys, rivers, beaches and so on. Divide the children into small groups and ask them to describe the landscape features of their own region. Ask them to include names, e.g. the Yorkshire Moors, in their description and, wherever possible, to give indications about direction and distance. Then provide them with pictures or photographs of the two other areas which contrast with each other and with your own region. Ask them to

**Figure 1**

| Number | City | County | Industry |
|--------|------|--------|----------|
| 1 | London | Greater London | Government/services |
| 2 | Bristol | Avon | Tobacco |
| 3 | Cardiff | South Glamorgan | Mining |
| 4 | Birmingham | West Midlands | Pottery, cars |
| 5 | Nottingham | Nottinghamshire | Mining |
| 6 | Sheffield | South Yorkshire | Steel |
| 7 | Liverpool | Merseyside | Chemicals |
| 8 | Manchester | Greater Manchester | Cotton |
| 9 | Leeds | West Yorkshire | Wool |
| 10 | Middlesbrough | Cleveland | Chemicals |
| 11 | Newcastle | Tyne and Wear | Shipbuilding/mining |
| 12 | Glasgow | Strathclyde | Shipbuilding |

possible reasons for geographical distribution of the various kinds of farming. (For example, sheep are good climbers and prefer well-drained land that does not stay wet. Sheep also prefer the short grasses that grow on hillside.)

*Gg AT1/2a,2e,4e,5b; AT2/2c,2d,3b,4d; AT3/3c*

# 3. What is it like living in another place?

## Group size
Pairs or small groups.

## What you need
An atlas and a road atlas of the UK, street maps of your area and two other chosen locations (to give a balance of rural, urban and coastal areas), a map showing the main roads and railway lines connecting the three locations, reference books on British industries.

## What to do
Ask the children to identify and describe the main economic activities in each of the three main areas. Discuss with them the reasons why these particular industries developed (e.g. wool and water supplies provided for the West Yorkshire carpet and textile industry), and the effects on people's lives and the environment. Ask them to draw pictures of typical urban industrial, rural farming and coastal environments and to describe characteristic features of each one of the locations (for example, industrial urban – pollution, workers housing estates, few open spaces).

discuss in groups what they can see in the pictures and to write descriptions of the physical features of both regions. Using an atlas, ask the children to locate the three regions and transfer the main physical features of each on to a blank map of the UK, using appropriate symbols and colours – green for lowland, brown for hills, blue for areas of water and so on. They can then mark on their map the names of these physical features. (The area covered on the map will be determined by the distances between the three locations).

## Content
Children need to be familiar with their home region and its main geographical features and be able to describe them using geographical terms and to indicate position and distance where appropriate, e.g., the River Trent flows south to north through the county of Nottingham. They also need to be able to locate their home region and its physical features on a suitable map. Identifying similarities and differences between their own regions is essential before wider and and more detailed chronicles of land use, economic activity and so on can be undertaken.

In choosing the contrasting locations, ensure that a wide variety of relief and other features are included.

## Further activity
Ask the children to use the class/school library to discover areas in the UK which specialise in different kinds of farming, such as sheep-rearing, dairy farming, arable farming. Ask them to locate these areas on the relief map in their atlases and to note down the differences. They should then be able to suggest

environmental issues related to each locality and identify any existing or potential threats to there environments, e.g. industrial waste, mining and quarrying, excessive use of fertilisers and pesticides and removal of hedgerows due to intensive farming.

## Content

This activity continues to develop the notions of environment influencing the quality of people's lives. Discussion should be aimed at enabling children to make rational decisions which take into account both advantages and disadvantages and balance variables such as absence of pollution, better job prospects and opportunities for certain kinds of leisure activities. They should also consider that some of the advantages, such as attractions of the seaside during the summer, are strictly short-term.

*Gg AT1/2a,2e; AT2/2b,2c, 2d; AT5/2a,2b,3a,4b,5a*

# 5. Do you feel European?

## Group size

The whole class, then pairs.

## What you need

One atlas per pair of children, a wall map of Europe, the European emblem, political maps of Europe showing countries of the European Community in outline, a recording of Beethoven's 'Ode to Joy', crayons, pens.

## What to do

Play Beethoven's 'Ode to Joy', to the children. This is the European national anthem. Show the European emblem of

# 4. The best place on earth is...

## Content

Key Stage 2 pupils are required to study their own locality and other contrasting localities in their home region and elsewhere in the UK. They should investigate similarities and differences between them and the effect different environments have on people's lives. They should note the decline of many traditional economic activities and the consequent changes in a locality. Ask them to look at an example of regions where traditional industry has declined and other activities, such as tourism, have developed. Ask them to produce a brochure attracting people to the area.

*Gg AT1/2a,2e; AT2/2c,2d, 3d,3e,3f; AT4/3b,4a,5c; AT5/2a,2b*

## Group size

Pairs or small groups, then the whole class.

## What you need

Ordnance Survey maps (1:50000) of the three localities identified in the previous activity, atlases, photographs, pictures and general tourist information about each locality.

## What to do

Ask the children to list, in two columns, all the advantages and disadvantages of living in each of the three localities. Tell them to decide which of the three localities they would prefer to live in and why they would not like to live in the other two. Organise a class debate to decide which locality is preferred by most children. They could consider the twelve gold stars on a blue background. Look at a large wall map of Europe and identify the twelve member states. Discuss the country the children are to study in more detail. Give out the political maps of Europe and ask them to colour the sea with blue crayon. It is important that they can differentiate the land from the sea and it will help them to become familiar with the shape of the coastline. They can then colour in each of the twelve countries in a range of colours and fill in the name of the country. Finally the children can identify and describe the location of each country in relation to Europe as a whole and its immediate neighbours. Encourage them to use appropriate directional vocabulary.

## Content

Children at Key Stage 2 need to become familiar with the names of the member countries of the European Community and their capital cities. It is also essential that they can identify Europe on a globe and a map, describe the location of the European Community member states relative to each other and mark the capital of each country on their maps.

*Gg AT1/2a,4e,5e; AT2/5a*

# 6. Which country will it be?

### Group size
The whole class and small groups.

### What you need
Atlases, blank maps and a wall map of the chosen European Community country or countries, posters, video tapes (holiday programmes offer a useful introduction to countries), information books, information packs from embassies or tourist information offices, holiday photographs brought in by the children.

### What to do
Decide which country or countries are to be studied. Create a display in the classroom to stimulate the children's curiosity. Ask them to share with the class what they already know about the chosen country. Show them the video and/or the posters and holiday photographs. Allocate a specific country to each group. Give out the blank maps of the country. Ask the children to find in the atlas the important towns, rivers and other physical features and mark them on the blank map.

Ask the children to identify one coastal area, one inland urban area and one rural location for further study. Shade these in different colours on the map.

### Content
During Key Stage 2 children are required to study localities in a European Community country outside the United Kingdom. This activity is concerned with identifying the position, shape and general characteristics of EC countries before contemplating further study of their human and economic geography.

| River | Source | Meets sea at | Total length | Tributaries | Countries | Major cities/ports |
|-------|--------|--------------|--------------|-------------|-----------|--------------------|
|       |        |              |              |             |           |                    |
|       |        |              |              |             |           |                    |
|       |        |              |              |             |           |                    |

**Figure 1**

## Further activity

Most EC countries have important rivers flowing through them. Ask the children to mark on an outline map of Europe the major rivers from their source to the sea. At the bottom of the map draw a grid displaying the statistical information about each river (see Figure 1 above). Ask the children to fill in the grid. Introduce and consolidate with children such vocabulary as source, tributaries and delta.

**Gg AT1/2a,2e; AT2/2c, 2d,3c; AT3/2b,3c,4c**

# 7. Up hill and over dale

## Group size
Pairs and small groups.

## What you need
An atlas, wall maps of the EC countries chosen in the previous activity, weather charts of your own region and of one chosen country, blank maps of the countries of the EC, reference material on each country.

## What to do
Give each group a blank map of the chosen country. Ask the children to identify from the atlas the main landscape features of the chosen country and draw them in on their blank map. Ask them to focus on the location in the chosen country that is most like their own, i.e., coastal, rural or urban. Tell the children to use their map, the atlas, reference material and information books to identify similarities and differences between the two locations.

Ask them to produce a large feature for the display board which presents the following information about both locations:
• average monthly temperature chart;
• average monthly rainfall chart;
• a description of general weather/climatic conditions;
• a description of the main landscape features with accompanying maps, pictures and photographs;
• an illustrated account of how these features have affected the lives of the people in the two locations, especially the work they do.

## Content
This activity reinforces and consolidates the use of maps of various kinds to investigate the physical characteristics of locations and to develop understanding of distribution patterns. The important understanding of the relationship between environment and land use which helps to explain cultural, economic and political differences is further refined in the process of presenting information in a variety of ways.

**Gg AT1/2a,2d,2e,4e,5b,5d; AT2/2c,2d,3d,3e; AT3/2a,3a,3c,5b**

# 8. People, people everywhere!

## Group size
Pairs.

## What you need

Reference books for countries in the European Community, atlases with population distribution maps, maps showing the three locations identified in Activity 6, information about the population in each of the three localities, information from embassies and/or tourist offices, sugar paper, pencils, paper.

## What to do

Ask the children to identify the population distribution in each of the three locations and produce a pie chart or a bar graph to show the differences between them. Using the reference books and the maps of the locations, the children should suggest which environmental factors affected each location's settlement and development. Tell the children to mount the maps of each locality on a large sheet of sugar paper and, using boxes and arrows, to indicate the factors they have decided upon.

## Content

Settlements develop for many different reasons. For example, Amsterdam was situated at a point of easy access to the sea and was therefore a suitable place to develop fishing and trading (see Figure 1). As industry developed in the hinterland, it grew as a port and trading centre. This required large numbers of workers and led to high population density.

## Further activity

Tourism has become an important industry in all the EC countries. Ask the children to identify and mark in one of their maps a holiday location, using shading and a key. Ask them to explain how it affects the population of the area and what are the disadvantages of a short holiday season. Suggest that they look through holiday brochures to identify how tourist centres try to extend the holiday season: for example, a mountain resort may offer skiing in winter and rock climbing in the summer.

*Gg AT4/4a,4b,5a,5b,5c*

# 9. Where in the world?

## Group size

The whole class, then pairs.

## What you need

Atlases, a globe, National Curriculum document, blank maps of the world, materials collected from embassies and travel agents. Children whose parents or grandparents were

**Figure 1**

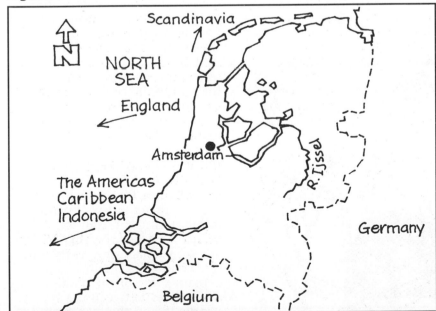

born in an economically developing country should be encouraged to bring photographs and artefacts.

### What to do
Discuss with the class what is meant by an economically developing country. Explain briefly how the occupations, land use and settlement patterns are related to the location and environment. Give examples using the list of countries on page 43 of the National Curriculum document and any of the reference material that will illustrate the main points. Ask the children to find the countries on the world map and copy their locations on to the blank map of the world.

Select an economically developing country to study or, if you have sufficient appropriate material, allow pairs to choose a country to study. Use the material available, together with charts, maps, drawings and pupils' descriptions, to prepare posters and displays which give the following information:
• location of the country;
• the continent it is part of;
• oceans and seas which surround it;
• monthly climatic charts;
• time zone(s);
• distance by air and sea from the UK;
• main economic activities;
• a range of goods/produce from the country that can be brought here.

### Content
Pupils need to be able to use maps and globes to identify places they are studying, so that they become familiar with the world map, the continents, seas and oceans. Before they begin to study in detail a locality in an economically developing country, an overview of the general characteristics of such countries is essential. Most of these countries lie between the tropics and have a high density of population, little development in terms of living and working conditions and an extreme climate.

*Gg AT2/5a*

# 10. Within the tropics

### Group size
The whole class, then pairs.

### What you need
Atlases, detailed maps of an economically developing country, outline maps of the same country, reference books.

### What to do
Choose an economically developing country. Explain to the children the reasons why you have chosen it, such as the ethnic origins of children in the class, export activities of local firms and so on. Give the children outline maps of the country and ask them to mark in the main physical features – hills, lakes, rivers, seas, valleys and the important towns and cities. Help the children mark in and name the central line of latitude and discuss the country's position in relation to the Equator and the tropics. Ask the children to use the display in Activity 9 in this chapter to identify and explain some of the main differences between the way people live in the tropics and

the way we live in this country. Compare such aspects as size and area of county (by measuring the coastline of each), population and language.

## Content
Allow the children to research widely and explore the full range of human activity to compare in each area. Use the word 'culture' and explain that it has to do with what people eat, wear, the work they do, the houses they live in as well as religion, traditions, customs and artistic achievement. Children should be encouraged to identify similarities with their country and to note changes in economically countries to avoid stereotyping.

*Gg AT1/2a,4e,5b,5d,5e; AT2/4e,5c; AT3/3a*

# 11. Paradise?

## Group size
The whole class, and then pairs.

## What you need
A wall map and outline maps of the chosen economically developing country, reference material (books, pictures, posters), atlases, maps of your own region, paper, pencils, pens.

## What to do
Choose a region in the economically developing country that is located in a similar position to your own region in the UK (rural/urban, inland/coastal). Discuss the similarities between the two locations with the class. Ask the children to use the atlas to identify features of the

landscape in both locations and to compare them. Record the information on maps and charts as appropriate.

## Content
In identifying similarities and differences between their localities, the children will come to understand the reasons for the differences in landscape, climate and vegetation, and eventually the impact of these differences on the cultures of different regions.

*Gg AT1/4e,5b; AT2/2c,2d, 3c,3d,4d,4e; AT3/3a*

# 12. Exciting for us, ordinary for them

## Group size
Pairs and small groups.

## What you need
An atlas, a good quality map of an economically developing

country known for its tourist attractions (e.g. Brazil, the Philippines, Jamaica, Mexico), reference material including pictures and travel brochures.

## What to do
Identify the main economic activities of the chosen country. Explain to the children that tourism can also be an industry if it is on sufficient scale. Ask the children to locate the main tourist destinations on the map. Discuss with the children the different types of tourist attractions such as beaches, historical sites, fine architecture, rare flora and fauna, a sunny climate and so on. The children should consider how some of these, for example, climate or

to describe the materials using two or three words for each and to write their descriptions next to the pictures on photocopiable page 193. A list of describing words such as, hard, soft, heavy, light, gritty, wet, dry, runny, shiny, dull, rough, smooth, could be displayed to help the children.

### Content
Children should be able to describe simple properties of familiar materials. They should be able to describe moist soil as gritty and wet, flour as soft and light and rocks as hard and heavy.

### Further activity
The children could group fabrics and other materials according to observable features such as shape, colour, texture and hardness. Using these and other materials, the children could attempt to relate their properties to their uses.

### Safety
Some materials may be sharp. Children should not put the materials in their mouths and should wash their hands after touching them. They should also be warned of the dangers of glass even though they will be investigating this material in a relatively safe context of a window pane.

*Sc AT3/2a,3a*

wildlife, may seem 'exotic' to Western visitors, even though they are quite ordinary to the country's inhabitants.

With the help of reference material, the children should find out which regions, cities and resorts are the most popular with foreign visitors. Working in pairs or groups, they should focus on one particular destination, describe what it has to offer to tourists and what sort of work tourism has generated for people who live there. Ask the children to consider mixed feelings that people in economically developing countries may have about Western tourists and their relative wealth. Encourage them to compare the tourist industry in such countries with that in Britain.

### Content
The children should become familiar with the different perspectives where economically developing countries are concerned. They should become aware of stereotypes of 'exotic' countries and their cultures and customs.

*Gg AT2/5c; AT4/2a,2b,2c, 3b,3c,4a,4d,5a,5c,5d,5e*

# 13. Simple materials

## Group size
Small groups

## What you need
Rocks, soil, sand, water, lemonade, flour, aluminium foil, bricks, coal, wood, wool and other fabrics, a polythene bag, a glass window; photocopiable page 193.

## What to do
Allow the children to touch the materials and talk about them to each other. Then ask them

# 14. Making concrete

## Group size
Groups or the whole class.

## What you need
Sand, gravel, cement powder, water, a mixing container,

spoons, card reinforced with tape to make a small concrete block mould. Thin disposable gloves would be useful but are not essential.

## What to do

Allow the children to investigate the properties of the materials by touching them (see Safety below). Get them to describe them accurately using such terms as 'soft', 'powdery', 'gritty' and so on. Ask the children to consider whether the materials are man-made from natural materials or whether they occur naturally.

Ask the children to mix the sand, gravel and cement powder together but not the water. Can they still identify the three components in the mixture? Have the three components changed in any way?

Now slowly add the water to the mixture, stirring to ensure even absorption. Spoon the concrete mixture into the card moulds. Wash the spoon and mixing container immediately before the concrete sets, ensuring that large amounts of water are washed down the sink. Allow the blocks to set, remove the cardboard mould and ask the children to observe and describe the properties of the concrete block. How is it different from the dry mixture of the ingredients? Is it similar in any way?

## Content

Concrete is a mixture of naturally occurring materials with useful properties of hardness, durability and inflexibility. Sand, gravel, cement powder and water have been converted into concrete by a chemical reaction, which unfortunately

cannot be seen. The children should understand that the materials in the dry mixture of sand, gravel and concrete powder have not changed and could be separated. The chemical reaction occurs when water is added, causing the cement powder to attach itself firmly to the sand and gravel. Cement powder is made by heating calcium carbonate (limestone) with clay.

## Further activity

The children could make miniature concrete beams, for example, for a motorway bridge. They could test the strength of these by hanging masses in a bucket on the beam, suspended between two tables. Different proportions of the ingredients should be used. This would offer the children the opportunity to formulate a hypothesis, to predict, to set up a fair test and record and make inferences from their results.

## Safety

It is important that the children do not put any of the materials near their mouths and eyes. Cement powder should be thoroughly washed off hands. The use of thin plastic gloves is preferable

*Sc AT3/3b,4b*

# 15. Constructing simple circuits

## Group size
Pairs.

## What do you need

Card, wood, adhesive and other construction materials, a variety of tools, batteries (cells) in a battery box, a lamp holder or a buzzer, connecting wires, crocodile clips, a bought

**Content**
The children will be able to use their knowledge of buildings to identify the need for electric lamps and buzzers. Using their knowledge and experience, they will generate a design indicating the required resources. They will plan and make their design using these resources and appropriate tools. During the design and construction phases, as well as after completion of their structure, they should be able to comment on the effectiveness of the materials used and the

**Figure 2**

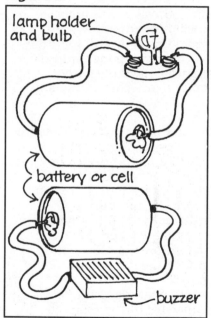

switch or one made out of two drawing pins and a paper clip mounted on soft board.

### What to do
This activity is based on work in technology when the children will be making a house, a garage, a lighthouse or Rudolph the reindeer for Christmas. Ask the children if they can think of any further work that needs to be carried out on their model. Hopefully they will suggest providing electricity to the house, garage and lighthouse, and even to Rudolph's nose. They will therefore require a lamp, although some children might want to have a doorbell on their house or garage, or a bell (hooter) on their lighthouse. Some children will want to control these devices using simple switches. A simple switch can be

constructed as shown in the illustration below (Figure 1).
Ask the children to design their building, incorporating the circuits into the design. When this has been successfully completed, start on the planning and making of the chosen project.
When it is complete, ask the children to justify the use of their materials.

**Figure 1**

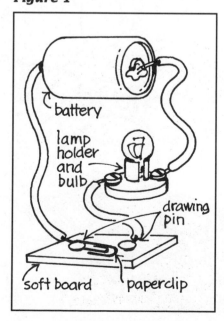

production process involved.
On lighting the lamp or getting the buzzer to buzz the children will have made a complete circuit. The lamp will only light and the buzzer will only buzz when a complete circuit is made (see Figure 2 above). While children may find this easy to accomplish practically, they will need to know that a complete circuit is needed for electrical devices to work and understand that a

'complete circuit' involves electric current passing from the battery or cell to an electrical component (lamp or buzzer) and back to the battery, without a break in that circuit.

Teachers should be aware that the lamp and the buzzer will not work together in a series circuit, even if a number of batteries (cells) are used. However, they can both be made to work if a parallel circuit is constructed.

### Safety
It should be stressed that while simple circuits used in school lessons are not dangerous and will not give shocks, the mains electricity at school, in the home and in the community is very dangerous. It is also worth noting that the components used in science activities can overheat causing burning, so due care and attention must be exercised when handling such components.

*Sc AT4/3a,4a*
*T AT1/3a; AT2/3b,3d,3e;*
*AT3/3b,3c; AT4/3b*

# 16. Fuels for heating and cooking

### Group size
Individuals, then large groups or the whole class.

### What you need
Posters, books, photographs and slides showing different fuels and their natural occurrence, crayons, pencils.

### What to do
Ask the children to find out at home and in reference books at school, the range of fuels used to heat and cook at home. Some of this information should come from first-hand experience but a group or whole class discussion would help to fill the gaps in children's knowledge. Ask the children to record their findings on a poster. Encourage them to find out where coal is mined in Europe, Where oil is extracted and from where we obtain our natural gas.

### Content
Children should be aware that there are a variety of fuels used in the home for heating and cooking. These include solid fuels such as wood, coal, coke and anthracite as well as gas and electricity. Coal, coke and anthracite are fossil fuels formed from the remains of trees, particularly in the Carboniferous era. Oil is also a fossil fuel formed from the remains of minute marine animals (zooplankton). Likewise, natural gas is a fossil fuel formed from the remains of marine organisms. Electricity is produced in coal, gas or oil-burning power stations and in nuclear power stations. Some electricity is produced in peak periods in hydro-electric power stations. Paraffin used in domestic and greenhouse heaters is produced during the process of refining crude oil.

*Sc AT4/3b*

# 17. Fuels, energy and waste gases

### Group size
The whole class or large groups.

### What you need
Pictures of power stations and chimneys and access to a car, a candle, matches.

## Further activities

Obtain a large peanut and attach it to the end of a needle mounted in wood. Light the peanut in the flame from the gas cooker or from a Primus stove (it will take a few seconds to ignite). Either watch the peanut burn (time it), or hold it over a test tube containing a small amount of water. With care, the water should boil. The peanut contains a large amount of energy in the form of fat, which is capable of heating water.

Compare the energy obtained from the candle, petrol in the car engine and the peanut with energy production in our own bodies. We take food which gives us energy due to a number of reactions in the body, and carbon dioxide is produced as a waste product.

This work could lead to a discussion of the greenhouse effect.

## Content

The combustion of fuels releases energy and waste gases. The paraffin wax of the candle melts and is drawn up the wick, where it burns in the oxygen in the air and vaporises. Energy is released and carbon dioxide gas is given off. Likewise, in the car engine, oxygen mixes with petrol and is ignited by a spark from the spark plugs. The energy so produced pushes the pistons up and down, and these in turn move the drive shaft which turns the wheels. Carbon monoxide and carbon dioxide gases are given off.

## What to do

Allow the children to look at the pictures, to see the candle burning and, if possible, to see exhaust fumes emitted from a car engine. Talk to the children about what is happening in the pictures. Ask them what the burning candle and the running car engine have in common. Try to help the children to think about energy and waste gases, as well as pollution.

## Safety

Great care should be taken when burning candles, using heating devices and when burning the peanut.

*Sc AT3/2b,4c*

# CHAPTER 8

# Food and farming

From an early age, most children are fascinated by farms, due to their association with young animals, large, powerful machinery such as combine harvesters, the food they produce and the bustle of the farmyard.

The Science, Geography and History National Curriculum documents each make references to 'food and farming'. The concepts, knowledge and understanding and skills associated with these curriculum areas may be grouped into cross-curricular projects for various ages and abilities. We have chosen for the focus of the 'Food and Farming' project the upper levels (3–5) of Key Stage 2. The obvious starting point for such a project is a visit to a working farm or farms or, if this is not possible, a trip to a City Farm or watching a relevant video. Classroom work could consider production of different categories of food such as cereals or dairy products, relating these to the food we eat. This would raise the question of famine in some countries of the world and the causes of food shortages. A major part of the geography component of the project would be to look at the location and optimum growing conditions for dairy farming, cereals, apples, potatoes and rice in the United Kingdom and other parts of the world.

Modern agriculture could be compared with agriculture through the ages, from the earliest historical evidence of cereal production in the Middle East and the Mediterranean to medieval farming, self sufficiency and crop rotation. Chronology may be enhanced by considering bread production from the time of the Corn Laws and Bread Riots to modern milling techniques.

Scientific activities consider farm produce and balanced diets, chemical changes during yoghurt making, dissolving various food products and using red cabbage to indicate whether solutions are acidic, neutral or alkaline. Children will have the opportunity to examine cereals as an example of a crop grown on a farm and to understand their importance as food for the human race. Many farmers rely on fertilisers to increase the yield of their crops and the children will be able to explore the use of different amounts of fertiliser. These activities associated with farming provide an excellent stimulus for challenging project work.

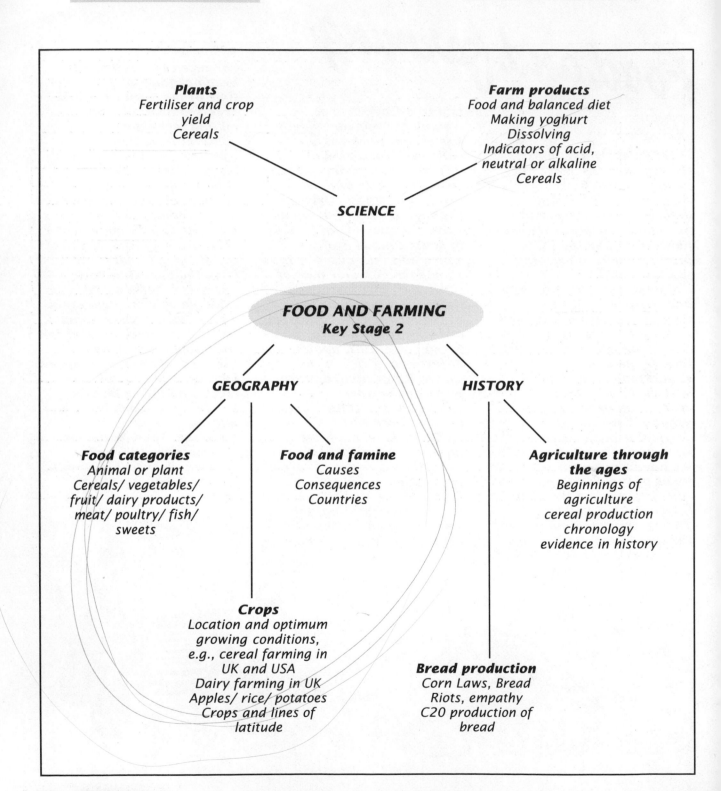

**Plants**
Fertiliser and crop
yield
Cereals

**Farm products**
Food and balanced diet
Making yoghurt
Dissolving
Indicators of acid,
neutral or alkaline
Cereals

**SCIENCE**

**FOOD AND FARMING**
**Key Stage 2**

**GEOGRAPHY**

**HISTORY**

**Food categories**
Animal or plant
Cereals/ vegetables/
fruit/ dairy products/
meat/ poultry/ fish/
sweets

**Food and famine**
Causes
Consequences
Countries

**Agriculture through
the ages**
Beginnings of
agriculture
cereal production
chronology
evidence in history

**Crops**
Location and optimum
growing conditions,
e.g., cereal farming in
UK and USA
Dairy farming in UK
Apples/ rice/ potatoes
Crops and lines of
latitude

**Bread production**
Corn Laws, Bread
Riots, empathy
C20 production of
bread

| Activity | Curriculum Area | ATTAINMENT TARGET AND LEVEL | | | | |
|---|---|---|---|---|---|---|
| | | AT1 | AT2 | AT3 | AT4 | AT5 |
| 1 | Science | | PoS(iii) | | | |
| 2 | Science | | PoS(i) | | | |
| 3 | Science | | | 4b | | |
| 4 | Science | 4b, 4c | 3c, 4b | | | |
| 5 | Science | 3, 4, 5 | 5d | | | |
| 6 | Science | | | PoS(i) | | |
| 7 | Science | | | 5b | | |
| 8 | Geography | 4e | 3a, 4e | 3a | 5c | |
| 9 | Geography | 3d, 5b, 5d | 2d | 5a | 5c, 5e | |
| 10 | Geography | 5b, 5d | 3f | 5a | 4c, 5c, 5e | |
| 11 | Geography | 4e, 5b, 5d | 2c, 4b, 5c | 4a, 5a | 5c, 5e | |
| 12 | Geography | 4e, 5b, 5d | 3a, 4b, 4e, 5c | 3a, 4e, 5b | 3d, 4e, 5c, 5e | 2b |
| 13 | Geography | 2a, 5b | | 3c, 4c | 3d, 4c, 4e, 5c, 5e | 2b, 4a, 4c |
| 14 | History | 3a, 3b, 3c, 4a, 4b, 5a | 4, 5 | 5 | | |
| 15 | History | 3a, 3b, 3c, 4a, 5b | | | | |
| 16 | History | 3a, 3b, 3c, 4a, 4b, 4c, 5a | | | | |
| 17 | History | 3a, 3b, 3c, 4a, 4b, 5a, 5b, 5c | 4 | 3, 4, 5 | | |
| 18 | History | 3a, 3b, 4b, 5b, 5c | 3, 4, 5 | | | |
| 19 | History | 3a, 3b, 3c, 4a, 4b, 4c, 5a, 5b, 5c | 3 | 4 | | |

# ACTIVITIES

## 1. Fertilisers: goodies or baddies?

### Group size
The whole class and small groups.

### What you need
Seed trays, cereal seeds, poor soil, fertiliser.

### What to do
Ask each group of children to set up two seed trays, one containing poor soil and another containing poor soil to which the correct concentration of fertiliser has been added. This will produce a reasonable-sized sample. Tell the children to plant the seeds, maintaining similar conditions of light, temperature and water, for the purposes of a fair test. Further applications of liquid fertiliser could be made to the one tray as the plants grow. Ensure that the children make regular measurements and observations of the plants. Which are taller? Which look healthier?

Alternatively, you could ask the children to research a hypothesis such as 'soil with fertiliser will grow better plants'. It will be necessary to establish what is meant by 'better'.

The activity could be continued over a longer term, perhaps even to maturity of the grain which could then be weighed. The children could go on to look at the effects of pesticides on plant growth and crop yield.

### Content
This investigation allows the children to study aspects of local environment affected by human activity, such as farming, and to consider the benefits and detrimental effects of this activity.

The children will investigate the benefits of fertilisers as well as the problems associated with fertiliser seeping into water-courses. Issues of higher yields could be discussed, along with the high costs to many poor nations of importing fertilisers and the subsequent long-term deterioration of the soil.

### Safety
Fertilisers contain potentially dangerous chemicals. Children must wash their hands thoroughly after handling them or preferably wear disposable gloves. Fingers should be kept well away from the mouth.

*Sc AT2 PoS(iii)*

## 2. Finding the balance

### Group size
Pairs or small groups.

### What you need
Labels from different foods, for example: cereal packets, tinned food, frozen foods; paper and pencils.

+ fertiliser

### What to do

Discuss with the children why we need food. Ask them to keep a record of everything they have eaten and drunk in one day. They can list the foods they had for different meals. At the end of the survey, talk to the children about the range of foods that they have eaten. Different types of food could be discussed, for example, dairy products such as butter, cheese, milk; bread, cereals, potatoes and rice; fruit and vegetables; meat. This is a good opportunity to introduce the concept of nutrients in the different kinds of food – carbohydrates, proteins, fats, vitamins and minerals. Talk about a balanced diet and the need for fibre and water to maintain good health.

Ask the children to bring in food labels from packaged and tinned foods. Working in pairs or small groups, they could look at the labels and write down the contents. Do all the foods contain a balance of carbohydrates, proteins and fats? Do some foods contain only fats? How much sugar do they contain? Is there anything else in the foods such as additives or preserving agents? Can these cause problems? (Think about allergies and hyperactivity.) Talk about the need for different types of food for different purposes, e.g., food energy, food for growth and repair, the need for water, fibre, minerals and vitamins to stay healthy.

### Content

Food is important to provide energy and materials for growth and repair, and to regulate the way our bodies work. There are different nutrients in food which serve

different purposes. In order to remain healthy we need to eat the right balance of different nutrients. A balanced diet must provide enough carbohydrates and fats for energy, proteins and minerals for growth and repair, vitamins to help with metabolism, water to transport materials and fibre to help the body to get rid of the waste. Balanced diets differ according to age, occupation and climate.

*Sc AT2 PoS(i)*

## 3. Milk and yoghurt

### Group size

The whole class, small groups.

### What you need

A range of different types of natural yoghurts from the supermarket, including a low-fat diet variety; a pint of full-fat fresh milk, other types of milk – semi-skimmed,

skimmed, dried, evaporated; sugar and salt; a yoghurt maker if available, a saucepan, a casserole dish, a wooden spoon.

### What to do

Most children are familiar with the wide variety of yoghurts that are available on supermarket shelves. Discuss with the children how yoghurt is made. What ingredients are needed to make yoghurt? What is yoghurt? If possible, the class could make some yoghurt. This is done simply in an electric yoghurt maker which consists of a number of jars inside a covered container. The container requires a supply of electricity which maintains a thermostatically-controlled temperature of 40ºC. Alternatively, you could make yoghurt by heating a pint of milk to boiling temperature, turning the heat down very low and simmering for two minutes. Leave to cool for about five minutes and, using a clean spoon, skim off all the skin which will have formed on the surface. Then mix the cooled milk with one tablespoon of natural live yoghurt (a commercial brand) in a clean casserole dish, earthenware if possible. Cover the dish and leave in a warm place for twelve hours. Then store in a refrigerator.

The children could compare the yoghurts they have made with the different types of milk: full-fat milk, skimmed milk, dried milk and evaporated milk. They could consider aspects such as consistency, smell and taste. What changes do they think have taken place in the milk to make the yoghurt? Does the addition of salt or sugar have any effect on the consistency? They could compare their yoghurt with the commercial brands of natural yoghurt.

### Content

Yoghurt is made from milk (full-fat, skimmed, evaporated or dried) by a process of fermentation. Milk is first sterilised by heating, then cooled and a prepared bacteria culture is added. It is then incubated at 40°C until the acidity reaches a certain level and clotting takes place due to the formation of lactic acid. After that, the yoghurt is cooled again, ready to be eaten. The acidity of yoghurt is due to the formation of lactic acid from lactose. The yoghurt is stored in the refrigerator to slow down the action of the bacteria.

### Safety

It is essential to keep all the utensils scrupulously clean.

Great care needs to be taken when boiling the milk. This should be done by an adult.

*Sc AT3/4b*

# 4. Breakfast time

### Group size
Small groups.

### What you need
Samples of different types of muesli from the supermarket, a range of cereal seeds – wheat, maize, barley, oats, rye, rice seed if possible (available from a local seed merchant or health food shop), small plant pots or seed trays, seed-bed compost, hand lenses, paper, pencils, a range of cereal plants (if it is not possible to obtain these, provide pictures of wheat, oats, maize, barley, rye and rice).

### What to do
Discuss with the children the type of cereal they have at breakfast time. What plants do the breakfast cereals come from? Show the children the cereal seeds that have been obtained from the seed merchant or health food shop and discuss with them the importance of cereals as food. Explain that cereals are members of the grass family. If possible, obtain samples of the cereal plants or their pictures and show these to the children.

The children should work in small groups and plant their cereal seeds in plant pots or seed trays. The seeds will need to be soaked in cold water overnight before they are sown. Only a few seeds should

be sown in each plant pot. Regular watering is necessary. The children can measure their rate of growth over a period of time. Did all the seeds which they have planted germinate? When the seeds have grown to a height of a few centimetres above the soil surface, they will need to be transplanted.

Using the information on the sides of the muesli packets, the children could record in a table the different cereal seeds which each muesli contains. They could also taste small samples of each muesli to decide which is their favourite and record their results graphically, for example, in a bar chart.

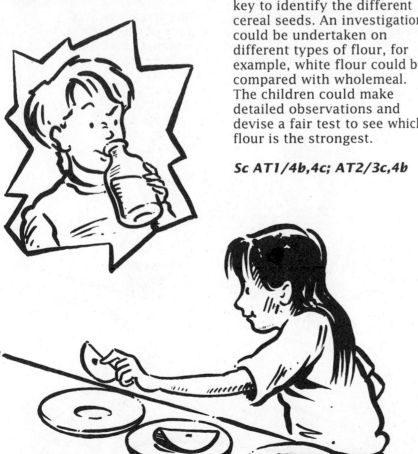

## Content
Cereals are members of the grass family which are grown for food. Examples are wheat, barley, rice, oats, maize. Wheat is made into flour and used for bread, pasta, pastries and cakes. Oats are used for porridge. Barley is used to make beer. Maize is used in breakfast cereals such as cornflakes. Rice is the staple food for much of the world.

## Further activity
The children could grow the seeds under different conditions to see the effect of light, temperature and moisture on growth.

They could make a simple key to identify the different cereal seeds. An investigation could be undertaken on different types of flour, for example, white flour could be compared with wholemeal. The children could make detailed observations and devise a fair test to see which flour is the strongest.

*Sc AT1/4b,4c; AT2/3c,4b*

# 5. Going off

## Group size
Small groups.

## What you need
A pint of fresh milk, two apples, five small shallow dishes, five small containers, weighing scales, clear food wrapping or polythene bags, paper, pencils, a knife, disposable gloves.

## What to do
Discuss with the children questions such as the following:
• Have you ever smelled sour milk?
• What has happened to it?
• How do we keep milk fresh in warm weather?
• What happens to food when it goes off?

If we keep fresh food too long, it sometimes goes off. What makes food go bad? The children can carry out investigations to find out. Disposable gloves should be worn. They should cut the apples up and put equal weights into identical dishes. They should investigate the effect of temperature, moisture and being open to the air. At the end of the investigation the pieces of apple should be re-weighed. Similarly, equal quantities of milk can be poured into small containers of the same size. The effect of temperature can be investigated by storing some of the containers in the refrigerator, and other containers outside and near a radiator in a warm room.

Ask the children to observe the apple and the milk over a period of several days and record any changes. This investigation is an ideal opportunity to consider fair testing and variables. What will the children need to keep the same, what will they need to change?

### Content
Factors influencing the process of decay include temperature, moisture, air, and exposure to micro-organisms.

### Safety
Care must be taken in disposing of the decaying material.

*Sc AT1/3,4,5; AT2/5d*

# 6. Dissolving

### Group size
Small groups.

### What you need
A range of foods from the kitchen cupboard, for example, white and brown sugar, flour, salt, curry powder, coffee, jelly, cornflour, custard powder; jam-jars, spoons, cold and warm water, a measuring cylinder; paper and pencils.

### What to do
Ask the children to examine the food closely and to record their observations. Colour and texture should be noted. The children are going to find out which of the foods dissolve in water. They will need to make sure they are carrying out a fair test. Variables such as the amount of solid, the volume of water and its temperature, and number of times the mixture is stirred with a spoon, should be considered. The children should first test whether the foods dissolve in cold water and then try warm water. Ask them to draw up a three-

columned table, headed 'Dissolves in cold water' 'Dissolves in warm water' and 'Does not dissolve' or alternatively, they could devise their own method of recording the results. Next to the name of each food substance they could stick a polythene bag containing a small sample of the substance.

### Content
Water will dissolve a variety of substances – they will disappear when added to water. When a substance dissolves in a liquid it is said to be soluble. Solubility increases with the temperature. Stirring helps the dissolving process.

### Further activity
The children could increase the amount of each substance to see if it will still dissolve in the water. If the children put a small amount of table salt

solution in a small, shallow dish and leave it in a warm place, the water will evaporate and the salt will be left behind as crystals. This evaporation process could take some days depending on the temperature.

*Sc AT3 PoS(i)*

# 7. Making good use of red cabbage water

### Group size
Pairs.

### What you need
Red cabbage water obtained by placing freshly cut red cabbage in warm water, test tubes and a test-tube rack or yoghurt pots, lemon juice,

Only safe, everyday liquids should be used. However, diluted solutions of hydrochloric acid and sodium hydroxide (alkaline) will increase the range of colours obtained. If these are to be used, they should be stored in a locked room in suitable conditions, handled by the teacher alone and washed down the sink with water after use. Spillages should be handled with care and splashes on clothing or skin rinsed immediately with quantities of water.

*Sc AT3/5b*

# 8. A food survey

## Group size
Initially individuals, then small groups.

## What you need
Small notebooks, pictures of undernourished children from an economically developing country, graph paper, coloured pencils, atlases, a globe, outline maps of the world.

## What to do
The stimulus for this activity could be a recent incidence of famine in an economically developing country. Show the children the pictures and discuss why children in some economically developing countries are short of food. Ask them to name all the different kinds of food they eat – make up a list on the chalkboard. Ask the children to keep a record of all the food they eat between getting up in the morning and going to bed in the evening. Once the children have recorded all their data, tell them to

colours obtained after addition of the liquids to acid (red/orange/yellow), neutral (blue/purple) and alkaline (green).

## Content
Some chemicals such as red cabbage water indicate whether a substance is acid, alkaline or neutral. We call these chemicals indicators and red cabbage is a very effective indicator. The children could also use Universal indicator, which gives a different but slightly more impressive range of colours.

## Further activity
The children could find out whether various soils are acid, neutral or alkaline. Mix the soil with water (preferably de-ionised), shake and leave to settle. Either decant the liquid into the red cabbage water or pour red cabbage water on to the soil solution. This could lead to a discussion about gardeners using peat to increase the acidity of soil and lime to decrease it.

lemonade, water, cola, vinegar, milk, other safe everyday solutions.

## What to do
Cut up the fresh red cabbage leaves and place them in water. If a blue/purple colour is not obtained, use hotter water and crush the leaves.

Ask the children to add small amounts of the liquids to be tested to the red cabbage water, decanted into test tubes or yoghurt pots. Remind the children to use equal amounts of liquid to make it a fair test. Ask them to record the results in a table and encourage them to see patterns.

Relate the three basic

categorise it under the headings shown in Figure 1. Put the resulting charts up on the display board, together with food wrappers brought in by the children. The food wrappers can be used to make a further categorisation of food produced in the UK and food produced abroad. Ask the children to describe and illustrate a typical day's food supply for themselves and compare it with what a child in a drought-affected country might eat in a day. Tell them to show the differences in quantities, varieties and, if possible, nutritional value.

| Food from plants | | | | | Food from animals | | |
|---|---|---|---|---|---|---|---|
| Food from cereal crops | Vegetables | Fruit | Dairy products | Sweets | Meat | Poultry | Fish |
| | | | | | | | |

**Figure 1**

## Content
Many people in the world are short of food. The reasons are frequently a combination of many factors, but adverse climatic conditions (drought, floods, hurricanes, and so on),

pests and diseases affecting crops and livestock and problems created by wars are the main causes. Help the children to understand the cycle of deprivation: poor harvest – no crops to sell – no money coming in – no new seeds, no machinery can be bought, and so on. The children need to identify and understand the causes and effects of the shortages of food in some economically developing countries.

## Further activity
Ask the children to research the origins of the foods they have and to mark on their outline maps of the world the country of origin and the food it supplies.

**Gg AT1/4e; AT2/3a,4e; AT3/3a; AT4/5c**

# 9. Bread – the staff of life

## Group size
Small groups.

## What you need
A good quality map of the UK showing the counties, aerial photographs of wheat fields, pictures of tractors ploughing fields and sowing seed, a picture of a combine harvester at harvest time; ears of wheat and flour; Photocopiable pages 194 and 195.

## What to do
Ask if any of the children have had the opportunity to make bread. Discuss the process of making flour from the wheatcorn. Ask the children to look at the pictures of wheat farming. What do they tell about the conditions needed for wheat farming?
    Give out photocopiable

pages 194 and 195 and ask the children to identify areas where the land is below 90 metres, rainfall is between 625 and 1000 mm per annum and summer temperatures average over 17°C. Ask them to shade in on the outline map the counties that meet these conditions and to name them. Ask them to label their map 'The wheat-growing counties of the United Kingdom'.

The children could go on to make a comparative study of another wheat growing area of the world such as Canada or Ukraine.

## Content

The main wheat-growing counties of the UK are Hertfordshire, Essex, Suffolk, Cambridgeshire, Buckinghamshire, Kent, Oxfordshire, Berkshire and Wiltshire. British wheat is not used to make the bread to which the British consumer has become accustomed, because it is 'soft' wheat. The climate in Eastern England is not dry enough to make the grain ripen fully, so the British wheat is used mainly in biscuit and cake making. Durum, or

| Map A: rainfall | 625mm light blue | 625 - 1000mm dark blue | over 1000mm purple |
|---|---|---|---|
| Map B: temperature | below 16°C yellow | 16 - 17°C orange | over 17°C red |
| Map C: relief | below 90m green | 90 - 360m brown | over 360m black |

Figure 1

'hard' wheat, used for bread-making, is imported from Canada.

Gg AT1/3d,5b,5d; AT2/2d; AT3/5a; AT4/5c,5e

# 10. Dairy products

## Group size
Pairs.

## What you need
Photocopiable pages 194, 195 and 196; atlases, pictures of dairy produce, coloured pencils; information pack from the Dairy Council (optional).

## What to do
Mount a stimulus display showing the main dairy produce and how it is produced. Include pictures of dairy cattle and discuss with the children how cattle are managed – how they are fed in summer and winter, how milk is collected from the farm and so on.

Explain to the children that dairy farming is normally only possible in areas which meet certain conditions. Set the children the task of finding out where these areas are in the UK. Give out maps A, B and C and ask the children to colour in the relevant areas as stipulated in Figure 1.

Ensure that the children complete the maps with the key marked on them. Then give out map E (photocopiable page 196) showing the main dairying areas in the UK. Figure 2 below combines the

Figure 2

| Name of area | Map A Rainfall (mm) | Map B Summer temps. (degrees Celsius) | Map C Relief (metres) |
|---|---|---|---|
| Ayrshire Plain | over 1000 | below 16 | below 90 |
| Lowlands of Solway Firth | over 1000 | below 16 | below 90 |
| Lancashire Plain | over 1000 | below 16 | below 90 |
| Cheshire Plain | over 1000 | 16 - 17 | below 90 |
| Vale of York | 625 - 1000 | below 16 | below 90 |
| Trent Valley | 625 - 1000 | 16 - 17 | below 90 |
| Welsh Lowlands | over 1000 | 16 - 17 | below 90 |
| Thames Basin | 625 - 1000 | over 17 | below 90 |
| The Weald | under 625 | over 17 | below 90 |
| The West Country | over 1000 | 16 - 17 | below 90 |

information shown in Maps A, B and C for the main dairy farming areas of the UK. Provide each pair with a copy of this table, but remember to leave the three columns blank so that the children glean the information for themselves.

Ask the children to fill in the table. Explain that good pasture land suitable for dairy cattle is normally found below an altitude of 90 metres, where the mean summer temperature is above 16°C and the rainfall is in excess of 625mm per year. Can they explain why some of the areas in their table do not meet all these criteria?

## Content
The central task of this activity is to identify those areas of the UK which have the best conditions for dairy farming. However, some areas which do not meet these conditions precisely are still areas of intensive dairy farming. This has to do with the influence of the sea on winter temperature, the proximity of conurbations providing suitable markets and the presence of clay soils which retain moisture.

## Further activity
Ask the children to look at Map F (photocopiable page 196) showing the names of towns and cities. From which areas shown on Map E are the following cities likely to obtain milk ?

| | |
|---|---|
| **1.** Glasgow | **6.** London |
| **2.** Liverpool | **7.** Cardiff |
| **3.** Leeds | **8.** Plymouth |
| **4.** Nottingham | **9.** Newcastle |
| **5.** Bristol | **10.** Norwich |

*Gg AT1/5b,5d; AT2/3f; AT3/5a; AT4/4e,5c,5e*

# 11. Apples

## Group size
Pairs and small groups.

## What do you need
Atlases, a globe, outline maps of UK counties (Map D on photocopiable page 195), outline map of the world, a variety of apples to taste, a knife, information packs and other reference material relating to apples and cider production, paper, pencils.

## What to do
Buy as wide a selection of apples as you can. Ask the children to study the varieties and note down differences. Then cut up the apples into small segments and give the children a segment each to taste. Ask them to comment on the apple tasted, rating it on a 1–5 scale for sweetness, texture and preference. Explain how apples are grown and what are the best conditions.

Give out the outline map of the counties of the UK and ask the children to shade in counties of Gloucestershire, Hereford and Worcester, Somerset and Devon. Using the relief, rainfall and temperature maps of the UK in their atlases, ask them to give the reason why they think these counties are the main apple producers.

Tell the children that not all apples are sold for eating. Slightly damaged and surplus apples are turned into apple drinks and cider.

Using all the available information ask the children to plan and produce a frieze along the classroom wall which shows the sequence of apple to cider production, starting with a picture of an apple

orchard with an explanation of the climatic conditions required.

## Content
In order to provide supermarkets and greengrocers with high quality apples that look and taste good, orchards are planted on slopes above valley floors to minimise frost damage. The fruit requires plenty of rain in summer to swell it and regular spraying with insecticides to reduce pest damage. The countries of the South West of England are most suitable because of the influence of the sea and prevailing south west winds which ensure mild winters and relatively warm wet summers.

## Further activity
Other countries supply the UK with apples including France and South Africa. Give out to the children an outline map of the world and ask them to shade in England, France and South Africa. Using an atlas ask the children to list all the countries that lie with lines of latitude 48°–53°N to 30°–40°S. Using their knowledge of the growing conditions required for apples and their atlases, ask the children to suggest which countries lying on the same lines of latitude might have the necessary conditions for apple growing i.e. freedom from severe frosts, proximity to the sea for providing suitable rainfall and so on.

*Gg AT1/4e,5b,5d; AT2/2c, 4b,5c; AT3/4a,5a; AT4/5c, 5e*

# 12. Potatoes or rice?

## Group size
Pairs.

## What you need
Atlases showing average temperatures and rainfall around the world, map G showing main potato growing areas of the UK (photocopiable page 197), map H showing main rice-growing areas of the world (photocopiable page 202); reference material on rice and potato production; potatoes and varieties of rice to add to a classroom display.

## What to do
Ask the children to list the various ways in which they eat potatoes. If possible, undertake a survey based on the school meals. Alternatively, ask the children to record the weight of potatoes used in meals at home, to provide figures for average consumption per child per week/month/year.

Give out copies of map G and ask the children to use their atlases to identify, mark in and name the main counties where potatoes are grown in large quantities. Explain to the children that Cornish and Channel Island potatoes appear in the shops earlier than potatoes from other counties, but are more expensive. Ask the children to imagine that they are Cornish farmers trying to sell their early potatoes to the supermarket chain. Ask them to write a letter to the supermarket buyer, explaining why their potatoes will sell well and justifying their higher price.

Explain to the children that rice is the staple food for many people in other countries. Draw on children's experiences of Chinese and Indian takeaway food. Ask them to look at the books and pictures about rice production and suggest why rice is not grown in this country and to speculate on the conditions needed.

Give the children a copy of map H and ask them to shade in the areas shown on the map between the tropic of Cancer and the tropic of Capricorn. Ask them to find out the names of the main countries where rice is grown and eaten. Against each country ask them to write down the average annual rainfall and the lowest and highest monthly temperatures. Can they now make a general statement such as 'Rice is grown mainly in those countries with about ____ mm of rain a year and where the temperature lies between ____ °C and ____ °C?

## Content
Potatoes and rice are the world's two main staple foods. Rice is a grass that thrives in water and is generally kept in a flooded condition during growth. The main variety of rice providing the staple diet of many tropical countries is the long-grained Indica rice variety. A shorter grained Japonica rice is now grown in more temperate lands, but this particular activity focuses on the long grained variety.

Potatoes grow best in a variety of climatic conditions, where the soil is sandy and therefore well drained. Potato-growing areas tend to be fairly flat and suitable for mechanised cultivation and harvest. Cornish and Channel Island potatoes mature earlier because of the more southerly and milder climatic conditions. There is high demand for limited supplies and this, together with the transport costs, pushes up their price.

*Gg AT1/4e,5b,5d; AT2/3a, 4b,4e,5c; AT3/3a,4e,5b; AT4/3d,4e,5c,5e; AT5/2b*

# 13. What to grow where

## Group size
Small groups.

## What you need
Photocopiable pages 198 and 199.

## What to do
Remind the children of the work they have done in previous activities and how they have discovered that the physical conditions in an area influence the choice of farming activity. Tell them that they are going to try to solve the problems that farmers face when they decide what to grow and where.

Give out the briefing sheet and the base map. Divide the children into small groups and ask them to deal with one or more of the areas of ABCD on the base map on photocopiable page 199. It may be useful to ensure that the children know how to interpret the base map, that they understand the symbols and are able to indicate the slope of the land. Work out with them simple cross-sections and explain how these provide further information.

Ask them to present their conclusions in the form of a report to the land owner. Encourage the children to justify each decision in terms of as many variables as is appropriate.

## Content
This is a problem-solving activity designed to provide children with opportunities to handle a range of variables simultaneously, to apply previously learned knowledge to new situations and to give

rational justification for their decisions. They will need to discuss each situation carefully in their groups, referring back to earlier work, e.g. the need for the farm to be above the flood plain and so on.

*Gg AT1/2a,5b; AT3/3c,4c; AT4/3d,4c,4e,5c,5e; AT5/2b,4a,4c*

# 14. Grind that corn!

## Group size
Small groups.

## What you need
The table below, showing the times when cereals were first farmed, pictures of examples of various cereals, a map of the world, large sheets of paper, coloured ribbon or thread, marker pins, rulers, felt-tipped pens, pencils, scissors.

## What to do
Show the children the table and ask 'How do we know that people farmed these cereals at these times?' Ask them to make a time-line showing the earliest farming times of the cereals. Display the finished time-line next to a map of the

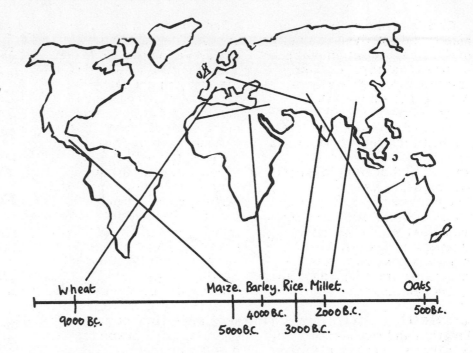

world. Use the coloured ribbon to connect the time-line with appropriate places on the map.

## Content
Archaeology has provided evidence of cereal farming in these periods. Burnt grain or impressions have been left on pottery excavated from various sites. Flint sickles have also been found bearing traces of plant remains. References in oral story-telling traditions and representations in art provide further clues. The reliability of these sources needs to be discussed. Our knowledge is fragmentary and limited; there may be much we do not know due to lack of evidence. The crops farmed would be the ancestors of those we now farm and have developed from wild grasses.

## Further activity
• Obtain wheat grain from a wholefood shop and grind it using a variety of implements (e.g., rolling pin, mortar and pestle, two stones). Ask the children to speculate about how the flour making process may have been discovered.
• Visit a working windmill or watermill and focus on the improvement in efficiency from hand-grinding to mechanised grinding.

*H AT1/3a,3b,3c,4a,4b,5a; AT2/4,5; AT3/5*

| Cereals - the first known farming times | | |
|---|---|---|
| **Crop** | **Region** | **Period** |
| Barley | Egypt | 4000 BC |
| Maize | Mexico | 5000 BC |
| Millet | China | 2700 BC |
| Oats | Asia/Europe | 500 BC |
| Rice | India | 3000 BC |
| Wheat | Mediterranean/Middle East | 9000/8000 BC |

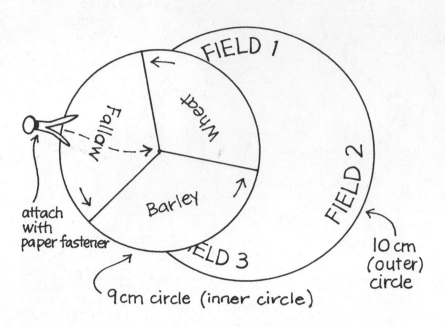

FIELD 1

Fallow

Wheat

Barley

FIELD 2

FIELD 3

attach with paper fastener

10 cm (outer) circle

9 cm circle (inner circle)

If possible, try to arrange a visit to Laxton in Nottinghamshire, to study the last remaining open-field system.

**H SSU A, AT1/3a,3b,3c, 4a,5b.**

# 16. Round and round again

## Group size
Small groups.

## What you need
Photocopiable page 201, two cardboard circles, one 9cm in diameter, one 10cm, a paper fastener, pencils and crayons.

## What to do
Ask the children to look at photocopiable page 201 and decide which of the two rotations they will make, either modern or medieval. The larger circle should have the fields labelled on its outside edge, and the inner circle should display the division of field use. The inner circle is attached to the outer circle with a paper fastener (see diagram above). The children should then compare the two rotations, focusing on key questions, such as the following:
• Why was there a need to improve rotation?
(Growth of towns and increased population.)
• How did people find new methods?
(Experimentation, applying scientific knowledge.)
• How else did farming become more efficient?
(Mechanisation, selective breeding.)
• How are the problems of soil fertility handled today?
(Chemical fertilisers.)

# 15. The medieval farming cycle

## Group size
Whole class in small groups.

## What you need
Photocopiable page 200, 'A medieval farming yearly cycle', paper, pencils and rulers.

## What to do
Ask the children in their groups to look at the farming cycle and discuss the purpose of each farming task. They should then list those things which people might have needed but could not produce themselves, e.g. salt, stone for building, metal for tools. Ask the children to compare their own diet with that of a medieval family and to record the similarities and differences in the form of a table. Children can then discuss the reasons for these in their groups.

## Content
Apart from salt, a family would be self-sufficient in food. Cereal crops would provide bread and beer, animals could be grazed on common land, and chickens kept and vegetables grown on land attached to cottages. Fruit and berries would also be gathered. Staple foods were much as they are today but there is now greater variety, especially in the way food is prepared and preserved. Focus on the reasons for this difference, particularly with reference to changes in trade and transport, preservation of food, population and mass production and the mechanisation of farming.

## Further activity
Children could create a model or collage of a medieval village and compare this with maps of a nineteenth- or twentieth-century village.

## Content

The medieval crop rotation worked successfully throughout the Middle Ages to support self-sufficient communities. The onset of the Industrial Revolution and a large rise in population created the demand for reform and improvement. Enclosures consolidated land into single farms and this organisation favoured experimentation and change. Landowners like Lord Townshend and Thomas Coke of Norfolk were key individuals in promoting new methods.

### Further activity

Ask the children to research other developments in agriculture e.g. selective breeding of cattle.

*H AT1/3a,3b,3c,4a,4b,4c,5a; AT3/3*

# 17. The farming museum

### Group size

The whole class in small groups.

### What you need

A visit to a farming museum, a camera, a collection of reference books on the history of farming, clipboards, paper, pencils.

### What to do

Ask each group to discover and record artefacts in the museum which relate to an aspect of the history of farming, e.g. ploughing, planting, reaping, threshing, grinding. The children can record their findings by taking notes, photographs (if the museum allows) or drawing.
   On returning to school, the children can work in groups to collate, organise and present their research. This could take the form of a group presentation to the class and/or a wall display.

### Content

It is advisable to visit the museum first and make sure information is readily available for particular themes. The children should be given time to look and question before they record. They will need to be encouraged to ask questions concerning physical features of the artefacts, how they were made, what they were used for, how the design was influenced by the purpose for which they were made and their value in terms of worth to the people who made and used them. They will also need to consider why changes took place and the effect these had on peoples' lives, relating changes to increased knowledge and new discoveries.

### Further activity

Create a class time-line showing technological development in farming.

*H AT1/3a,3b,3c,4a,4b,5a,5b, 5c; AT2/4; AT3/3,4,5*

# 18. The price of a loaf

### Group size

The whole class.

### What you need

The children will need to have some prior knowledge of the causes of poverty, and be familiar with the Corn Laws and the Bread riots of the late eighteenth and early nineteenth century.

### What to do
Introduce the motion for debate: 'This house believes the poor were justified in rioting in protest at the price of bread'. The proposers and opposers could be individuals, pairs or small groups. In any case they will need time to prepare their arguments. Conduct the session as a formal debate.

### Content
Bread was the staple diet of working people. Several factors gave rise to high corn prices: the Napoleonic wars, bad harvest and the Corn Laws. Poverty was exacerbated by new machinery, the overburdening of the Speenhamland system of poverty relief and the unemployment of soldiers returning from the war. There were serious riots in 1795 (rioters siezed food and sold it to the poor), 1816 (firing of ricks and barns) and 1830 (Labourers Revolt and Captain Swing). Issues children will need to consider include the point of view of farmers and landowners; possibilities of other means of protest (the poor were not enfranchised); emigration; punishments (transportation, hanging); fear of revolution.

### Further activity
Ask the children to write an imaginary diary account of a labourer transported for rioting at this time. Find out about how the local area was affected during this period.

**H SSU A, AT1/3a,3b,4b, 5b,5c; AT2/3,4,5**

## 19. Into the twentieth century

### Group size
The whole class in small groups.

### What you need
Information books on twentieth-century farming, paper, pens.

### What to do
Give each group one of the following themes to research in relation to the twentieth-century production of bread:
• the effect of mechanisation;
• the effects of war;
• the advance of science (freezing, insecticides and fertilisers);
• the developing world and famine;
• developments in trade and transport;
• the European Community.
  Make sure the children work through a structured process finding books, reading books and discussing, asking key questions, taking notes, producing tables, diagrams and illustrations, collating information, presenting information in the form of a wall collage.

### Content
The most significant influences on the production of bread in the twentieth century have been increased mechanisation (combine harvester and tractor), two world wars, scientific advances (chemical fertilisers and insecticides), the European Community, the development of large overseas producers (Canada and USA) and the plight of the developing countries. Children need to examine these issues critically, discussing controversies (insecticides, fertilisers and environmental issues), distinguishing between factual information and points of view.

### Further activity
Use one of the researched areas as a focus for debate, e.g. chemical versus organic farming.

**H AT1/3a,3b,3c,4a,4b,4c, 5a,5b,5c; AT2/3; AT3/4**

# CHAPTER 9

# On the move

This project, based on the upper levels of Key Stage 2, explores the dynamic nature of life and involves children in a wide range of firsthand experiences, and individual and group activity. Crucial to the National Curriculum geography studies is an understanding of maps, their interpretation and their value in indicating place, direction, distance and route. This project leads children through map-reading skills relating to local, regional, national and international journeys. At the same time, the notions of population movement, immigration, invasion and settlement are explored through the history activities. The search for evidence and the development of ideas such as cause and consequence in the context of the movement of individuals and groups, are explored through the children's own family and neighbourhood. Through these activities, children will begin to understand their national heritage and origin, as well as the similarities between the movement of people in historical time – the Vikings, the Romans, the Normans – and the more recent growth of ethnic groups within their own country.

These are the beginnings of very important ideas which will facilitate increased understanding and development of appropriate attitudes. However, the best starting point for the topic is probably the idea of physical movement of our own bodies and the way in which people initiate, control and use movement in their daily lives. The activities range from movement through air and water to investigations of plant and animal movement.

# BACKGROUND

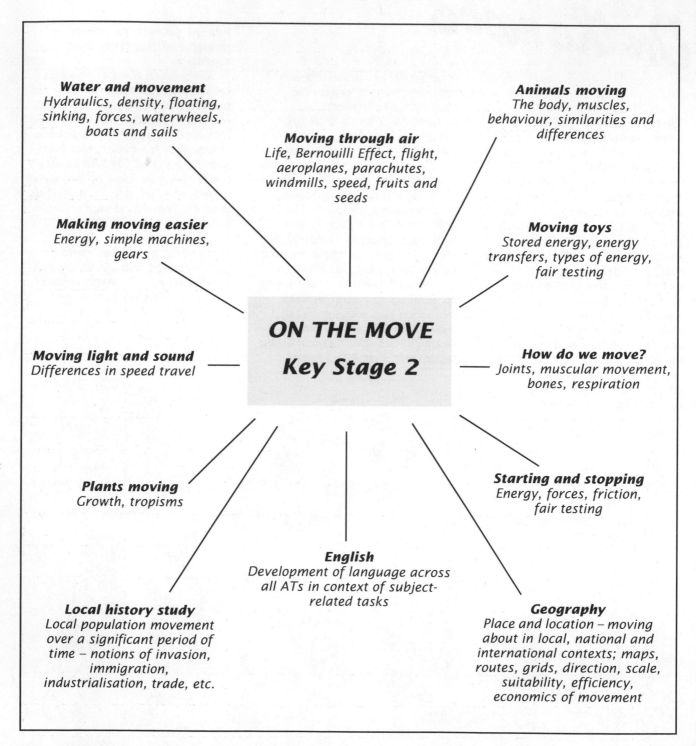

**Water and movement**
Hydraulics, density, floating, sinking, forces, waterwheels, boats and sails

**Moving through air**
Life, Bernouilli Effect, flight, aeroplanes, parachutes, windmills, speed, fruits and seeds

**Animals moving**
The body, muscles, behaviour, similarities and differences

**Making moving easier**
Energy, simple machines, gears

**Moving toys**
Stored energy, energy transfers, types of energy, fair testing

**ON THE MOVE
Key Stage 2**

**Moving light and sound**
Differences in speed travel

**How do we move?**
Joints, muscular movement, bones, respiration

**Plants moving**
Growth, tropisms

**Starting and stopping**
Energy, forces, friction, fair testing

**English**
Development of language across all ATs in context of subject-related tasks

**Local history study**
Local population movement over a significant period of time – notions of invasion, immigration, industrialisation, trade, etc.

**Geography**
Place and location – moving about in local, national and international contexts; maps, routes, grids, direction, scale, suitability, efficiency, economics of movement

| Activity | Curriculum Area | ATTAINMENT TARGET AND LEVEL | | | | |
|---|---|---|---|---|---|---|
| | | AT1 | AT2 | AT3 | AT4 | AT5 |
| 1 | Science | | | | 3c, 4c, 5d | |
| 2 | Science | | | | 3c, 4c, 5d | |
| 3 | Science | | | | 3c | |
| 4 | Science | | 3a | | | |
| 5 | Science | | 3c | | | |
| 6 | Science | 3c, 4b, 4c | | | 3c | |
| 7 | Science Technology | 4f | | | 3c, 4c, 5b, 5d 4c, 4d, 5c | |
| 8 | Science | 3b, 4b | 3a | | | |
| 9 | Science | | 4c | | | |
| 10 | Science | 4c | | | 4d | |
| 11 | Science Technology | | 3a, 4b, 4c, 5d | 3a,b,c, 4ab, 5d | 3a, 4b, 5b, 5d 3b, 4b, 5a, 5b | |
| 12 | Science | 4a, 4b | | | 4b, 4c, 5b, 5d | |
| 13 | Geography | 3a, 3b, 3c, 4a | 1a,1b,1c,3c,3f | 3c | | |
| 14 | Geography | 3a, 3b, 3c, 3d, 4a, 4b, 4c | 2b, 3e, 3f | | 1a, 1b, 1c | |
| 15 | Geography | 4b, 5c | 3b, 3c, 3f, 4b, 4c | | 4a, 4c, 4d, 4e | 3b, 4a |
| 16 | Geography | 5a, 5b, 5c | 3c, 3f | 3b, 4c | | 5a |
| 17 | Geography | 4b, 4e, 5a, 5b, 5c | 3b, 3c, 3d | | 3b, 4d, 5b | |
| 18 | Geography | 4b, 4e | 5c | 3a | 5c | |
| 19 | History | 3b, 3c, 4a, 5b | | | | |
| 20 | History | 3a, 4a | 3 | 3 | | |
| 21 | History | 3a, 3b, 4a, 4b, 5a, 5b | | 3, 5 | | |
| 22 | History | 3a, 3b, 3c, 4a, 4b, 4c, 5a, 5b | 3 | 3, 4 | | |
| 23 | History | 3a, 3b, 3c, 4a, 4b, 5a, 5b | | 3, 4, 5 | | |
| 24 | History | 3a, 3b, 4a, 4b | | | | |
| 25 | PE Science | statements a,c,e | | | 2c, 3c | |
| 26 | PE Science | statements d,e | | | 2c, 3c, 4c | |
| 27 | PE Science | statements a,c,f | | | 2c, 3c, 4c, 5d | |

# ACTIVITIES

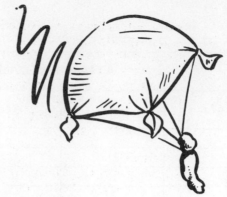

## 1. Dropping in – make a parachute

### Group size
Pairs.

### What you need
Cotton and other types of fabric offcuts, cotton thread, cotton reels, Plasticine, paper, tissue paper, scissors, stop-watches.

### What to do
Ask the children to make a parachute.

Cut a square of material approximately 12cm by 12cm. Twist each corner and tie an equal length of cotton thread (about 20cm) to each one. Tie the ends of the threads together, taking care not to get them tangled up. Make a parachutist out of Plasticine (or use a cotton reel instead). Fasten the parachute to the Plasticine. Launch the parachute folded or lightly crumpled up with the Plasticine weight in the middle. Time its fall with a stop-watch. Design a fair test to discover whether the time it takes for the parachute to fall depends on the type of material used (try other fabrics, paper and tissue paper), the size of the parachute, the size of the load. Does cutting a small hole in the middle of the parachute make any difference to speed and direction of the fall? Vary the position of the hole.

### Content
When a parachute is falling at a steady speed, the downward force of gravity on it, called weight, is balanced by the upward force of the air resistance, called drag. When the parachute first starts to fall, the weight is greater than the drag, so it has a resultant downward force on it and so it accelerates. As it speeds up, the drag increases more and more until the drag equals the weight. Then it no longer accelerates but falls with a constant speed. The speed for a man falling without a parachute is about 120 miles per hour (mph), but with a parachute it is about 20mph.

### Safety
Children should take care when using scissors.

*SC AT4/3c,4c,5d*

## 2. Spinning

### Group size
Individuals or pairs.

### What you need
Pieces of stiff paper 20cm by 10cm, paper-clips, scissors, a stopwatch.

### What to do
Ask the children to make a spinner as shown in the diagram below.

They should then bend the 'wings' of their spinner in opposite directions. If they put a paper-clip on the bottom of the spinner to weight it, they can fly the spinner by throwing it up into the air. Tell the children to time how long it takes to reach the floor. Can

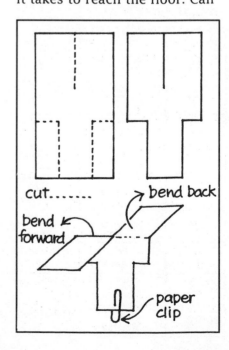

cut.......
bend forward
bend back
paper clip

they make it turn to the left and the right? Can they slow down the fall?

## Content
See 'Dropping in' on page 144.

## Further activity
The children could experiment with the following variables:
• the thickness of paper;
• the size and shape of the 'wings';
• the number of paper-clips – two instead of one?

If possible, ask the children to collect some sycamore fruits which are natural spinners. Discuss seed dispersal with them.

## Safety
Children should take care when using scissors.

*Sc AT4/3c,4c,5d*

# 3. Lift up

## Group size
Individuals.

## What you need
A4-sized paper, pieces of stiff paper 20cm by 10cm, adhesive, sticky tape, thin string, drinking straws, scissors.

## What to do
Give the children the following instructions.

Hold a piece of A4-sized paper so that the shortest side is nearest to you. Gently blow across the top of the paper. What happens?

Fold a piece of paper 20cm by 10cm in half. Stick the free ends together with adhesive or sticky tape. Make a small hole (just wide enough to insert a drinking straw) through both thicknesses of the paper a few centimetres from the folded end. Put a drinking straw through the hole and glue it into place. Thread a piece of thin string through the hole. Hold the string taut. Blow across your model wing and watch what happens.

## Content
These activities demonstrate the Bernouilli Effect. Air travels farther and faster over the upper surface of the wing than the lower surface. This causes a reduction in air pressure above the wing and the wing lifts. An aircraft wing is usually curved on the top and straight underneath.

## Further activity
Relate these findings to aeroplane and bird flight.

*Sc AT4/3c*

# 4. The push test

## Group size
Small groups.

## What you need
Bathroom scales, paper, pencils.

## What to do
Give the children the following instructions.

Stand the bathroom scales upright against a wall. Lie on the ground and push one foot against the scales as hard as you can. Ask a member of your group to take the reading on the scales. Repeat the experiment with the other foot. Which foot produced the highest reading on the scales?

Each member of the group should do this activity. Record your results in a table. Who pushed harder with the right foot? Who pushed harder with the left foot? Which muscles do you think you are using when pushing?

## Content
When children push with their legs on the bathroom scales, they use their calf and thigh muscles. Muscles are joined to bones and pull the bones to move them. When the arm is bent, the muscle contracts. To pull the bone back, another muscle comes into operation.

and gravity. Green plants need light to photosynthesise, that is to make their own food. If the light is coming from only one direction they will grow towards it.

## Safety

Children should take care when using scissors.

*Sc AT2/3c*

# 6. Water and movement

## Group size
Small groups.

## What you need
Guttering, water, a battery-operated fan, a stop-watch, three different boat shapes, a cardboard sail.

## What to do
Pour water into the guttering until the boats float. Attach the sail to one of the boats and place it at one end of the guttering. Ask the children which boat will travel the quickest down the length of the guttering when the fan is switched on. Can the children devise a fair test? The table below might help them. Do they appreciate the need for a starting point and a finishing point for each trial? Do they appreciate the need to time each trial? Ask the children to record their results in an

## Further activity
Ask the children to make a model of the arm using cardboard cut-outs, paper fasteners and elastic bands. The elastic bands represent the muscles of the arms and the paper fasteners the joints. The children can raise and lower the parts of the arm by pulling on the elastic bands, to see how the muscles work in pairs. Ask the children to look at their own arms and to feel the muscles move as they bend their arms.

*Sc AT2/3a*

# 5. Plants and light

## Group size
Small groups.

## What you need
A shoe-box with a lid, a small polystyrene tray, cress seeds, blotting paper or cotton wool, scissors, water.

## What to do
Give the children the following instructions.
Line the polystyrene tray with some blotting paper or cotton wool. Dampen the paper or cotton wool with water and sprinkle some cress seeds evenly over the surface. Place the tray in a light place. When the seeds start to grow, place the tray containing the seeds at one end of the box. Put the lid on the box and make a hole in the middle of the other end. Put the box on the window ledge so that the hole is facing the light. Keep watering the seedlings when necessary. Check the box after a few days. What has happened to the seedlings?

## Content
Plants are sensitive to a variety of stimuli, in particular to light

| What I want to find out | • The fastest boat<br>• How long it takes to travel down the guttering |
|---|---|
| What I must keep the same | • Shape of the sail<br>• Starting position<br>• Position of the fan |
| What I must vary/change | • Shape of the boat |

appropriate table and to draw a suitable conclusion. What did they do if the boat touched the sides of the guttering? Did they keep the fan in one place? Did they take just one reading for each boat shape or did they repeat it three times and take an average?

They should go on to consider what kind of design would produce a faster boat. They could look at aspects such as shape, material, finish and so on. How different is it to the original?

## Content
The shape of the boat affects its speed through water. The less resistance provided by the boat's contact with the water, the faster the boat will go. Ships and boats generally have a pointed front to lower the water resistance, allowing them to 'cut through' water. The children will be hypothesising, designing a fair test, collating results and drawing inferences from their results.

## Safety
Always take care to keep water away from electrical apparatus and sockets.

*Sc AT1/3c,4b,4c; AT4/3c*

# 7. Water and movement: water-wheels

## Group size
Small groups.

## What you need
A cork with straight sides, a piece of guttering, six to eight strips of plastic from a detergent bottle or a yoghurt container, a piece of dowel or a knitting needle, a cork borer, Plasticine, adhesive, scissors.

## What to do
Drill a hole through the centre of the cork so that when the dowel or knitting needle is inserted, the cork moves freely. Cut six to eight thin grooves into the cork at equal distances from each other. Cut six to nine strips of plastic the same length as the cork and glue these in position in the slots. Pass the dowel or knitting needle through the cork, sticking a small piece of Plasticine at each end of the cork to stop it slipping. Hold the water-wheel under the running tap. Can it be made to turn both clockwise and anti-clockwise? In what position does it move the fastest? How does the flow of water affect the movement of the water-wheel?

A piece of guttering could be used to make a mill-race. By modifying the apparatus with the use of gears, the water-wheel may be used to drive a millstone.

## Content
The force of water causes the water-wheel to turn. As the flow, and hence the force of water, is increased, the speed of the turning wheel should increase too.

In past times, including the early part of the twentieth century before the invention of electricity, wind and water power were used to produce movement. Wind- and water-mills were common sights in towns and countryside. Today, we use electricity and complex mill machinery to grind cereal grains, rather than using cheaper, readily available but less 'efficient' forms of power such as wind and water. Today, technology has been used to solve the problem of harnessing energy to drive machinery.

This activity could be easily incorporated into topics on the seaside, fairgrounds, water-mills and the United States of

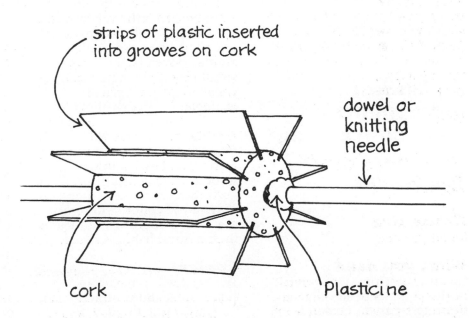

strips of plastic inserted into grooves on cork

dowel or knitting needle

cork

Plasticine

these may be heard as the animal moves over paper. Movement is one of the basic life processes common to humans and other animals.

### Safety
Ensure that children treat all animals with respect. Do not let the animals dry out as both earthworms and woodlice need a moist surface to obtain oxygen. If children have handled the animals ensure that they wash their hands afterwards.

*Sc AT1/3b,4b; AT2/3a*

America (the Mississippi River and its paddle boats).

### Safety
Plastic edges from containers can be sharp. Take care always to keep water away from electrical apparatus and sockets. Cutting and drilling should be supervised closely or done by the teacher.

*Sc AT4/3c,4c,5b,5d*
*Tech AT1/4f; AT4/4c,4d,5c*

# 8. Animal movement: 'Slowcoach', said the woodlouse to the worm

### Group size
Pairs.

### What you need
Earthworms from which most of the soil has been removed, woodlice, paper, a ruler, a stop-clock or a stop-watch.

### What to do
Ask the children to observe the earthworms and to record their findings. How do the earthworms move? How do the children describe the movement? In a quiet corner, place an earthworm on a piece of paper and ask the children to listen carefully. Can they hear anything?

Now ask the children to observe and record the movement of a woodlouse. How is this similar to and different from the earthworm's movement? Tell them to carry out a fair test to see which animal moves faster. They should then calculate the speed of both animals for example, 12cm per minute. **NB:** Can the children think of any other creatures which move in the same way as the worm (e.g. snail) and the woodlouse (e.g. centipede)?

At the end of the activity, remind the children to return the worms and the woodlice to their natural habitats.

### Content
The earthworm moves by expansions and contractions of its body. Little bristles (chaetae) grip the surface and

# 9. Animal movement: migration

### Group size
Individuals or pairs.

### What you need
Map of the world, secondary sources on migration of animals such as swallow, swift or martin, wildebeest or monarch butterfly.

### What to do
Using secondary source materials and a map of the world, the children can trace the path of migration of one of the animals, including the times of the year when they begin their migration and the direction of this movement. The research should include the reason(s) for this movement. As many children are familiar with the comings and goings of the summer migrant birds to Great Britain (e.g., swallow), it would seem logical to select this familiar species as a prelude to studies of more exotic ones such as wildebeest.

## Content

Animals (and plants) are influenced by environmental conditions, including seasonal change, and by competition for scarce resources. Swallows, swifts and martins migrate to Britain to take advantage of the relatively cool (though warm), climate and the plentiful supply of food (insects) which it produces. In the autumn these birds head south to Africa to avoid cold winters when few insects are on the wing.

## Further activity

Allow the children to research more examples of migration or to consider how daily changes in the environment affect animals and plants. How would *Homo sapiens* have been affected by climate and resources thousands of years ago?

*Sc AT2/4c*

# 10. Moving sound and light: which travels faster?

### Group size
Small groups.

### What you need
A torch and an electric bell, a musical instrument or two blocks of wood.

### What to do
This activity will be difficult to carry out in schools which do not have particularly generous playing areas. It could be carried out on an occasion when children are away from school, possibly on a visit.

Organise the children into sets of two groups of three.

The first group should decide upon a 'starter'. a 'flasher' and a 'noise-maker'. Give the torch to the 'flasher' and the electric bell to the 'noise-maker'. Send this group to one side of the school field. Locate the second group as far away from the first group as possible, (preferably at a distance of 100 metres or more), and ask them to observe carefully what happens. As directed by the 'starter', the light is switched on and the sound produced together. The observers should decide whether they heard the sound first or whether they saw the light first. Repeat the investigation three times in all and then let the two groups exchange roles. Consider the class set of results. Encourage the children to interpret their findings.

## Content

Sound travels more slowly through air than does light. Sound travels through air at 330 metres per second, while light travels at 300,000 kilometres per second. Thus, the torchlight should be seen

'immediately', while there should be a slight delay between the noise being produced and being heard.

## Further activity

The time delay can be made visible by banging two sticks together and hearing the sound after having seen contact being made. Children could try to investigate the time it takes for sound to travel. It can be calculated by starting the stop-watch as the two sticks make contact and stopping it when the sound is heard. For 100m distance the expected time delay would be approximately 0.3 seconds. In reality the operational error and reaction times will be such that greater time intervals will be suggested.

*Sc AT1/4c; AT4/4d*

The electric motor is being driven by a 1.5V battery which produces a small electrical current. This is not dangerous but should be compared with the electric current at home and at school.

*Sc AT4/3a,4b,5b,5d;*
*T AT2/3a,4b,4c,5d;*
*AT3/3a,3b,3c,4a,4b,5d;*
*AT4/3b,4b,5a,5b*

# 12. Moving toys: a balloon bullet

### Group size
Pairs.

### What you need
Balloons, a pump, cotton thread, gut or plastic wire, a plastic drinking straw, sticky tape.

### What to do
Ask the children to pump up a balloon and then release it. Does it move far? Does it move in the same direction each time? Does a round balloon move in the same way as a long one? The children can

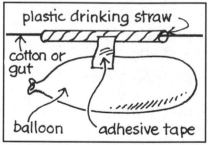

then set up the items shown in the diagram above. They should thread the drinking straw on to the cotton and fix the cotton across a corner of the classroom. Then they can attach the deflated balloon to the straw with sticky tape, and blow into the balloon, pinching the neck between their fingers

# 11. Gear up for movement

### Group size
Pairs.

### What you need
Materials to build a vehicle, for example, Jinks Construction Techniques, 1cm pine or Malayan jelutong wood, dowelling, cardboard, a junior hacksaw, photocopiable page 203, junior glue gun or strong adhesive, a 1.5V battery, a battery box, two wires, a worm-gear, an electric motor, a gear wheel, plastic tubing, washers or grommets between wheels or chasis.

### What to do
Ask the children to construct a vehicle using the instructions on photocopiable 203. This could involve precise measurements for the wood used (minimum 20cm by 9cm rectangle chassis). Ensure that the gear is attached to the front axle before you attempt to secure the motor. The amount of tension between the worm-gear and the axle-gear is important for movement. Too little or too much tension will lead to little or no movement. The worm-gear might have to be placed slightly off centre from the axle-gear. It is important that the motor is rigidly attached to the vehicle or vibration will prevent movement of the axle.

### Content
Chemical energy in the battery produces electrical energy. This electrical energy is converted into movement energy in the motor which turns the motor spindle. This movement energy is in turn transferred to the worm-gear and axle-gear which causes the axle to rotate and ultimately the wheels and... movement!

### Further activity
The gears could be replaced by a pulley on the motor spindle and a pulley on the axle driven by a belt (elastic band).

until they are ready to let go. Ask them to make some predictions about the movement of the balloon which could be tested, such as 'the more puffs of the balloon, the further it will go'. How many puffs are needed to make the balloon travel one metre, two metres, five metres, and so on? Children could go on to design and make a balloon-powered boat. Other toys with stored energy can be found on pages 58 and 59 of *Inspirations for Science*.

## Content

Energy is stored in the balloon. Movement is in the opposite direction to the thrust of the air escaping. A similar phenomenon, with forces acting in opposite directions, causes movement in a space rocket or jet engine. The size and direction of a force on an object affects its movement.

## Safety

A cotton or gut line is almost invisible and is potentially dangerous. Set it up in the corner of a classroom, above head height.

*Sc AT1/4a,4b; AT4/4b,4c, 5b,5d*

# 13. On foot

## Group size

Initially individuals, but children who follow the same route to school can be grouped together.

## What you need

A large-scale street plan of the locality with a covering grid showing number/letter co-ordinates. The map must include the catchment area of the school and the nearest high street or shopping area. A4-sized paper, pencils.

## What to do

Ask the children to close their eyes and imagine they are about to set off for school from home. Help them to visualise the route they will take by giving verbal clues, for example, 'You have just closed the door behind you. Think carefully what you will do next. Which direction will you take – right or left? What buildings do you pass – are they houses, shops, factories? What are the names of the streets? Do you pass any open spaces – playgrounds, playing fields, parks?' and so on.

Give each child a piece of paper. Make sure they think carefully about where on the paper they are going to start. Tell them they have to draw in as much detail as they can of what they can see as they walk to school. Explain to them that they are drawing a picture map.

## Content

A route map of this kind is a progression, on a larger scale, of simpler plans and maps.

Initially such maps can present an elevation view and later become two-dimensional. Discussion with the children needs to focus on such ideas as scale and distance between features on the map; the important features to include and how they will be symbolised; how to orientate the map and describe direction.

## Further activity

Using the large-scale map, ask the children to locate their own house and school and to mark or trace with their fingers the route shown in their drawings. Remind them to check their maps as they walk to and from school, adding, removing and correcting the siting of features, distances and direction. Other tasks, such as the route to the playground or other shop, can be completed in the same way.

*Gg AT1/3a,3b,3c,4a; AT2/1a,1b,1c,3c,3f; AT3/3c*

selected features on their journey into town. This can lead to a discussion about the location of buildings and land use in relation to human activity, for example, the location of the bus station in relation to shops.

**Gg AT1/3a,3b,3c,3d,4a,4b, 4c; AT2/2b,3e,3f; AT4/1a, 1b,1c**

## 15. 'A day in the country'

### Group size
Pairs.

### What you need
A road atlas covering the area from your locality to the chosen destination, e.g. a country park or a large park within a city; string, scissors.

### What to do
Tell the children that they are to plan the route for a family day out in a large park. Using the road map, help them to find the shortest car route from your location to the chosen destination. Plan the return journey via a different route. Ask the children to list the towns/districts they will pass through and the roads they will travel on. Calculate the distance the car is likely to travel, using the atlas and string.

Tell the children that the family are going to leave the car in an area adjacent to the park and hire bicycles. With the help of the map and string, the children should calculate the distance the family will have to cycle to get to various landmarks/points of interest (which should be selected before the activity). Ask them to plan a different cycle route

## 14. Downtown

### Group size
Pairs.

### What you need
An enlarged street map of the area around the school, stretching to the city or town centre, a reduced copy (A4 size) of the above map, an aerial photograph of part of the city or town centre, paper, pencils.

### What to do
Tell the children to imagine that they and their parents are taking a bus to town to book a holiday. At the bus station, the family decide that they also need to stop at the bank, call in at the shoe shop and the department store. Ask the children to decide on a route and write down directions, for example, 'The bus continues along Church Drive; at the main junction, it turns left into Wilford Lane'.

Now ask the children to look at the enlarged street map and locate the nearest bus stop to their house. The map will also show the bank, the travel agents and the shops and department stores. Remind the children to use the letter/ number co-ordinates to locate positions. They should then plan the shortest route for the family that will allow them to call at all the shops they wanted to visit and return to the bus stop closest to home. The children can mark their route on the reduced photocopies of the street map.

### Content
This activity takes the children on from freehand maps where scale, distance and location are relative and imprecise, to seeing maps as accurate tools for representing an area. The skills of map interpretation will be developed, using the key to interpret symbols, appreciating differences in scale, giving and following directions precisely, so that some of the purposes of maps begin to be appreciated.

### Further activity
Ask the children to compare the aerial photograph and the street map, picking out

back to the car. Is this way longer or shorter?

## Content
An important skill for children to develop is using a scaled map to measure distance from one place to another and interpreting it on the scale. Notions of distance 'as the crow flies' and effects on routes of intervening physical features ought to be part of the discussion about journeys and routes.

## Further activity
Discuss with the children why the park/country park was established and why that particular site was chosen. Through role-play, they should consider the reasons for different views being held about building a country park (or any other development) at a particular place. Ask the children to design and display posters or a brochure explaining why the development took place and the advantages claimed for it.

*Gg AT1/4b,5c; AT2/3b,3c,3f, 4b,4c; AT4/4a,4c,4d,4e; AT5/3b,4a*

# 16. Cruising down the river

## Group size
Small groups.

## What you need
A road atlas covering the area from Shardlow to Newark (1cm:4km) or similar region with a canal/waterway; 1:50,000 Ordnance Survey map of the route (reduced); picture of a narrow boat or cruiser, views of the River Trent and canal locks, a reel of cotton or some string.

## What to do
You may wish to use this activity as it is or to substitute details of a local river/canal waterway.

Show the children the photographs of a canal or river and boats and locks. Lead the children in discussing general aspects of boats and canals, changes in traffic and the reasons why rivers and canals are still used. Ask the children to measure distance 'as the crow flies' between Shardlow and Newark with a ruler, using the scale to convert into miles and/or kilometres. Then ask them to use the cotton or string to measure the water course distance. Why are the two measurements different? Ask the children to find places where the route has been canalised using grid references. Ask them to try to find out from the map the reasons for this. Ask the children to calculate how long the journey from Shardlow to Newark would take – a barge travels at an average speed of 3mph downstream. The return journey will take longer – ask the children to explain why. Can they tell from the map which way the river is flowing?

## Content
As well as measuring distance on a wide variety of scaled maps, children need to be able to indicate precise location using four-, then six-figure grid refrences. They should also be able to find locations using such references. It is also important to provide experience in reading contour lines and getting a picture of the slope of the land. Following the route of a river and using such terms as upstream and downstream are important aspects of map interpretation. The activity should include discussions of the reasons why some parts of rivers may not be navigable by boats and barges.

## Further activity
Ask the children to follow the river/canal route on the map, looking for signs of industrial activities along the waterway, for example, power stations or factories. Help the children to interpret map symbols and to locate the industries accurately. Encourage them to give reasons for their location as well as their effect on the environment.

*Gg AT1/5a,5b,5c; AT2/3c,3f; AT3/3b,4c; AT5/5a*

Ask the children to design, write and illustrate a brochure advertising Anglesey as a popular holiday resort, indicating its main attractions and what people will be able to enjoy if they go there.

*Gg AT1/4b,4e,5a,5b,5c; AT2/3b,3c,3d; AT4/3b,4d,5b*

# 18. Flying high – Viva Espana!

### Group size
Pairs.

### What you need
A school atlas, copies of map B or E (see National Curriculum Statutory Orders Geography), copies of a larger-scale map of Spain; pictures of an aeroplane (with details of air speed), an airport and a typical Spanish seaside resort, e.g. Malaga; a temperature chart and hours of daily sunshine for the summer months for the UK and the selected resort (available from travel brochures).

### What to do
Ask the children to imagine they are going on holiday to Spain flying from East Midlands airport which is just south of Derby. The route the aeroplane will fly will take it southwards over Southampton, The Channel Isles, Nantes, Bilbao, Madrid and on to Malaga. Ask them to measure the distance with a ruler, using the scale to convert the distance into miles and/or kilometres. If the aeroplane flies at an average speed of 450 mph, can they work out how long it will take to get to Malaga? Approximately how many miles of north/south is

# 17. A journey on the train

### Group size
Pairs.

### What you need
1:50,000 Ordnance Survey Landranger 114/115; a copy of the area between 5366 eastings and 7083 northings, (one copy per pair); an atlas; pictures of Beaumaris and Nottingham castles, and of Menai Bridge; street maps, town guides, reference books relating to the two locations.

### What to do
You may wish to use this activity as it is or replace Nottingham with your own town or area.

Tell the children that they are going by train to visit a relative who lives in Beaumaris on the Isle of Anglesey. The children will need to locate Anglesey in their atlas. How far is it 'as the crow flies' from Nottingham to Beaumaris? Use compass points as reference to locate direction. On the journey the train stops at the following stations: Derby, Stoke, Crewe, Chester, Conwy, Bangor (this is their destination) before reaching its final destination at Holyhead. Using a ruler and the scale on the atlas, the children should convert the measurements of the train's route into miles or kilometres. Ask the children to compare the result with 'as the crow flies' measurement. Can they suggest why the train's route is so much longer?

### Content
Work with atlases is often neglected and yet in many ways the atlas is more important than the larger-scaled Ordinance Survey maps, particularly for longer journeys and larger areas. Modern school atlases provide excellent representation of the environment in ways that Ordnance Survey maps cannot do. Development of a child's mental construct of the landscape, better understanding of scale of the relationship between location and site and of transport and communication systems can only be achieved through the use of atlases.

Spain and how long will the aeroplane take to fly the distance between Bilbao and Malaga?

Show the children the photographs of typical Spanish seaside resorts. Ask them to describe the photographs and compare what they see with their own locality, giving reasons for identifiable differences in architecture and occupations.

## Content
An important aspect of geography is concerned with how people are influenced by their environment and how they seek to modify it so that it provides a better standard of living. The relationship between these two factors – environmental influence and modification – is fundamental to geographical understanding. It is essential that the children examine this relationship, especially in areas that they are likely to visit. The National Curriculum requires that pupils compare their own locality with other contrasting locations from such points of view.

## Further activity
Ask the children to study the two weather charts carefully and to describe the main differences in temperature and rainfall. Ask them to research how the different weather conditions affect the day-to-day lives of local people, the kind of work they do, their clothes, food, housing and leisure activities. Ask the children to record and illustrate their research and mount a display entitled 'How the weather affects our lives'.

*Gg AT1/4b,4e; AT2/5c; AT3/3a; AT4/5c*

# 19. People on the move

## Group size
The whole class and individuals.

## What you need
A globe or an atlas, wall maps of the British Isles and the world, one or two pieces of paper per child, crayons, pencils, felt-tipped pens, thick coloured thread, coloured board pins, scissors.

## What to do
Children will need to find out about the birth place of their parent(s).

Discuss the maps with the children, making sure that they can identify their locality and the UK. Ask one or two children to identify the birthplace of their parent(s). Raise the questions: when did they come to live here and why?

Ask the children to draw a picture of their parent(s) on the paper and cut round the outline. They can then place the pictures around the edge of the appropriate map and use a piece of thread to link the parents with the birthplace. Suitable labelling can be added to the display.

## Content
Care obviously needs to be taken to consider the feelings of children with absent parents. Other family members can be used where necessary. Encourage the children to find out more about their family history. It is important to stress the idea that population movement is a key feature of human history and to expore the reasons behind this. Stress should also be placed on the notion that population movement encompasses mass migration as well as shorter journeys from village to local town, or even from one area of a town to another.

*H AT1/3b,3c,4a,5b*

# 20. Oral history: asking the questions

## Group size
Small groups.

## What you need
A large sheet of paper per group; felt-tipped pens or pencils; sheets of A4-sized paper; clipboards.

A meeting will have to be arranged with a local person whom the children can interview.

## What to do
Tell the children some brief details about the person who is going to visit them at a future date, e.g. name, birthplace, job and so on. Explain that they are going to interview this person to find out more about the 'journey' of their life, for example, what brought them to this locality? The children can then brainstorm in groups, formulating the kind of questions they will need to ask. When they have a complete list, they need to make a selection of five to ten questions to make up an interview schedule.

## Content
The emphasis of this activity needs to be on the formulation of questions – encourage the children to ask a range, e.g. what, when, why, how, where, who? It may be useful to get the children to consider the best order in which to ask the questions.

The children could formulate an interview schedule for a famous traveller or exile from the past, e.g. Sir Francis Drake, Marcus Garvey, Marco Polo. Alternatively they could interview each other about their own pasts.

*H AT1/3a,4a; AT2/3, AT3/3, PoS SSU B, Links with SSU A: Domestic life, families, and childhood*

# 21. Oral history: finding the answers

## Group size
The whole class or groups.

## What you need
A tape recorder, a blank tape, an interviewee and interview schedules.

## What to do
Introduce the interviewee to the class and let the children take turns to ask questions from the schedule. This session should be taped.

## Content
Do not worry if the schedule is not rigidly adhered to – questions are bound to arise which were not considered earlier. This also shows that the children are thinking on their feet. Make sure that the children do find answers to all of their questions. A follow up session will be necessary to bring out the main historical issues:
• that there are reasons behind population movement;
• that these reasons can be personal or part of wider social, political movements such as war, oppression or economic change.

## Further activity
The children can illustrate the 'journey' of the interviewee's life. Another interview could be set up with a different person and comparisons made between the two experiences.

*H AT1/3a,3b,4a,4b,5a,5b; H AT3/3,5 PoS SSU B, links with SSU A: Domestic life, families and childhood*

# 22. Push or pull?

## Group size
Small groups.

## What you need
A collection of books on particular groups of settlers,

e.g., Romans, Normans, Anglo-Saxons, Afro-Caribbeans, Asians, Poles, Jews; photocopiable page 204, felt-tipped pens, pencils, notepaper.

## What to do
Provide each group with the photocopiable page 204 and a set of books relating to a particular settlement group. Explain that they are to study this group, using the question sheet as a guide. Each group can record their findings on a large sheet of paper and then report back to the whole class. Encourage them to identify similarities and differences.

The children could go on to write up and illustrate individual accounts of a particular immigrant experience. A wall frieze could then illustrate the variety of settlement experience.

## Content
It is important to emphasise the push/pull factors in population movement.
• PUSH – over-population, famine, religious or political persecution.
• PULL – job opportunities, family, exploration, conquest, trade, search for resources. Individual decision making needs to be stressed, as well as social and political pressures. Use should be made of local experience where possible and links made with current world events. Terms such as 'host population', 'immigrant' and emigrant' need to be fully explained. Discussion should take place about the kind of problems which may arise when people from different cultures are brought together.

*H AT1/3a,3b,3c,4a,4b,4c, 5a,5b; AT2/3; AT3/3,4*

# 23. A local trail

## Group size
The whole class or groups.

## What you need
A local map with route marked or your own home-made route map, clipboards, paper, pencils, crayons.

## What to do
You will need to have researched and planned a local trail which provides evidence of local settlement. Explain the purpose of the trail to the children – they are to look for and record evidence of immigrant settlement in the area in the past and at present. Walk the trail, recording any evidence with notes, drawings or rubbings. Back in the classroom the findings can be collated and displayed on a wall frieze.

## Content
The trail needs to be carefully researched by the teacher and key sites marked on the map. Key evidence in the environment could include Saxon/Norman churches, temples or mosques, restaurants, shops, Roman sites, place-names, buildings and so on. Evidence of population movement away from the locality such as war memorials can also be noted.

*H AT1/3a,3b,3c,4a,4b,5a,5b; H AT3/3,4,5 CSU 1 CSU 4 SSU B, Links may be made with SSU A Houses & Places of Worship*

# 24. Imagine!

## Group size
Individuals.

## What you need
Books on Saxons and Vikings; pens, pencils, paper; spelling cards containing key words.

## What to do
Revise or explain the historical context of the Viking raids. Ask the children to imagine the following scenario:
'You are the son/daughter of a Saxon farmer. A Viking raid is expected – a village down the coast has already been attacked. Your family

decide to leave and move somewhere safer. How do you feel? What can you take with you? What must you leave behind? What happens? How do you feel leaving home? Where will you go to now?'

Ask the children to write a story from the point of view of the Saxon child.

## Content

This activity will be most effective if the children are relaxed with their eyes closed and the scene then depicted as vividly as possible. Make sure the children understand the context of the raid – that the raids were part of an expansionist process, the search for land, trade and raw materials – and appreciate the effects this had on the lives of ordinary individuals. Children with literacy difficulties could tape or illustrate their stories.

*H AT1/3a,3b,4a,4b CSU 1*

# 25. Athletics: push power

### Group size

The whole class to begin with, then dividing into groups of four. (This could be done as an unsupervised group activity.)

### What you need

Hall, playground or playing field, one cane, four bean bags and a metre rule or measuring tape for each group, photocopiable page 205.

### What to do

Ask the children to experiment with different ways of pushing with their legs to propel themselves quickly along the floor. They should try jumping, hopping, bounding and possibly bunny jumps.

Ask the children to practise single jumps from two feet to two feet – rehearse with them the techniques for increasing the length of the jump. They can then work in pairs, advising a partner how to improve his or her technique. Talk to the children about the basic jumps. Give them an opportunity to try out each one. Hand out photocopiable page 205 to each child. Arrange the children in groups of four and give each group a cane (for a take-off line), a bean bag for each child (for a personal marker) and a metre rule.

Explain the activity on the photocopiable page. Work through the first two activities if you feel this is necessary. It is important that all the children estimate and measure the first jump, so that future estimates are based on knowledge of previous results.

## Content

Appropriate warm-up is very important – feet, ankles, knees and hips need warming and suppling, progressing gradually to vigorous footwork activities. Large muscle groups in upper leg need stretching with slow, high knee lifts, 'stork stands' (stand on right leg, grasp left foot with left hand and pull heel into seat) and reaching for the feet with legs straight.

The basic jumps/hops used are simple to perform but for the children to achieve their potential look for:
• a standing start;
• a balance between the height and length to achieve the greatest distance;
• a powerful arm swing to assist with overcoming the initial inertia.

It is usual, when measuring jumping events, to measure from the front edge of the take-off line to the heels of the jumper.

The 'five basic jumps' used in this activity are:
• two feet to two feet;
• two feet to one foot;
• one foot to two feet;
• one foot to the other foot;
• one foot to the same foot.

Jumping involves a pushing force.

### Further activity

This could be based on linking combinations of three or more basic jumps together, e.g. hop/step/hop; jump, step, hop, hop, and so on. This work requires concentration, co-ordination and considerable energy. The children will experience running out of energy as the final jump in a long sequence is executed. Encourage the children to investigate the correlation between the length of the jump and the height of the performer and the length of his or her legs.

*PE KS2 Statement a, c, e; Sc AT4/2c,3c*

# 26. Floaters and sinkers

### Group size

Sixteen to twenty.

### What you need

Sufficient water space – the activity is easier in deeper water but use of this obviously depends on the ability of the children; photocopiable page 206.

### What to do

Conduct this activity for only part of a swimming session. It is important that the children do not get cold.

Space the children across the pool, either standing on the bottom or treading water. On a signal, they must take a large breath, tuck in their heads, draw up their knees and grasp their shins with their arms. The children will float in a mushroom shape. Those with good floatation will form large 'mushrooms' high in the water. Some may float submerged – these are the 'sinkers'.

Repeat the activity several times until the children are confident. Using photocopiable page 206, one person (either the teacher or a pupil who is not taking part) should record the group's level of floating ability.

Divide the children into two groups, trying to include a range of floaters and sinkers in each group.) Take it in turns for each group to watch the other from the side of the pool. Ask the observers to form opinions as to why some children float more easily than others. Ask the swimmers to experiment floating – stretched out long and thin and stretched in a star shape.

Some children will float horizontally, others will show varying degrees of sinking of the hips and legs. Ask the children why they think this happens.

Put all of the children into the water, starting with a quick warm-up if necessary. Ask what will happen if they breathe right out before they begin floating. Working in pairs, the children could devise a fair test to discover whether their predictions were correct. Continue the lesson with vigorous activity.

**NB:** Once back in the classroom the children can discuss what happened and fill in their photocopiable sheets

using the information which the teacher recorded at the pool.

## Content
(This work supports classroom work on flotation.)

The ability of the human body to float in water depends on its density, i.e., the relationship between its mass (or weight) and its volume (mass:volume). The greater the density, the poorer the floating ability. Density depends upon gender and body composition.

|  | Density |
|---|---|
| Fat | 0.90 |
| Females | 0.97 |
| Males | 0.98 |
| Water | 1.00 |
| Bone | 1.85 |

Good floaters have an even density distribution. throughout the body. Poor floaters tend to have high density (muscular lower trunk and legs). Filling the lungs with air increases the volume of a body without an appreciable increase in mass –

the body density thus decreases and the floating ability increases. The force from the water (upthrust) helps the body to float.

*PE KS2 Statement d, e; Sc AT4/2c,3c,4c*

# 27. Gymnastics: pushing and pulling

## Group size
The whole class and apparatus groups.

## What you need
A clean floor and at least one apparatus arrangement, arranged to provide raised, horizontal and variously inclined surfaces (beams, bars, benches and planks).

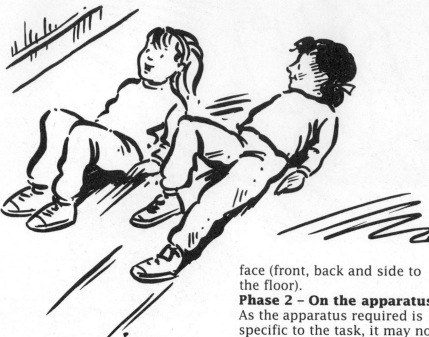

Encourage the children to express themselves in terms of force, gravity and friction. In order to make the best use of valuable hall time do not engage in lengthy discussion – put the emphasis on the *doing*. Use their activities as an introduction or a follow-up to, classroom-based work.

## Content
Through sliding activities along horizontal and inclined surfaces, concepts of pushing and pulling as forces, gravity, friction and starting and stopping are reinforced.

On horizontal surfaces a range of variations can be achieved – back, front or side towards the floor; feet leading the way, head leading the way; feet pushing/pulling; hands and arms pushing/pulling.

To achieve quality of movement good body tension needs to be maintained and all pushes and pulls should be performed to their full extent.

Most of the above activities can be performed on raised and inclined surfaces – but not all. It is important for the children to attempt the transfer from floor to apparatus and to reject for themselves those they find inappropriate. Discussion of problems encountered is most important.

## Safety
This activity is suitable as part of a gymnastics session. It must be balanced with vigorous activity to provide contrast with the slow, sustained effort required. As children will be using benches and beams, it is important that cushioned matting surrounds all equipment.

*PE KS2 Statement a, c, f; Sc AT4/2c,3c,4c,5d*

## What to do
**Phase 1 – On the floor**
Ask the children to lie on their backs and practise propelling theselves along the floor by pushing with their feet. They will produce actions with both feet moving simultaneously and with feet moving alternately. Draw the children's attention to the slight sideways movement resulting from the latter and discuss 'direction of forces'. Ask the children if they can use their feet to produce a pulling action.

Encourage the children to find a different way of sliding by using pushing and pulling movements. Ask if they can suggest why some ways are easier than others – arm and leg strength and the degree of contact with the floor are significant.

Develop a short sequence involving push and pull with arms and legs and a change of face (front, back and side to the floor).

**Phase 2 – On the apparatus**
As the apparatus required is specific to the task, it may not be possible for every group to work on sliding at the same time. Ensure that a rotation takes place, but that each group is able to spend a worthwhile amount of time experimenting with the effect of the different gradients and the narrow surfaces of the bars and beams. Gravity will be much in evidence here! Suggest the following activities:
• Compare the amount of effort needed to pull or push yourself up the different slopes. Which is easier, pushing or pulling? Which feels safer?
• What happens when you slide down a slope? What do you need to do to control the movement?
• Why do you need to use more energy going up the slope?
• What do you notice about pulling or pushing yourself along a narrow beam or a bar (lying along the top or supended underneath – 'monkey climb')?

# CHAPTER 10

# Mini-projects

In addition to developing a grid that is part of a whole-school approach to planning, there may be projects which are particular to an individual class, school, or time of year, and teachers may wish to include these in their planning. In this chapter you will find some ideas for such projects.

The chapter offers a range of projects which may be taught as short 'one-off' projects at various appropriate times in the school year. There is a planning web shown for each project, identifying the key curriculum areas which could form part of the project. Activities relating to the National Curriculum requirements are suggested within each curriculum area.

Many of the activities described earlier in this book could be built into the projects.

## Maths
Measurement
Time/speed/distance
Graphs

## English
Different sports:
descriptions of events
poetry
discussions
Favourite sports
Commentaries

## Science
Health and diet
Keeping fit
Pulse rate/heart rate
How far can I jump? – fair test
The body: muscles

## A SPORTING EVENT

## History
History of sports
Ancient Greece:
Olympic games
Athens
Sparta

## Technology
Design of sports facilities,
e.g. golf course
Data base
Design of equipment
Design of games

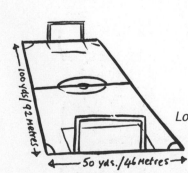

## Geography
Location of sports facilities:
choosing a suitable site
Weather and sport

## Music
National songs
Rhythms

**Maths**
Thermometer – temperature
Weather data
Graphs/histograms

**Science**
Friction
Melting and freezing
Temperature measurements
Keeping warm/insulation
Snow and ice
Fuels
Energy
Ice balloons

**English**
Imaginative writing:
Stories
'The big freeze'
Winter poems
Winter holidays
Descriptions

**FREEZE UP**

**Technology**
3-D models
Design of a sledge
Overcoming friction in design
Design of garments for
protection from the cold
Design of buildings

**History**
Past events:
Great freeze ups
Weather data from previous
years

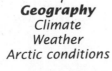

**Geography**
Climate
Weather
Arctic conditions

**Music**
Winter music

**Maths**
Weight
Prices of bread,
fruit and vegetables
Using the calculator
Shopping

**Science**
Making bread
Conditions for yeast to grow
Wind and water-mills: gears
Flours – an investigation
Cereals
Growing plants/seeds
Fruits and vegetables
Forces: levers/pulleys
Preserving and storing food
Fertilisers and pesticides

**English**
Story: 'Little Red Hen'
Harvest poems
Posters
Discussion/debates

**HARVEST**

**Technology**
Windmills
Packaging
Technological change:
farming tools
efficiency

**History**
Origin and history of festivals
Storage of food in the past
Technological change

**Geography**
Harvest in different countries
Climate/temperature/rainfall
Tropical harvest time
Drought
Fruits from other countries
Staple foods

**Music**
Harvest songs

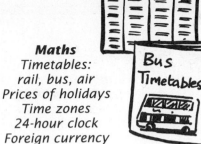

**Maths**
Timetables:
rail, bus, air
Prices of holidays
Time zones
24-hour clock
Foreign currency

**Science**
Weather and weather
instruments
Study of different habitats:
marine and freshwater
Keeping cool
Keeping warm

**English**
Holiday brochures:
design/information
retrieval
Descriptions of resorts
Information skills:cities
countries of the world
Postcards
Accounts of holidays
Writing letters
Visit to travel agent:
interviews

**History**
Leisure and pastimes
Development of transport and
the growth of towns:
Victorian Britain
Public health

**HOLIDAYS**

**Technology**
Teletext information science
Designing holiday brochures
Interviews/questionnaires:
holiday needs

**Music**
Holiday songs
Making musical instruments to
accompany roleplay/drama

**Geography**
Maps:scale/distance/latitude/ longitude
Planning routes and journeys
Transport: rail, road, air
Tourism: local, national, international
Climate
Other localities: holiday photographs and postcards
Environmental features of resorts

**Maths**
Ticket prices
Graphs: favourite rides
Board games
Probability

**English**
A visit to the fair – a story
Posters and advertisements
Favourite ride
Poems
Fairground food: descriptions,
tastes

**Science**
Light/electricity: circuits
Levers/pulleys
Friction
Forces Gears

**THE FAIR**

**Technology**
Designing and making:
rides, 3-D models
Questionnaires:
favourite rides
favourite food at the fair

**History**
Origin of fairs
Leisure and pastimes

**Music**
Fairground music
Fairground sounds

# CHAPTER 11

# Assessment and record-keeping

Evaluation, assessment and testing have become an increasingly important part of a primary teacher's role. The implementation of the National Curriculum brought with it the notion of formal testing, and fears that seven- and ten-year-olds would be put through a process which would promote anxiety, lower their self-esteem or label them in psychologically harmful ways. And, while no teacher would wish such consequences on his pupils, it is vital that all teachers are able to check children's progress through appropriate assessment.

Such assessment serves a double purpose – it indicates both the child's and the teacher's performance, as well as providing the necessary information for reporting to parents or other teachers. The National Curriculum has provided teachers with a common language for assessment of performance and progress across the entire range of curricular activities.

The first part of this chapter seeks to provide such a language – a general set of criteria that will help teachers to make credible judgements about the simple question 'How are my children getting on? Does the work they have done show knowledge and understanding? Does it exemplify skill? If it does, then how much knowledge and understanding, and how much skill?' This type of analysis shows each child's specific response to the task, as well as their more general strengths and weaknesses, which is surely a major function of assessment. Equally important, however, is the fact that such an analysis can be used to remedy learning difficulties, and to increase, even for the brightest child, understanding of the ideas being learned and the ability to reason about them and apply them skilfully. In this context, then, the purpose of finding out how a child is 'getting on' is related to future planning and to the achievement of aims and objectives, particularly those concerned with understanding ideas.

Evidently, evaluation and assessment do not stand alone but are an integral part of a cyclical process.

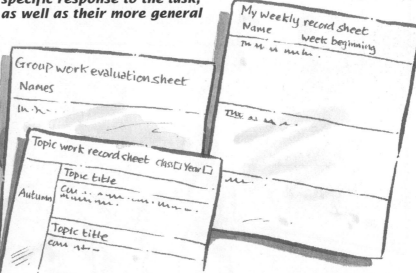

# BACKGROUND

There is a close relationship between each stage of the process – for example, assessment can only be effective if it is clear that the learning objectives are. Assessment will be easier if objectives are precisely stated. It will also be more informative and valuable if it is continuous, with frequent opportunities to apply the chosen criteria. This does not make the task onerous. Teachers can and do make assessments each time they look at a child's response to a task, both formatively as the task is being carried out and summatively, when it has been completed. Indeed, having the criteria available makes the teacher's intervention more relevant and more effective, since the advice for

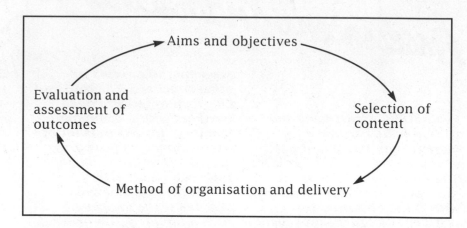

improvement and the praise for achievement will be from a more considered and consistent base.

Of course, the extent to which children can achieve a learning objective will depend upon two of the other stages of the curriculum process – the extent to which they have had access to appropriate content and the methods the teacher has used to get the children to think about and manipulate that content.

Let us take a specific example: Attainment Target 4 in National Curriculum for Geography (Human Geography) sets the achievement target that children in Key Stage 2/Level 4 should be able to 'explain why few people live in some areas and many in others'. It also suggests that the content should include an investigation of urban and rural areas of the United Kingdom. Here we have the basis for an objective, or a set of objectives, for a lesson or teaching sequence, including

tasks that will aim to provide opportunities for children to show that they:
• know the different population distribution patterns between area A and area B;
• are able to explain those differences, giving cause and effect.

The National Curriculum documentation gives no direct guidance as to what quality of explanation is expected and is satisfactory for a child at Level 4. It is left to the teacher to make that decision, based on her knowledge of what the statement of achievement demands in terms of children's knowledge and understanding. Clearly there are many variables to be taken on board. The teacher must decide how many and which, and care is needed in getting the balance right. The more teachers talk about such matters, the more they look at the work done by other children working with other teachers and the more they moderate work across class groups and schools, the easier it will become to find the right level and balance.

A quality explanation to the geography question at this level is likely to include reference to population density being affected by such things as:
• climate and weather;
• physical features;
• resources and the opportunities for work;
• the development of transport systems and other forms of communications;
• access to markets;
• the extent to which the particular environment can be improved, e.g., building a bridge or motorway or deepening a harbour may significantly affect the population density in an area.

Understanding some of the relationships that exist between the various factors form the content and strategic development of the lesson(s). This provides for the statement of attainment to be achieved. However, such understanding will not come –

nor can it be evaluated – unless teachers can ensure the following conditions:
• that they themselves are aware of the crucial relationships between the variables. This means teachers knowing what worthwhile ideas and generalisations are inherent in this achievement objective. The generalisation that where people live and how they live is influenced by the environmental conditions is one aspect that teachers should recognise in this context and aim to help their children to recognise. They should also accept and intend to apply the notion that children will not recognise and tease out relationships by being told about them, but by thinking about the information they have – making inferences, predictions and so on.

• that children have access to a wide range of experience and appropriate information. This will include opportunities to look at pictures and maps of regions with differing population densities, recalling things they have seen and heard about, going on educational visits, listening to people, watching television and videos, researching information from books and documents and so on. Teaching children research skills is very important. Clearly, there is a limit to what teachers can provide in any given situation, but without carefully managed opportunities to acquire a range of appropriate information, little that is rigorous and in-depth is likely to develop.

• that children process the information. Information on its own is of little *lasting* value – it only becomes valuable when used to exercise and develop skills and understanding. These will evolve as the information is reorganised and used to answer questions and solve problems. Information that is re-presented to the teacher in the same form in which it was found has not taken the child any further forward. Tasks must provide opportunities for children to think about an idea in as many different ways, and from as many different points of view, as possible. Such tasks are likely to start off by asking children, as appropriate, to describe and re-present information, but then move on to classifyng and categorising; to interpreting and explaining, identifying similarities and differences; to predicting and

inferring, to making extrapolations, evaluating, giving opinions and making judgements. There is no particular order suggested here and such tasks might require the full range of responses – talking, writing, drawing, role-playing, making something, having a discussion and so on.

If teachers can guarantee the above conditions, the quality of both teaching and learning will be enhanced and evaluation will be both easier and more meaningful.

Let us go back to the attainment target. Given that the teacher has played his part, it is reasonable to expect that a child's performance in the task can be judged against the following criteria.

• **Variables included:** the concern here is with whether children have considered all the appropriate variables they have had reasonable access to. In explaining why area A has a different population pattern to area B, have they considered climate, physical features, available resources, ease of communication, access to markets, environmental improvement and so on? The child who has included them all has produced an answer of better quality that the child who has only considered two of these factors. There are always likely to be a number of variables involved in answering a good question – better answers will consider more rather than fewer of them. Knowing this helps the teacher not only to assess and evaluate in a summative sense, but also to help the children improve their performance whilst the answer is still in the formative and unfinished stage.

• **Detail of response:** this simply means giving more detail in connection with each item included in the response. A child who suggests that climate is a factor in determining population distribution would be elaborating the response by saying why, by giving examples, by comparing one section with another and so on. We ought to expect this of all children at all ages at an appropriate level. A very young child at Key Stage 1 might clearly be able to suggest that not many people live in desert regions because there is no water supply. The child who can elaborate on this by suggesting that this also means that it is difficult to grow crops, rear animals and will have improved the quality of her answer significantly. If we do not expect this elaboration, many children will never do it. If it is a criterion and we consistently apply it, the child will increasingly, respond to it.

• **Concrete to abstract:** this is the extent to which the child is beginning to move away from the immediate and concrete, towards thought about qualities or conditions without tangible elements. For example, a child who suggests that people may not wish to live in very dry areas because their standard of living might not be very high, because of the difficulty in getting water, or that the area became more prosperous after the harbour had been developed, is showing clear signs of abstract thinking. Again, this kind of thinking need not be confined to older children – younger 'juniors' and even infants are capable of it. If it is in the teacher's mind, if it is looked for and encouraged, it is even more likely to occur more frequently.

• **Tentativeness:** this criterion can be applied to all those responses where there are possible limitations to the

available information and/or the child's ability to interpret it and therefore to the conclusions the child is arriving at. Tentativeness contrasts with uncritical, assertive responses that young and/or unthinking children are prone to give. Tentativeness

(a)

shows a willingness to qualify and temper conclusions and is an indication of more sophisticated thinking. So the child who identifies possible problems of living in a desert area but indicates that irrigation could significantly improve the situation is exhibiting a willingness and ability to think about both sides – indeed, all sides of a

situation – before drawing conclusions.

These criteria, consistently applied, provide a useful basis for looking for signs that a child is making progress in terms of developing ideas and thinking processes. Tables a)–d) provide further examples of the way in which these criteria might be applied using some of the tasks set in several of the themes developed in this book.

| Theme | Activity | Variables included | Detail | Concrete to abstract | Tentativeness |
|---|---|---|---|---|---|
| How people live | 7. Up hill and over dale | Do their accounts include all the variables they have researched from the reference material, e.g. location – urban, rural, coastal; climate; physical features; availability of resources which affect work patterns, e.g. fish from the sea, good farm land, tourist facilities, and so on? | Do they indicate the need to take into account other geographical factors (that they can reasonably be expected to be aware of), e.g. differences in lattitude? | Do they move from descriptions of weather towards reasoning about about mean or average climate conditions or about such factors as supply and demand with regard to seasonal patterns of work? | Do they show an understanding that people are not only influenced by their environment, but also modify it in order to enhance work opportunities, e.g. by damming rivers, providing irrigation and artificial climate conditions for cash crop agriculture? |

(b)

| Theme | Activity | Variables included | Detail | Concrete to abstract | Tentative-ness |
|---|---|---|---|---|---|
| How people live | 8. People, people, everywhere! | Have the pupils included in their answer:<br>• initial physical influence – access to the sea for fishing and trade;<br>• subsequent control of the environment (reclaimation of land and construction of a canal). | • Do they suggest that the initial settlement provided for the immediate needs, but access to deep water meant that the volume of trade was increased (more workers, people became more prosperous and so on)? | • Do they indicate that they understand and can apply to the situation important environmental generalisations. e.g. 'the environment influences what people do'? | |

(c)

| Theme | Activity | Variables included | Detail | Concrete to abstract | Tentativeness |
|---|---|---|---|---|---|
| Local study | 38. Then and now | In the first of the tasks in this activity, have the children identified the full range of differences from the maps?<br>• Number and density of houses in the area;<br>• Other building development or reduction, including farm building and industrial building;<br>• Increased size of shops, schools and so on;<br>• Reduction of agricultural land;<br>• Changes in field layouts;<br>• Removal of hedges etc.;<br>• Development of roads;<br>• Development or decrease in rail transport. | This criterion applies to the final task in this activity. Have the children tried to explain the differences, e.g. 'fields have become bigger because farmers now have large machines that operate best in large fields', or 'the village has more houses than before because people travel to work to the nearest town?' | Watch for signs of and encourage use of such ideas (however expressed) as, for example:<br>• efficiency (a big combine harvester can work more efficiently in large fields);<br>• life cycle, food chains (destroying hedgerows has had a bad effect on the wildlife)<br>• commuter belt, inner city. | • In making explanations and expressing opinions, do they see both sides of the issue, e.g. the farmer who wants to use machinery efficiently and the conservationist who wants to protect wildlife? |

(d)

| Theme | Activity | Variables included | Detail | Concrete to abstract | Tentativeness |
|---|---|---|---|---|---|
| Local study | 20. My house | • Have the children included in their comparisons the full range of differences – size, location, shape, construction materials, technology, rooms and furniture? | • Did they go on to explain the differences as being related to such factors as weather, availability of construction materials, wealth of owner and so on? | • Are they beginning to use phrases such as 'comfortable', 'labour-saving', 'standard of living' or make references to such ideas in what they say or write? | • Do they avoid suggestions that their house is best but try to show the advantages of both kinds of houses in their contexts? |

These criteria form the basis not only for evaluations, but also for teaching intervention and feedback to children about the quality of their work, which is an important teaching skill. There will be, of course, no dramatic change in children's responses from being less to more inclusive, from providing little to much elaboration and so on. Teachers will need to make many interventions and provide frequent feedback including appropriate references to the criteria. 'Can you think of another...?', 'Can you explain why...?', 'What would be the result of...?', are the kind of questions which will, gradually, persuade children that they need to think more comprehensively about the task – that the expectations for the task are such that limited and superficial answers are not acceptable. If this is done in a context of positive reinforcement of what has been done and supportive exhortation for what might still be achieved, children will, sooner or later, respond to the extent that they, as well as the teacher, have the criteria in mind as tasks are undertaken. These criteria are useful in that they have universal applicability and can be used across not only a variety of tasks but across curriculum areas and are therefore especially useful in a thematic approach. They also provide evidence of progression in terms of:

• knowledge – the extent to which a child is able to use activity, experience, research and so on to accumulate appropriate information.
• intellectual skill – the extent to which the child can process information within the context of a range of thinking skills to identify and tease out the relationship within a conceptual framework.
• understanding – the extent to which those relationships are used to explain situations,

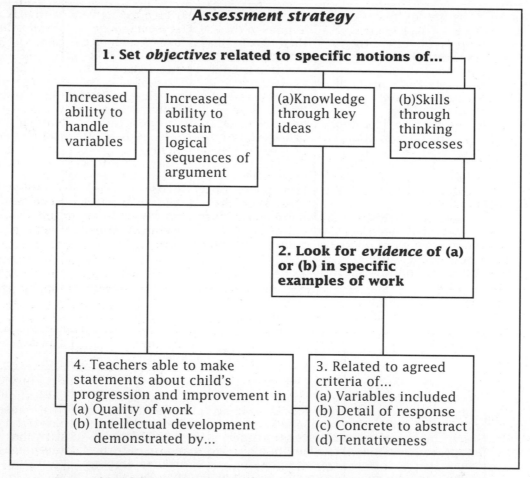

(Reproduced from *Equal Opportunities in Schools* Antonouris and Wilson (1989) Cassell)

solve problems and generalise across situations.

The diagram on the page opposite indicates how those two dimensions of objectives and outcomes fit into the overall assessment cycle.

## Record keeping

A key element in any whole-school curriculum planning is the design of an effective record-keeping system. Record keeping must not be an end in itself but only part of the assessment process.

Record-keeping systems serve a number of purposes and it is important to recognise these when designing a system that will be useful and effective.
• They identify the attainment targets and statements of attainment which a child has studied.
• They record a child's level of attainment and progress.

• They provide teachers with information which will enable schemes of work to be evaluated and which can be passed on when children change schools.
• They provide evidence for parents about their children's achievement.
• They ensure progression and continuity.

A record-keeping system must be manageable and simple and should lead to a response. The collecting and recording of evidence is not an end in itself but should inform future practice. Records must be key to the decision-making processes concerning:
• individual needs;
• curriculum coverage;
• curriculum planning;
• development and continuity;
• classroom organisation.

A record-keeping system should be easy to interpret

and should enable those who read it to gain the information they require. It should include information which is required by schools, and local and national bodies. An effective record-keeping system should also provide feedback for the children to reflect on their progress with the teacher.

A whole-school recording policy is required. Consideration within this must be given to such questions as:
• Why do we record?
• What do we record?
• How do we record?
• How is continuity and progression shown?
• How is the information collected, stored, retrieved, and transferred?

## Cross-curricular projects: keeping a record

In any project, it is important to identify both the generic skills (the intellectual skills which are cross-curricular) and skills which are specific to a project. There are a number of statements of attainment which will be addressed within each project and these must be identified within the record-keeping system. Have the children addressed the statement? Is it understood?

The **long-term planning** will have identified the projects to be covered in a year (or two years, see Table 1). This could also provide an audit of the sequence through which the various attainment targets and different levels are addressed.

When an individual project is being planned in the **medium-term planning**, each activity included in the project should be identified with the appropriate attainment target level and statements of attainment in a whole-class teaching plan and record. Table 2 shows an example of such a record for part of the project 'On the move'. Provision can then be made in the **short-term planning** for evidence of the children's achievements. It is important when planning individual activities that there are ample opportunities to introduce children to ideas, so that they can gain full understanding of them. The criteria listed on pages 172–173 of this chapter could be the basis on which observations are made to

record achievements.

Individual children's record sheets (see Table 3) may be used for each project. These would include all the statements of attainment covered in a project in all of the curriculum areas included in that project. Each box could be cross-hatched when experienced and coloured in when achieved. This gives a picture of those attainment targets and statements of attainment which have been covered and achieved and those which need to be addressed in future projects. These are just some possibilities for recording children's achievements in cross-curricular work. They can be adapted to individual situations and developed as appropriate.

**Table 1**

| | Record sheet: long-term planning | | | | | |
|---|---|---|---|---|---|---|
| Date....................... | | | | | | |
| | **Autumn term** | | **Spring term** | | **Summer term** | |
| **Reception** | Myself | Night and day | Pets | Families | Water | Holidays |
| **Year 1** | The senses | Celebrations | Forces | The garden | The seaside | Animals and plants |
| **Year 2** | Vikings | Food | Keeping warm | Space | Farms SATs | Local study |
| **Year 3** | The seasons | Ancient Greeks | Plants and growth | On the move | Homes | Buildings |
| **Year 4** | Materials | How we live | Water | Tudors and Stuarts | Local environment | Local environment |
| **Year 5** | Ourselves | Ancient Egypt | Weather | Victorian Britain | Pollution | Pollution |
| **Year 6** | Communi-cation | Explorations and encounters | Change | Life processes | EC countries SATs | The environment |

**Table 2**

| Whole-class teaching plan and record | | | | | | |
|---|---|---|---|---|---|---|
| On the move | | | | | | |
| Class 5W   Spring term   Date............ | | | | | | |
| **Curriculum area** | **Details of work to be undertaken** | **Attainment targets and level** | | | | |
| | | **AT1** | **AT2** | **AT3** | **AT4** | **AT5** |
| Science | Making a parachute | | | | 3c, 5d | |
| Science | Plants moving towards the light | | 3c | | | |
| Science | Making a water wheel | | | | 4d | |
| Science | Observing animal movement | | 3a | | | |
| Geography | Planning a route to school | 3a, 3b, 3c, 4a | 3c, 3f | | | |
| History | Local trail with historical sites | 3a, 3b, 3c, 4a | | 3, 4, 5 | | |
| History | Understanding Viking raids | 3a, 3b, 4a, 4b | | | | |

## Table 3

| Individual record sheet for a project | | | | | |
|---|---|---|---|---|---|
| School:<br>Name:<br>Date of birth: | | | Title of project: | | |

| | Level | | AT1 | AT2 | AT3 | AT4 | AT5 |
|---|---|---|---|---|---|---|---|
| **SCIENCE** | Level 1 | a | | | | | |
| | | b | | | | | |
| | | c | | | | | |
| | | d | | | | | |
| | Level 2 | a | | | | | |
| | | b | | | | | |
| | | c | | | | | |
| | | d | | | | | |
| | | e | | | | | |
| | Level 3 | a | | | | | |
| | | b | | | | | |
| | | c | | | | | |
| | | d | | | | | |
| | | e | | | | | |
| **GEOGRAPHY** | Level 2 | a | | | | | |
| | | b | | | | | |
| | | c | | | | | |
| | | d | | | | | |
| | | e | | | | | |
| | Level 3 | a | | | | | |
| | | b | | | | | |
| | | c | | | | | |
| | | d | | | | | |
| | | e | | | | | |
| | | f | | | | | |
| **HISTORY** | Level 4 | a | | | | | |
| | | b | | | | | |
| | | c | | | | | |
| | Level 5 | a | | | | | |
| | | b | | | | | |
| | | c | | | | | |

# PHOTOCOPIABLES

**The pages in this section can be photocopied and adapted to suit your own needs and those of your class; they do** **not need to be declared in respect of any photocopying licence. These photocopiable pages relate to specific activities in the main body of** **the book and the appropriate activity and page references are given at the top of each page for quick reference.**

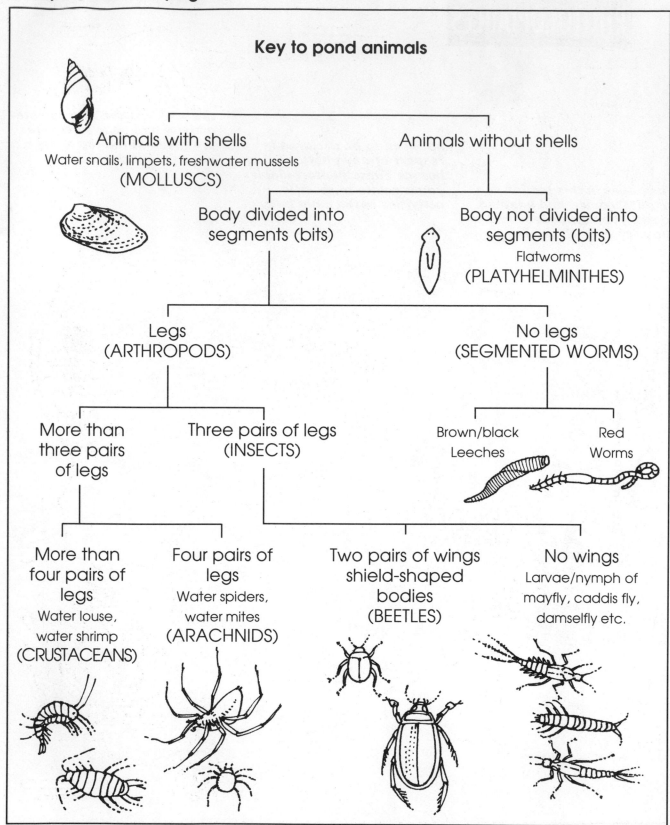

# Key to pond animals

**Animals with shells**
Water snails, limpets, freshwater mussels
(MOLLUSCS)

**Animals without shells**

**Body divided into segments (bits)**

**Body not divided into segments (bits)**
Flatworms
(PLATYHELMINTHES)

**Legs**
(ARTHROPODS)

**No legs**
(SEGMENTED WORMS)

**More than three pairs of legs**

**Three pairs of legs**
(INSECTS)

Brown/black
Leeches

Red
Worms

**More than four pairs of legs**
Water louse, water shrimp
(CRUSTACEANS)

**Four pairs of legs**
Water spiders, water mites
(ARACHNIDS)

**Two pairs of wings shield-shaped bodies**
(BEETLES)

**No wings**
Larvae/nymph of mayfly, caddis fly, damselfly etc.

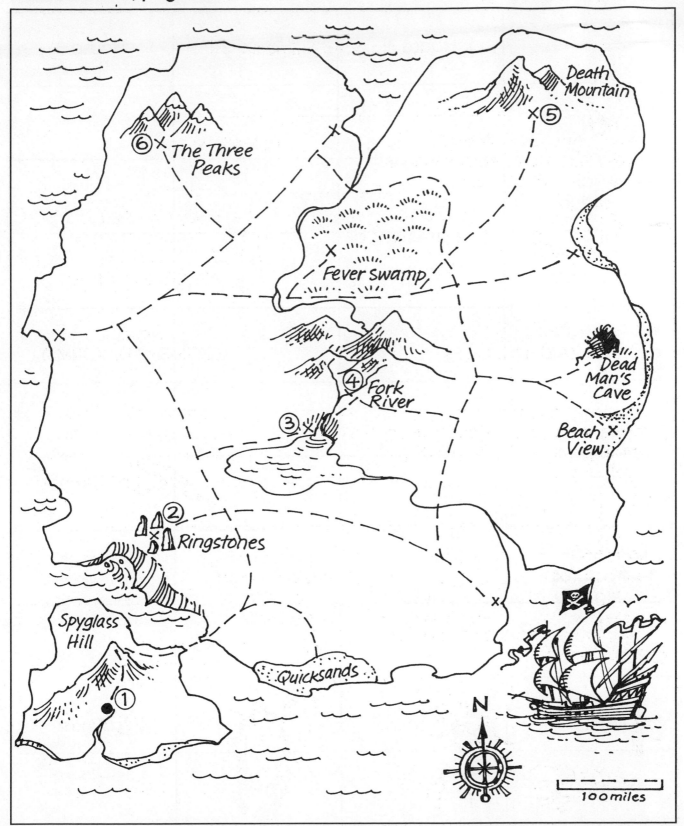

**Dig that style! page 60**

|  | House 1 | House 2 | House 3 |
|---|---|---|---|
| Age |  |  |  |
| Building materials |  |  |  |
| Roof - material and style |  |  |  |
| Walls - material, patterns, bonds |  |  |  |
| Windows |  |  |  |
| Doors |  |  |  |
| Decorative features |  |  |  |
| Alterations and renovations |  |  |  |
| Garden |  |  |  |
| Boundaries |  |  |  |

# A place to pray, page 61

| Name of building | |
|---|---|
| Religion | Age of building |

Which of these activities or events takes place in the building?

| | | | |
|---|---|---|---|
| Praying | ☐ | Christenings | ☐ |
| Singing | ☐ | Funerals | ☐ |
| Worshipping | ☐ | Festivals | ☐ |
| Weddings | ☐ | Other | ☐ |

Has the building always been used as a place of worship?

Look at the building carefully. Put a ring around the things you find there.

| Inside | | Outside | |
|---|---|---|---|
| aisle | font | tower | porch |
| altar | tomb | spire | main doorway |
| seats | windows | | |
| bell | statues | dome | minaret |
| chancel | nave | gargoyle | clock |
| pulpit | pictures | | |
| patterns | dates | headstone | dates |

In the desert daily heating and nightly cooling of rocks causes them to break up.

Water gets into the crack and freezes. As it freezes it expands and splits the rock. Eventually a large crack or fissure is formed and rocks fall from the cliff.

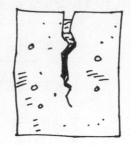 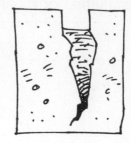 

The roots and trunk of a tree can split up rocks and cause screes.

Acid rain dissoves away limestone rocks. This, together with soil erosion from over-grazing of cattle and sheep causes the limestone paving seen at places such as Malham Tarn.

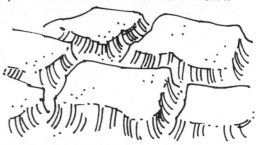

What has happened to the surface of the statue? Is this similar ro what happens to gravestones?

The path is much wider than last year. You could hardly see any of the stones in it then.

Can you read the writing on old gravestones?
What has happened to them?

**Speedy winds, page 88**

| | Beaufort wind scale | | |
|---|---|---|---|
| Beaufort number | Description | Wind speed (km/hr) | Description of effects |
| 0 | Calm | 0-1 | Smoke rises vertically. |
| 1 | Light air | 2-5 | Wind direction shown by smoke, but vanes do not move. |
| 2 | Light breeze | 6-11 | Leaves rustle, wind felt on face, vanes move. |
| 3 | Gentle breeze | 12-19 | Leaves and small twigs move, light flags are extended. |
| 4 | Moderate breeze | 20-28 | Dust and paper rise, small branches sway, flags flap. |
| 5 | Fresh breeze | 29-38 | Small trees sway, crested waves on inland waters. |
| 6 | Strong breeze | 39-49 | Umbrellas difficult to use, large branches sway. |
| 7 | Near gale | 50-61 | Trees sway, hard to walk against wind. |
| 8 | Gale | 62-74 | Twigs break off trees, very hard to walk into wind. |
| 9 | Strong gale | 75-88 | Slight damage to buildings, chimney pots and slates are removed. |
| 10 | Storm | 89-102 | Trees uprooted, serious damage to buildings. |
| 11 | Violent storm | 103-117 | Widespread damage. |
| 12 | Hurricane | 118+ | Disaster, terrible damage. |

# The water cycle, page 92

Clouds produce rainfall.

Evaporation from the river.

The heat from the sun causes water in the sea and other areas to evaporate as water vapour.

The rain finds its way into streams and rivers.

Evaporation from the sea.

As water vapour rises it is cooled. The water vapour condenses into tiny drops of water which form clouds.

Some water is used by man but most returns to the rivers or evaporates.

Rivers flow into the sea.

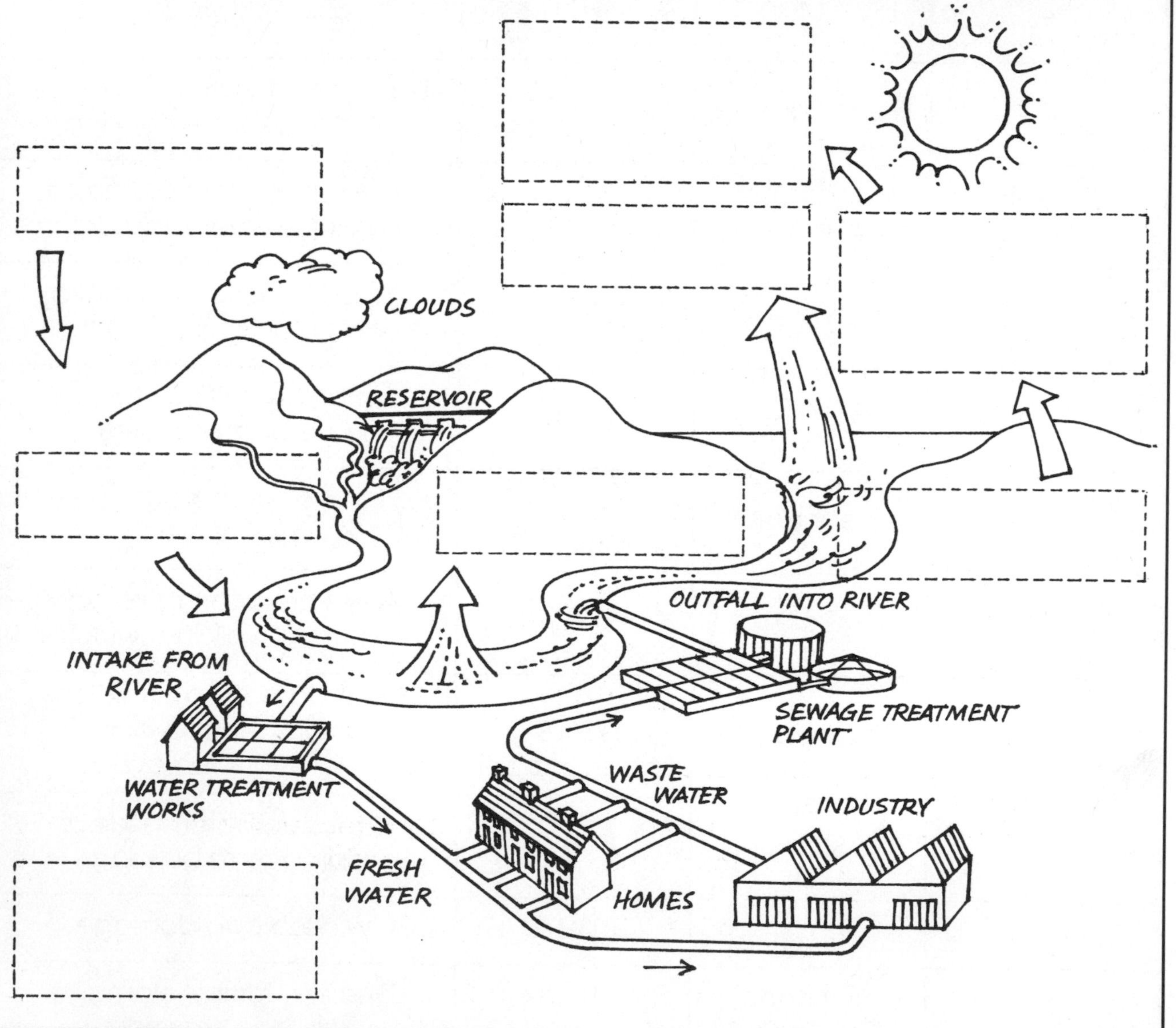

CLOUDS

RESERVOIR

OUTFALL INTO RIVER

INTAKE FROM RIVER

SEWAGE TREATMENT PLANT

WATER TREATMENT WORKS

WASTE WATER

INDUSTRY

FRESH WATER

HOMES

# A family tree, page 96

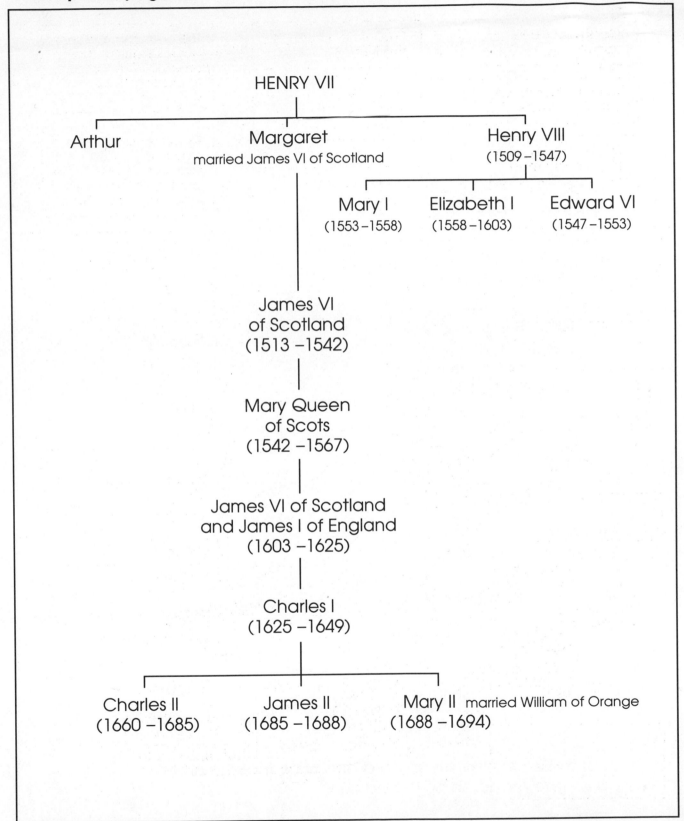

HENRY VII

Arthur

Margaret
married James VI of Scotland

Henry VIII
(1509 –1547)

Mary I
(1553 –1558)

Elizabeth I
(1558 –1603)

Edward VI
(1547 –1553)

James VI
of Scotland
(1513 –1542)

Mary Queen
of Scots
(1542 –1567)

James VI of Scotland
and James I of England
(1603 –1625)

Charles I
(1625 –1649)

Charles II
(1660 –1685)

James II
(1685 –1688)

Mary II  married William of Orange
(1688 –1694)

# A family tree, page 96

| | |
|---|---|
| I am Henry VIII's father.<br>My family name is Tudor. | (Henry VII) |
| I am Henry VII's son.<br>My family name is Tudor. | (Henry VIII) |
| I am male.<br>My father is Henry VIII. | (Edward VI) |
| My sister is Elizabeth.<br>My brother is Edward. | (Mary I) |
| I am female.<br>My sister is Mary. | (Elizabeth I) |
| My family name is Stuart.<br>My son is Charles I. | (James I) |
| I am male.<br>My father is James I. | (Charles I) |
| My father is Charles I.<br>My family name is Stuart. | (Charles II) |
| My brother is Charles II.<br>My daughter is Mary II. | (James II) |
| My father is James II.<br>I am married to William of Orange. | (Mary II) |

Mount these statements on card and write the name of the appropriate monarch on the back.

Henry VIII had six wives.

Henry VIII was a bad king.

Henry VIII married Anne Boleyn in 1533.

Henry VIII was very rich.

Henry VIII had two of his wives executed.

Henry VIII was a cruel king.

Henry VIII was unkind to his daughter.

Henry VIII died in 1547.

Henry VIII enjoyed hunting.

Henry VIII was a great king.

**From the inventory of John Herries, 1599**

| | |
|---|---|
| A frying pan, a pair of tongs and a roasting iron | |
| 1 little kettle | 1s 6d |
| and 3 pewter spoons | |
| 3 little bowls | 2s 6d |
| 1 kettle, 1 pot spoon | 1s 0d |
| 2 wooden platters | 1s 0d |
| and 5 dishes and 2 earthen pots | 8d |
| 5 stoneware pots | 4d |
| 2 salt boxes | 1s 0d |

**Total value 8s 0d**
(in modern money about £48)

**From the inventory of William Hobby, 1597**

| | |
|---|---|
| 2 brewer's vats, a bough, a brewing vessel, | 10s 0d |
| 3 pails, 1 churn | |
| 3 brass pans, 2 brass kettles, | |
| 2 little cauldrons, 6 brass pots, | |
| a chafer, 2 frying pans, a dripping | |
| pan, a grid iron, 2 pairs pot hooks, | £2. 0s 0d |
| 3 spits | |
| A basin and an ewer, 9 plates, | |
| 14 pewter dishes, 6 saucers, | |
| 6 porringers, 3 pewter salt cellars, | |
| 1 pewter cup, 5 brass | £1 3s 0d |
| candlesticks | 1s 0d |
| 13 spoons | |

**Total value £3.14s 0d**
(in modern money about £384)

**kettle** – used for cooking food, not just boiling water
**chafer** – a container for hot charcoal to keep food warm at table
**gridiron** – utensil for grilling meat
**spit** – rod on which meat is skewered and roasted over a fire
**platters** – plates
**ewer** – jug
**porringer** – soup bowl

Musketeer

Cavalier

Pikeman

*1666*

| | |
|---|---|
| *2nd September* | *Jane [a maid] called us up, about 3 in the morning, to tell us of a great fire they saw in the City. So I rose, and slipped on my nightgown and went to the window. (...)* |
| *[Morning]* | *Jane comes and tells me that she hears that above 300 houses have been burned down tonight by the fire we saw, and that it was now burning down all Fish Street by London Bridge. Walked to the Tower. There I did see the houses at that end of of the bridge all on fire, and an infinite great fire on this and the other side the end of the bridge. The lieutenant of the tower told me that it begun this morning in the King's baker's house in Pudding Lane. So I down to the water side and there got a boat and through bridge, and there saw an awful fire. Everybody trying to move their goods, or fling them into the rover or bring them to boats. Poor people stay in their houses until the fire touches them. Then they run into boats or clamber from one pair of stairs by the water side to another.(...)* |
| *[That night]* | *To my boat, and there upon the water again, and to the fire up and down, it still increasing and the wind great. So near the fire as we could for smoke. And all over the Thames, with one's face in the wind, you were almost burned with a shower of fire drops — this is very true — so as houses were burned by these drops and flakes of fire, three or fire, nay five or six houses, from one another..., the churches, houses and all on fire and flaming at once, and a horrid noise the flames made, and the cracking of houses at their ruin.* |
| *4 September* | *Walk into the garden and saw how horrible the sky look, all on fire in the night.* |
| *5 September* | *Walked into Moorfields. Our feet ready to burn, walking through the town among the hot cinders.* |
| *7 September* | *Up by 5 a-clock and, blessed by God, find all well, and by water to St Paul's wharf. Walked from there and saw all the town burned , and a miserable sight of St Paul's Church, with all the roofs fallen and the body of the choir fallen into St Faiths.* |

From the diary of Samuel Pepys

| Item | What it feels like | Item | What it feels like | Item | What it feels like |
|---|---|---|---|---|---|
| flour | | wool | | | |
| lemonade | | wood | | | |
| water | | coal | | | |
| soil | | brick | | glass window | |
| rock | | aluminium foil | | polythene bag | |

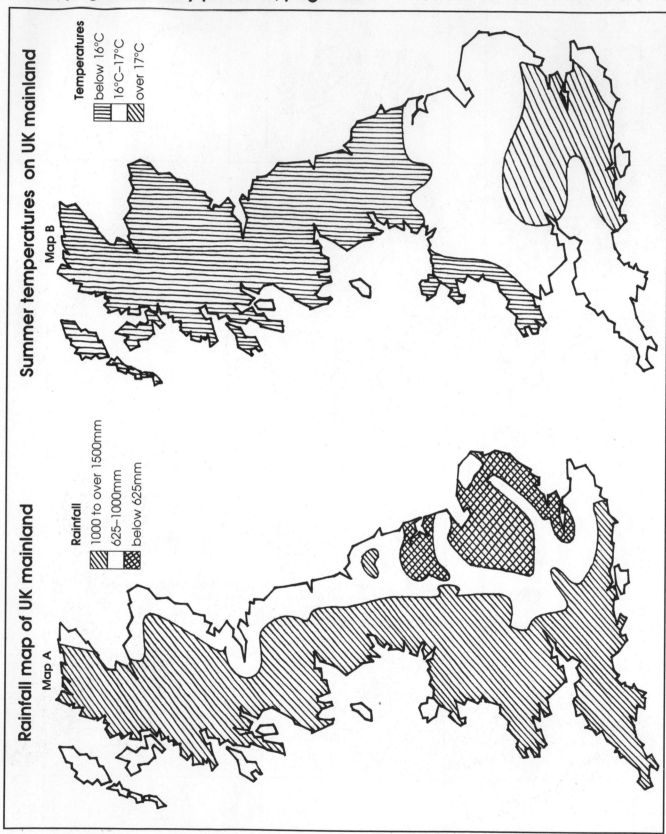

**Rainfall map of UK mainland**

Map A

**Rainfall**

1000 to over 1500mm

625–1000mm

below 625mm

**Summer temperatures on UK mainland**

Map B

**Temperatures**

below 16°C

16°C–17°C

over 17°C

Bread, page 132, Dairy products, page 133, Apples, page 134

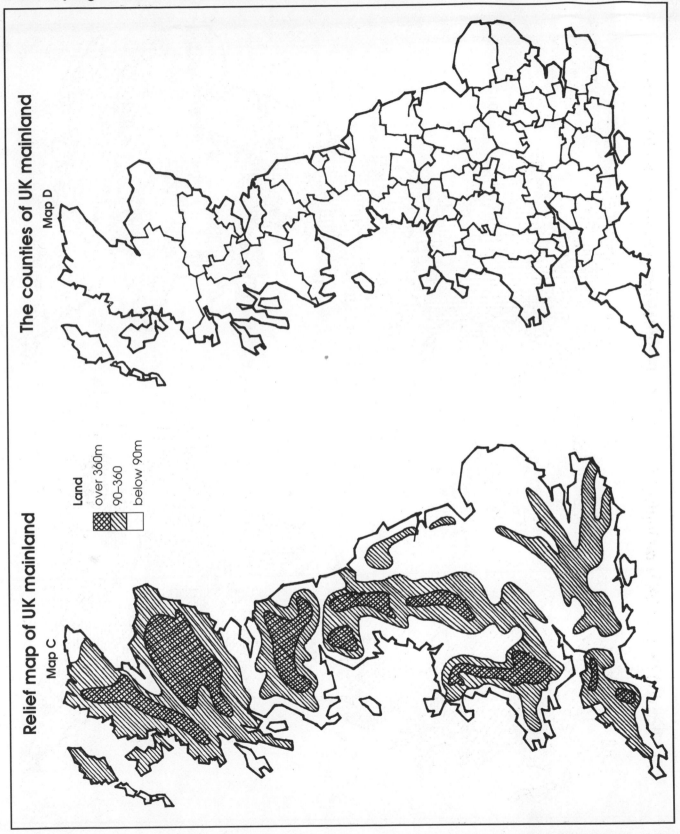

The counties of UK mainland

Map D

Relief map of UK mainland

Map C

Land

over 360m

90–360

below 90m

# Dairy products, page 133

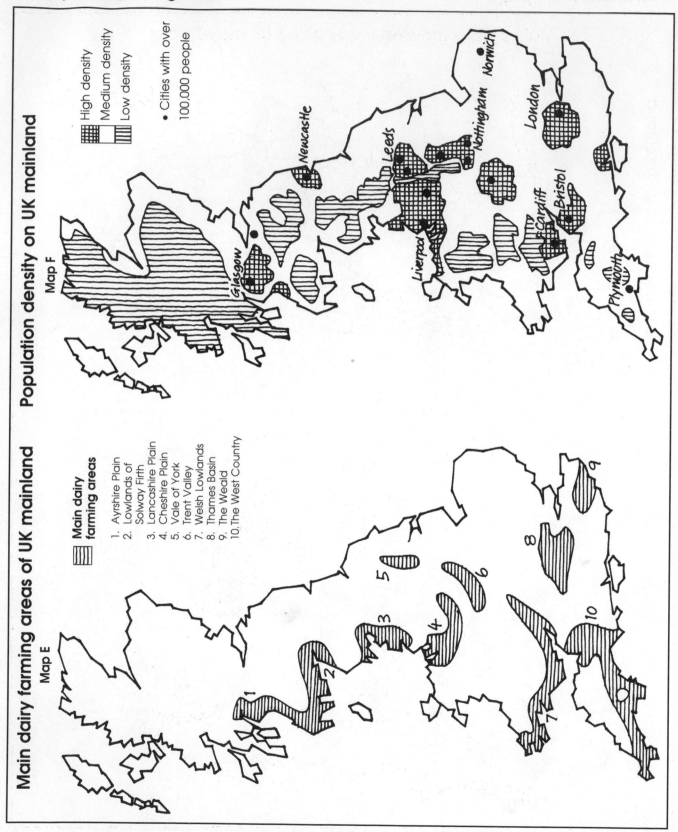

## Main dairy farming areas of UK mainland

Map E

**Main dairy farming areas**

1. Ayrshire Plain
2. Lowlands of Solway Firth
3. Lancashire Plain
4. Cheshire Plain
5. Vale of York
6. Trent Valley
7. Welsh Lowlands
8. Thames Basin
9. The Weald
10. The West Country

## Population density on UK mainland

Map F

High density
Medium density
Low density

• Cities with over 100,000 people

Newcastle
Leeds
Nottingham
Norwich
London
Liverpool
Cardiff
Bristol
Plymouth
Glasgow

## Main potato growing areas of the UK mainland

Map G

Main potato growing areas

## Briefing sheet

Your group have been invited by a local landowner to advise him on how he can make his land productive once again. The land covered by the map has not been cultivated for more than 50 years because it has been used by the Ministry of Defence for army training. Using your extensive farming knowledge, you must decide what crops to plant and which animals to rear in the most appropriate places. The landowner would like to live off the land and be self-sufficient in the staple foods, as well as have a surplus to sell. He also wants to build a farm. Where would you build one?

Physical conditions in areas A, B, C and D:

| Area | Height | Average temperature | Rain | Soil |
|------|--------|---------------------|------|------|
| A | 0–50m | 18°C | 750mm | moderate |
| B | 0–150m | 20°C | 1000mm | good in valley bottom up to 100m |
| C | 0–200m | 16–18°C | 1500mm | poor |
| D | 0–100m | 25°C | 500mm (rain shadow) | good |

The map covers an area of 400km$^2$ and prevailing wind is from the west. Suggest which of the following should be cultivated in the above areas:

**Daily cattle** – not too steep, moderate rainfall, warm temperatures, milked twice a day.

**Cereals** – low-level, best soil, warm and dry weather, good access for machinery.

**Rice** – fertile soil, land easily flooded, warm temperatures.

**Potatoes** – sandy, well-drained soil, good rainfall in summer.

**Grapes** – south-facing valley slopes, well-drained soil, hot summer weather.

**Apples** – valley slopes.

**Vegetables** – dry, warm weather, close to water with good access for machinery.

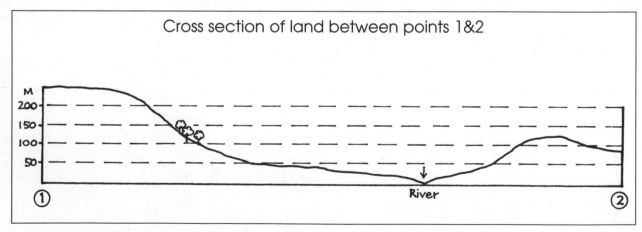

Cross section of land between points 1&2

# What to grow where, page 136

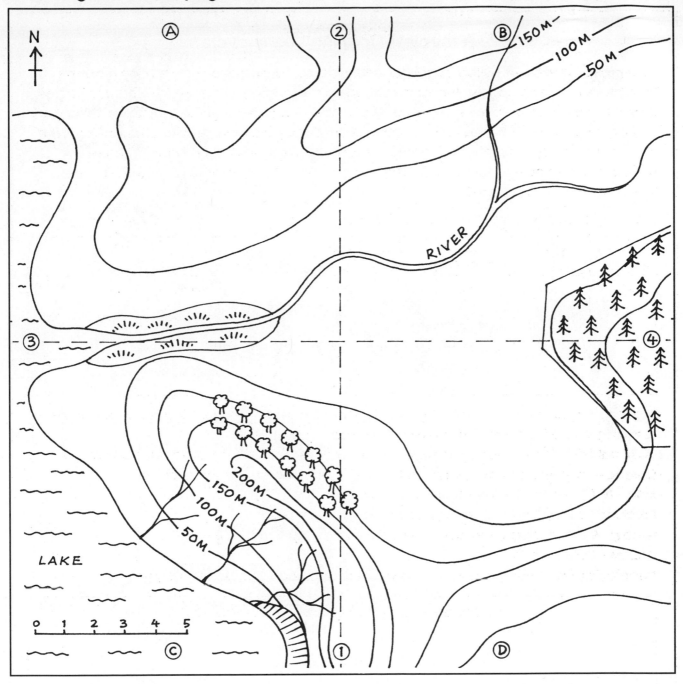

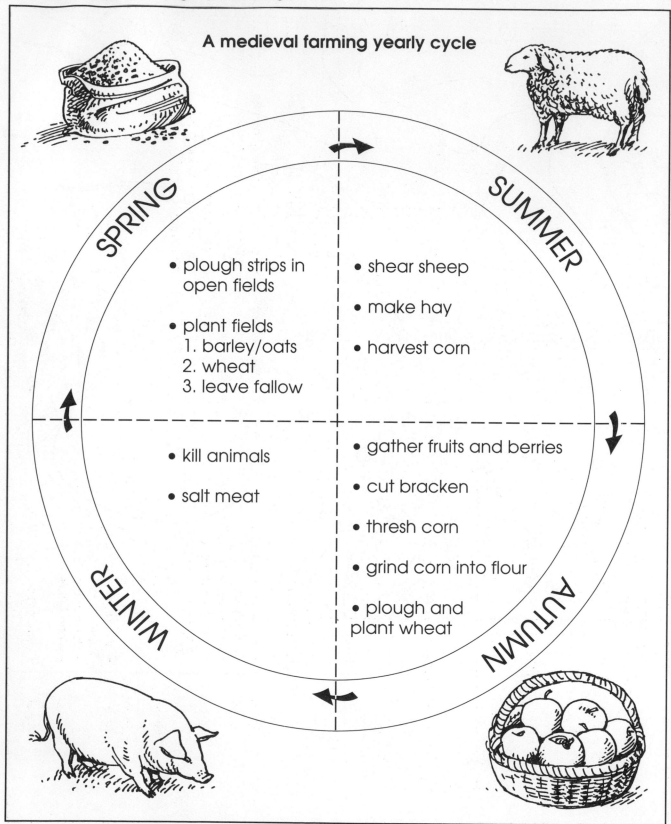

A medieval farming yearly cycle

**SPRING**

- plough strips in open fields

- plant fields
  1. barley/oats
  2. wheat
  3. leave fallow

**SUMMER**

- shear sheep

- make hay

- harvest corn

- gather fruits and berries

- cut bracken

- thresh corn

- grind corn into flour

- plough and plant wheat

**AUTUMN**

- kill animals

- salt meat

**WINTER**

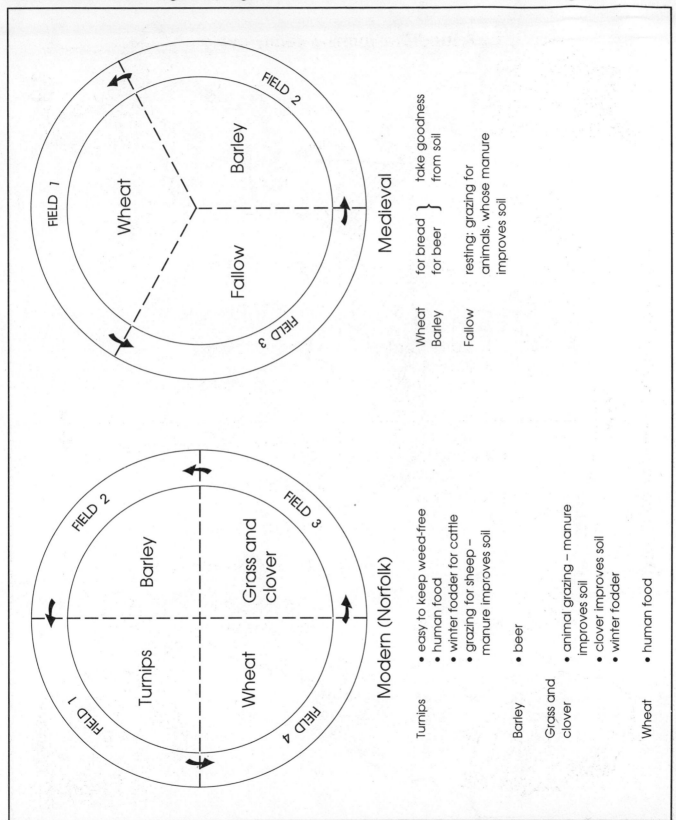

**Medieval**

Wheat — for bread } take goodness
Barley — for beer } from soil

Fallow — resting: grazing for animals, whose manure improves soil

**Modern (Norfolk)**

Turnips
- easy to keep weed-free
- human food
- winter fodder for cattle
- grazing for sheep – manure improves soil

Barley
- beer

Grass and clover
- animal grazing – manure improves soil
- clover improves soil
- winter fodder

Wheat
- human food

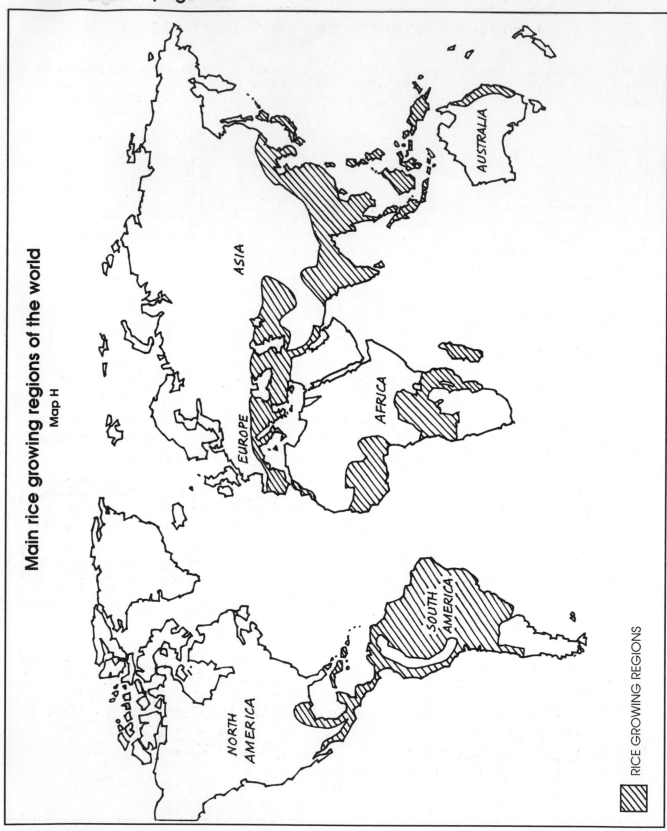

## Main rice growing regions of the world
### Map H

ASIA

AUSTRALIA

EUROPE

AFRICA

NORTH AMERICA

SOUTH AMERICA

RICE GROWING REGIONS

# Making a moving structure from softwood and card

1. Make a rectangular frame by sticking four pieces of wood together with adhesive.

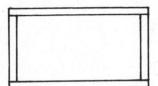

2. Draw a square on cardboard, divide it with two diagonal lines and cut it into four triangles.

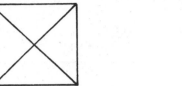

3. Reinforce the corners of the rectangular frame by sticking a cardboard triangle on to each corner with adhesive.

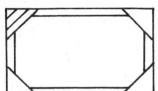

4. Cut out four larger triangles made from a card square and cut a hole in each one to take the wheel axles.

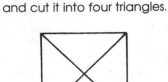

5. Stick the axle supports to the chassis with adhesive.

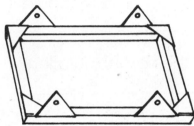

6. Cut out eight wheels from card.

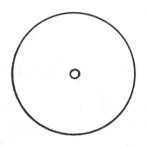

7. Support the card wheels by sticking a lollipop stick, card or offcuts of wood to each wheel.

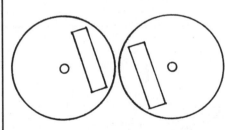

8. Stick pairs of wheel cards together by sticking the lollipop sticks/offcuts of wood to the card with adhesive.

9. Attach dowel for the axles to the wheels and thread through axle supports.

10. Add the motor and battery.

*hardboard*

*wormgear attached to motor*

*gear attached to axle*

*motor* — *battery*

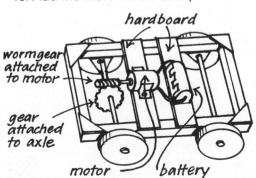

11. Gear attached to axle

*battery and battery box*

*gear attached to axle*

*hardboard*

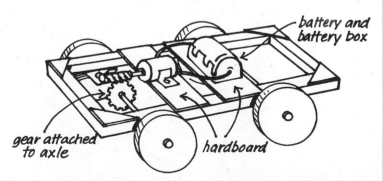

**Push or pull? page 156**

| |
|---|
| Name of the settlers |
| Where did they come from? |
| Why did they come to Britain? |
| When did they come to Britain? |
| How were they different from the host population? |
| Were they welcomed by the host population? |
| What kinds of problems did they have? |
| Are they still here? |
| What evidence do we have of their settlement? |

## Push Power

Which jump will carry you the furthest?

I think jump number ................ will carry me the furthest.

Can you explain to your group why you think this jump will carry you the furthest?

| Type of jump | Estimate | Measurement |
|---|---|---|
| 1. Two feet to two feet | | |
| 2. Two feet to one foot | | |
| 3. One foot to two feet | | |
| 4. One foot to the other foot | | |
| 5. One foot to the same foot (hop) | | |

What to do:

• Use the cane as the starting point and the bean bag to mark where you land.
• You should estimate how far you think you will jump for number one jump. Write your estimate on this sheet.
• Take it in turns to jump and measure, and record your measurements.
• Continue until you have completed all the five jumps.

# Floaters and sinkers

Use the data collected by your teacher at the swimming pool to help you do the tasks below.

| Girls' names | Good floater | Medium floater | Sinker | Height | Weight | | Boys' names | Good floater | Medium floater | Sinker | Height | Weight |
|---|---|---|---|---|---|---|---|---|---|---|---|---|
| | | | | | | | | | | | | |

## Tasks

1. Working in groups of four to six children, first weigh each other, then measure each other. Record your results of the chart.
2. Share your results with the rest of the class and record everyone's weight and height.
3. Look carefully at the heights and weights of the good floaters – can you make a statement about them?
4. What can you say about the poor floaters?
5. Is there any difference between the way boys and girls float?
6. Write a sentence about people and floating.

# ACKNOWLEDGEMENTS

*We gratefully acknowledge the help given to us by Di Billups and David Lea of Humberside LEA primary advisory team and by the headteachers and staff of the Willows Primary School, Grimsby and Grange Lane Infants School, Scunthorpe.*

*We also wish to acknowledge the contributions of Anna Disney, Kate Hunt (Senior lecturers in Primary Education) and John Moore (Principal Lecturer in Primary Education), all of The Nottingham, Trent University, in designing and developing the history, physical education and geography activities respectively.*